Lifelong Learning in Public Libraries

Principles, Programs, and People

Donna L. Gilton

THE SCARECROW PRESS, INC.
Lanham • Toronto • Plymouth, UK
2012

Published by Scarecrow Press, Inc.
A wholly owned subsidiary of The Rowman & Littlefield Publishing Group, Inc.
4501 Forbes Boulevard, Suite 200, Lanham, Maryland 20706
http://www.scarecrowpress.com

10 Thornbury Road, Plymouth PL6 7PY, United Kingdom

British Library Cataloguing in Publication Information Available

Library of Congress Cataloging-in-Publication Data

Gilton, Donna L.
  Lifelong learning in public libraries : principles, programs, and people/
Donna L. Gilton.
     pages cm
  Includes bibliographical references and index.
  ISBN 978-0-8108-8356-7 (pbk.) — ISBN 978-0-8108-8357-4 (ebook)
  1. Libraries and continuing education—United States. 2. Information
literacy—Study and teaching—United States. 3. Public libraries—Aims and
objectives. 4. Libraries and education. I. Title.
  Z718.8.G55 2012
  025.5—dc23

                                                                  2011044181

Printed in the United States of America

To the memory of the public librarian who taught me, Helen Cammett, Children's Librarian, Shute Branch, Lynn, Massachusetts, Public Library, 1954–1981.

Dedicated to my mother, Hattie Franklin Gilton.

To the memory of Norman Horrocks, who mentored me in publishing.

To the memory of E. J. Josey, "The Father of Modern Black Librarianship," who promoted librarianship as a field of mission in preserving our democracy.

With appreciation to Nadine Mitchell, Director, Lynn Public Library.

Contents

1

The World of Information Literacy Instruction (ILI)

Public librarians have always instructed their patrons on the use of information, but their style is so informal, personal, indirect, and basic and so tied to guidance, it is not always recognized as instruction, either by public librarians or by their peers in academic settings. It is a thesis of this book that public librarians should teach more, but that this instruction should be on their own terms, taking their own histories, philosophies, traditions, and characteristics into account.[1]

Public libraries exist to strengthen democracy by promoting an informed citizenry. By combining their own traditions with more elements of Information Literacy Instruction (ILI), public librarians can contribute to the information enfranchisement of their patrons, further fulfilling many of their traditional goals and purposes.

This book will give an overview of the ILI field for public librarians; describe all aspects of ILI; discuss many ways that ILI can be used in public libraries; consider the history, philosophy, and traditions of public library service; establish a framework for planning instructional programs, activities, and outreach from public libraries; and describe and summarize needs of diverse users and developmental theories. It will not attempt to give detailed information on topics already well discussed elsewhere but will give brief summaries and refer readers to other sources of information.

Several articles have mentioned the need for public librarians to receive much more training on how to instruct.[2] The present situation is very similar to trends affecting academic librarians before the Association of College and Research Libraries (ACRL) created the Institute of Information Literacy (IIL). It is a goal of this book to give public librarians an overview of this complex field and to enable them to pursue goals and strategies useful to them. It is hoped that this book will act as a "portable IIL" for this group, along with a forthcoming book, *Creating and Promoting Lifelong Learning in Public Libraries: Tools and Tips for Practitioners*, which will elaborate much more on specific instructional practices. These works will not only demonstrate the wide variety of instructional activities already performed by public librarians and what makes many of these activities unique but will also show that there are many ways of viewing, designing, and evaluating instructional programs.

Information enfranchisement represents a paradigm shift. It is no longer just a goal in itself but a means to an even nobler end—an informed citizenry, which has long been a traditional aim of public librarians. Promoting information enfranchisement *for all people* strengthens our democracy, promoting social capital, social inclusiveness, and community building. This attitude will also encourage the survival of the concept of "the common good" as well as help public librarians to deal with challenges from the information industry and the private sector.[3] The research reported here will probably raise more questions than answers, encouraging the creative research and work of both library scholars and professionals.

This chapter will define and describe Information Literacy Instruction, elaborate on the history of the movement in all kinds of library settings, and mention unique aspects of public libraries and their instructional activities. Chapter 2 will illustrate current developments in public library instruction as well as the state of the literature on this topic.

WHAT IS INFORMATION LITERACY INSTRUCTION?

Information Enfranchisement = Public Libraries + Information Literacy Instruction

Most definitions of information literacy focus on the characteristics of information literate individuals. Paul Zurowski's original definition of such a person is anyone who uses a wide variety of information sources to solve work-related and other daily problems.[4] Patricia Breivik, Carol C. Kuhlthau, Hannelore Rader, Christina S. Doyle, Christine Bruce, and other experts on ILI mention many other traits of information literate people, including the ability to define their information needs, their knowledge of a variety of information sources and information-seeking techniques, patience, flexibility, attention to detail, and the use of critical thinking to evaluate materials. Michael Eisenberg and Bob Berkowitz as well as American Library Association (ALA) organizations like ACRL or the American Association of School Librarians (AASL) have set many criteria to determine who is information literate.[5] According to the ALA Presidential Committee on Information Literacy, a person knowledgeable in ILI is "an individual with the ability to recognize an information need and can locate, evaluate and use that information effectively. People who know how to learn."[6]

A definition of library instruction or user education that is very useful for public libraries is the following: "activities such as providing library tours; delivering classroom lectures, presentations, or demonstrations on information gathering skills and resources; developing and teaching credit and noncredit library courses; co-teaching or providing course integrated library instruction; developing print, media, and multimedia library instructional materials; and even creating and implementing library signage systems."[7] Other definitions of information literacy can be found in works by Barbara Humes, Robin Angeley and Jeff Purdue, Lori Arp, Shirley Behrens, Loanne Snavely and Natasha Cooper, and Joanna Burkhardt, Mary C. MacDonald, and Andree Rathmacher.[8]

Most of these goals center around the personal goals of individual users of information, but one can question whether information literacy goals should always or usually be personal. How does information literacy affect society as a whole and how should it? Can and should information literacy instruction be used to empower individuals, promote the development of society, and promote democracy? These goals are part of the standards created by AASL,[9] and they are promoted in the United Kingdom, Australia, and other countries. It is certainly an implied goal in South Africa as public libraries there have promoted ILI to support such movements as Curriculum 2005 and to help their country recover from apartheid.[10]

None of the definitions of ILI are as straightforward as they appear. Every word in the phrase "Information Literacy Instruction" can be questioned and interpreted in a number of ways. First, what is *information*? What do people really need to know to be independent learners? Not all agree, and depending upon available technology, definitions of information literacy can be very fluid.

How much do people need to know to be *literate*? Even the criteria for basic literacy (the original meaning of this word) has changed greatly over time.[11] At the turn of the twentieth century, basic literacy was defined as the ability to sign one's name. It was later defined as the ability to sound out words, and by the 1930s, the ability to write down one's own thoughts. The National Literacy Act of 1991 defines literacy as the ability to "read, write, and speak in English," to be able to solve problems well enough to function at work, and to be able "to develop one's own knowledge and potential"—a definition that is also part of information literacy.

The National Assessment of Adult Literacy now measures literacy on three scales: prose, documents, and quantitative. Prose literacy is the ability to understand everyday popular literature. Document literacy is the ability to find and use information on forms, schedules, maps, tables, and other documents. Quantitative literacy is the ability to do everyday arithmetic with bank deposit slips and other forms. With the rise of digitalization, which "blurs the lines between text, voice, video, and data," definitions of basic literacy may soon change again. In addition, most people will need to know how to read some scholarly information for both work and more personal purposes.

There are several kinds of literacies that overlap with each other and yet have their own distinctive characteristics, including reading literacy, numeracy or literacy in mathematics, media literacy, cultural literacy, computer literacy, and information literacy. How all of these literacies are determined can change over time. Public libraries promote general literacy in reading through literacy programs as well as story hours, summer reading programs, book discussion groups, family literacy programs, and other activities that promote books and reading. Public librarians promote cultural literacy through story-telling, book lists, Great Books and other book discussion groups, and current affairs groups. In addition, book discussion and current affairs groups can promote critical thinking, another major goal of information literacy.

Many public libraries now instruct adults of all ages on computer use, promoting several literacies. The basic computer instruction on parts of a computer, how to use a mouse, how to do word processing, and how to send e-mail is computer literacy. Information on how to create newsletters, how to use PowerPoint, and how to send pictures online to grandchildren is media literacy. However, when librarians teach patrons about how Internet search tools are constructed, how to search those, how to evaluate the findings, how to evaluate websites, how to navigate the library's website, how to use the databases there, and how they differ from Internet search tools, we are dealing with some serious information literacy instruction!

For public librarians, there are a number of major questions. What counts as *instruction*? How is teaching defined? Must instruction always be direct or synchronous? Synchronous instruction is done either with a live class or in an Internet chat room and is interactive. As the teacher presents information, he or she can get direct and immediate feedback from students. With asynchronous or indirect instruction, the instructor creates handbooks, bibliographies, signage, "point of use" instruction, exercises, tutorials, and other instructional materials, either in print or online, which are meant to be used by patrons later. Users usually do not have the opportunity to give instant and direct feedback to instructors. Much of the instruction that has always happened in public libraries has been asynchronous and not considered instruction.

Must instruction always happen in a class or in a group and be formal? A lot of public library instruction has been informal and "one on one" in the form of instruction at the reference desk, reader's advisory services, bibliotherapy and other bibliographic counseling, and help for independent researchers, scholars, and learners. Should and can individualized instruction count? If so, to what extent and in what ways? *Creating and Promoting Lifelong Learning in Public Libraries: Tools and Tips for Practitioners*, the companion volume to this book, will explore these and many other issues in more detail.

Another issue is the role of cultural programs in public libraries. How do these programs relate to instruction? Can and should they intersect or should they always be on parallel tracks? What is the impact of extended ILI on more traditional public library activities? Chapter 7 of this volume will discuss this issue in more detail.

Many goals of ILI tie in nicely with traditional roles of public libraries. Public libraries promote informal education designed to supplement the more formal education in schools and colleges. At their best, they also promote equality and opportunity for everyone. Many aspects of ILI can be used to help public libraries improve what they have *always* done.

However, this influence does not have to be all one way, with public librarians always borrowing from their academic counterparts. Public librarians can also contribute to the field of ILI in general through marketing instructional services to a very diverse population, using many more approaches to instruction to serve this population, outreach to diverse groups, public relations, creativity and experimentation, a sense of mission, and the idea of "information enfranchisement" as a further goal of information literacy.

School and academic librarians have followed in the footsteps of public librarians. In the 1970s, some school libraries and media centers had story hours, book talks, and other cultural programming for their students. Karen Downing, Barbara MacAdam, and Darlene P. Nichols, in their 1993 work *Reaching a Multicultural Student Community*, examined how academic librarians can apply methods pioneered by public librarians, including community analysis, networking, marketing, and public relations, to an academic setting.[12] In the early 1990s, the University of California at Santa Cruz recruited a librarian who had been doing children's work and outreach in an urban public library. A major responsibility of her new job was to do similar outreach to diverse college students in their dormitories.

More recently, some academic librarians have taken their computer laptops to student unions and other locations around campus to do basic reference and instruction at these locations, echoing school visits that public youth librarians have always made (and some public library programming like story hours in the park). Librarians at the University of Buffalo have been experimenting with "office hours" at the departments that they serve and providing reference and instructional services onsite.[13] The rest of this chapter will describe the history and development of ILI in other library settings before looking at public library history and unique aspects of public library instruction.

EARLY INSTRUCTION IN ACADEMIC LIBRARIES

Academic libraries have done by far the most extensive work in ILI. However, instruction as a general phenomenon was not widespread in these libraries until the 1970s. This section will discuss the many isolated activities that eventually led to a formal Bibliographic Instruction (BI) movement in the 1970s, how BI developed, and how ILI emerged.

Very Early Instruction

The earliest academic library instruction on record occurred in German universities in the 1700s.[14] In the late nineteenth and early twentieth centuries, a number of U.S. universities offered courses on library use that combined the history of books and libraries with basic library research strategies and the critical evaluation of materials. However, in the early twentieth century, the quantity and quality of these courses declined. Full courses on evaluating library materials changed to more shallow instruction on library research techniques. By the 1920s, any kind of library instruction was rare.[15]

Library instruction on information use would remain rare until the 1970s. Developments in 1920–1970 had been important to both the history and the future of teaching about information, but these developments had little effect on most libraries at that time. Three of the most important were the bibliographic instruction program carried out by B. Lamar Johnson, the publication of Louis Shores's article about "library colleges," and the publication of *Teaching with Books* by Harvie Branscomb.[16]

B. Lamar Johnson organized an instructional program at Stephens College, a small Missouri women's college, in 1931–1950.[17] He prefigured the bibliographic instruction movement of the 1970s and 1980s by offering orientations, instruction in the use of basic reference tools, point-of-use instruction, individualized instruction, course-related instruction, and full courses.

Louis Shores believed that libraries should be the center of colleges, that students should be educated by doing independent studies in libraries, and that the professors should be "librarian-teachers."[18] His "library college" idea would directly influence leaders and their programs in the 1960s. This concept survives in public libraries—the people's universities—as public librarians work with all varieties of independent adult learners and promote lifelong learning. Shores's ideas were very influential in the work of the founders of Bibliographic Instruction (BI). Harvey Branscomb's 1940 *Teaching with Books* offered ideas that were very similar to Shores's, but Branscomb had a slightly different approach to the roles of teachers and librarians.[19]

The Bibliographic Instruction Movement

During the 1960s, two academic library programs based on Shores's "library college" concept would be major catalysts to the development of a full-scale Bibliographic Instruction movement in the 1970s. One was the unsuccessful Monteith Experiment, led at Wayne State University by Patricia Knapp in 1960–1962, which was the most important attempt up to that time to integrate Bibliographic Instruction into a college curriculum. The program lasted only a short time because of resistance from students and faculty, but Evan Farber was inspired to try something similar at Earlham College, a small Quaker college in Indiana that is managed by administration, faculty, and student consensus. The program proved so successful there that Farber made a presentation at the American Library Association in 1969 that helped to spark the national movement for Bibliographic Instruction.[20]

The idea of Bibliographic Instruction in academic libraries was ignited by the events of the 1960s and a major generational shift in the American Library Association. Young people entering the library field during this time were less conservative than their elders and not content with the status quo. The BI movement of the 1970s was a grassroots movement led by new librarians with little or no power in their organizations. A number of young faculty with PhDs who were unable to get teaching positions or tenure also became librarians, with strong backgrounds in their original fields. They really wanted to teach. In any case, young librarians trying to start instructional programs in information use first had to convince their often skeptical bosses and administrators. Doing this would prove to be an uphill battle.[21] Joining Farber were librarians such as Hannelore Rader, Carla Stoffle, Sharon Hogan, and Miriam Drake. Another factor sparking this movement, in addition to democratization, curricular changes, and generational issues, was the increasing complexity of libraries because of technology and automation. These technological developments would definitely help to spark the birth of the BI movement, but they played a more defining role in the transition that libraries later made from BI to information literacy.

The most important events in the 1970s were the formation by the Library Orientation Exchange (LOEX) of collections and conferences, the establishment of the Instruction Section of the Association of College and Research Libraries, and establishment of the Library Instruction Round Table (LIRT) within ALA. There were many local, regional, and national workshops, conferences, papers, articles, and books. An important early title was *Educating the Library User* by John Lubans.[22]

Most academic library instruction at this time consisted of tours and orientations. When librarians discovered that these activities were not enough to really teach students how to use libraries, they started to design more detailed and formal instruction. At first, this consisted of diluted versions of the reference classes that librarians themselves took in library school. Librarians would talk to students about one source after another. In the 1980s, the instruction would take more of a pathfinder approach with an emphasis on research strategies and other conceptual frameworks. Promoting the use of search strategies enabled librarians to tie their instruction to the research goals of their users, whether that was doing a term paper, doing genealogical research, or checking out companies to invest in or to work for. Early works include Pamela Kobelski and Mary Reichel's "Conceptual Frameworks for Bibliographic Instruction" and *Learning the Library: Concepts and Methods for Effective Bibliographic Instruction* by Anne Beaubien and others.[23]

More recently, academic librarians have been using concept mapping, paper trails, and other approaches to help students plan, conduct, evaluate, and use their own research. Concept mapping is a form of brainstorming helpful to individuals and especially groups of students looking for a research topic. Paper trails are diaries expressing what students are thinking or feeling as they do their library research.

Bibliographic Instruction matured in the 1980s when instruction librarians were concerned not only with conceptual frameworks and research strategies but also with learning theories. They used all of these approaches to improve their instruction. Materials reflecting the maturation of BI at this time include *Bibliographic Instruction: The Second Generation* by Constance Mellon and *Theories of Bibliographic Education: Designs for Teaching*, edited by Cerise Oberman and Katina Strauch.[24] The periodical *Research Strategies* was started in 1983 and existed until 2005. The librarians who started BI in the late 1960s and early 1970s were now moving into middle age, management, and more influential positions at their libraries and in the professional associations. Being able to teach about information became an important qualification for reference librarians entering the profession or changing jobs.

Components of traditional BI in academic libraries included library tours and orientations; formal instruction in the form of course-related instruction, course-integrated instruction, and full courses; informal instruction for interested individuals or groups; point-of-use instruction; creation of bibliographies, pathfinders, and other guides; and public relations efforts to promote the knowledge of library use. Pathfinders (also known as tracer bullets) are mini-bibliographies on a subject. They are often organized to encourage users to use research steps and to use groups of sources in a particular order. However, the biggest event of this decade was the emergence of a related but separate information literacy movement, which would absorb Bibliographic Instruction in the 1990s.

FROM BIBLIOGRAPHIC INSTRUCTION (BI) TO INFORMATION LITERACY INSTRUCTION (ILI)

From the Modern Second Wave to the Postmodern Third Wave

In 1945–1981, the United States was gradually changing from a modern industrial society to a postmodern information-based one. By the early 1980s, Daniel Bell and Alvin Toffler would be publishing books on this phenomenon, after describing a first wave agricultural society that existed for everybody until the nineteenth century and a second wave industrial society that existed from the industrial revolution until the end of World War II.[25]

Computers were doing for and to the world what automobiles did a century before. Manufacturers were replaced by information and service companies. A new information industry that used computers as a driving force emerged. Computer users could now send and receive messages from anywhere (with connections) to anywhere (with connections) and do it twenty-four hours a day. The implications of these developments for education, library services, and teaching about information have been staggering and sometimes shattering. Everything about these fields is now rapidly changing, and the end is not in sight.

The mass society is now in decline. People watch specialized television stations and read specialized periodicals. They can design blogs and Web portals exclusively for themselves. The standardization, centralization, and hierarchy of modern, industrial, second wave society is giving way to diversity, decentralization, flattening of hierarchies, and development of managerial teams in the postmodern, information-based, third wave society.

Education at all levels has been thoroughly decentralized. The big, traditional, modern campus was mostly inhabited by full-time residential students aged 18–22. But universities and colleges today consist of students of all ages who live all over the place and may never appear on campus. With computer-assisted distance education, students in a given program can take courses from around the world, and they often do! Decentralization on the K–12 level is seen in the charter school and home schooling movements. In addition, there has been a gradual worldwide shift in teaching methods from rote learning from a teacher and textbooks to students constructing their own learning. Students would now teach themselves by taking several steps to do research and by using and analyzing multiple sources in the process. These developments led to a need for librarians to do more ILI in academic and public libraries.

Libraries have been automating and using technology like the Online Computer Library Center (OCLC) cataloging system to do traditional jobs quicker and better. They once used the OCLC databases to do interlibrary loan and to answer reference questions. Now, new technologies, like the Internet, are redesigning the nature and purpose of work. Libraries are also now competing with an aggressive information industry, and their survival is no longer assured. Everything about modern, twentieth-century librarianship is being seriously questioned and is up for grabs.

The shift from printed information to electronic information has changed collection development policies and methods, reference services, and modes of instruction. In the case of collection development, a boasting twentieth-century librarian may have said to a colleague from another library, "My collection is bigger than yours!" Now she would be more likely to say, "My library is more connected than yours!" In addition, hierarchies have been flattened in many libraries, with librarians now operating in teams. There is also a blurring of distinction between paraprofessionals and professionals and librarians and technical people.

All of these developments have led to many changes in reference services. Professionals are asking whether these are still needed and if so, in what form? In some libraries, the central "reference" or "information" desk is being replaced with tiered services, "roving reference," appointments, and other experiments. Information is much more fluid, ever changing, and available in many forms.

Both reference and instructional services are moving into the "24/7" world of the Internet. Changes in library users may be the biggest change of all. Much reference work is now done online in the form of virtual and other services, as well as in person and by telephone, and these changes have raised users' expectations. Twenty-first-century users who have always known computers may see print as old fashioned and inaccurate. Users need to be able to find information, but also to define their needs ahead of time, and evaluate and properly use their research results afterward. As a result, there has also been a shift in instruction from the onsite, book-based instruction of traditional BI to instruction in more varied settings, with an emphasis on electronic and indirect or asynchronous instruction.

The Emergence of ILI

Unlike the BI movement of the 1960s and 1970s, information literacy is a "top down" movement led by education, library, and other leaders from a wide range and variety of organizations, including accrediting agencies and state legislatures. Many of the librarians involved in information literacy either represent the second or third generation of instructors, or they were there from the beginning of the BI movement, but are now at or near the end of their careers, often as administrators and leaders in the library profession.

Several events led to the foundation of information literacy instruction. *A Nation at Risk*, published in 1983, identified the management of information in electronic and digital forms as an important skill in a "learning society" without mentioning libraries or information resources in K–12 education.[26] Several researchers from the school media field published research on this topic important to all. For example, Jacqueline Mancall, Shirley Aaron, and Sue A. Walker, members of the National Commission on Libraries and Information Science (NCLIS), contributed "Educating Students to Think," a 1986 concept paper that defined information skills. In 1987, Carol Kuhlthau published *Information Skills for an Information Society: A Review of Research.*[27]

Another contribution was *Libraries and the Search for Academic Excellence*, a 1988 report co-sponsored by Columbia University and the University of Colorado.[28] It stressed the importance of information literacy and laid the foundation for ILI in higher education. The ALA Presidential Committee on Information Literacy was established at the same time. *Information Literacy: Revolution in the Library*, by Patricia Breivik and E. Gordon Gee, was published in 1989.[29]

All of these developments precipitated the formation of the National Forum on Information Literacy (NFIL) in 1990, which includes ninety-three professional associations, including the Association of College and Research Libraries (ACRL), the National Education Association (NEA), and the American Federation of Teachers. NFIL examines the role of information in libraries; integrates information literacy into their programs; supports, initiates, and monitors information literacy programs in the United States and abroad; encourages the creation and adoption of information literacy guidelines; and works with teacher education programs to make sure new teachers incorporate information literacy into their teaching.

Another organization that has emerged as a result of the information literacy movement has been the Institute of Information Literacy (IIL), a part of ACRL. IIL was created in 1997 by Cerise Oberman, who noted articles on the subject by nonlibrarians and also noted that library science faculty and academic librarians were reluctant to embrace it as a core competency. IIL offers an immersion program for academic librarians on how to teach about information. This program has four tracks: a basic teacher track for those "interested in enhancing, refreshing, or extending their individual instruction skills," a program track for librarians interested in managing instructional programs, an assessment track for those who want to assess and improve "both classroom and program assessment," and an intentional teacher track for those who want to "become more self-aware and self-directed as teachers. The last two tracks are for librarians with five or more years of experience.[30]

CURRENT INSTRUCTION IN ACADEMIC LIBRARIES

Since the early 1970s, academic librarians have created and used standards, objectives, guidelines, learning theories, and conceptual frameworks to create a variety of instruction, which has included tours and other forms of orientation; classes in the form of course-related and course-integrated instruction and full courses; and indirect instruction in the form of electronic and printed handouts, library signage, and the use of other media. Forms of electronic instruction include PowerPoint presentations in electronic classrooms, instruction on and about the Web, video conferencing, and the use of Blackboard, Sakai, and other forms of distance education technology. All of these techniques are used to teach research processes and strategies; the use of catalogs and classification systems in libraries; Online Public Access Catalog (OPACs); periodicals and their databases; critical thinking; evaluating general research results, websites, and search engines; and ways to share information and do ethical research.

An emerging academic trend that can lead to a reorganization of instructional services, and to a reorganization of libraries, is the rise and development of information commons, which exist on two different levels. One level is an online environment where a "variety of digital services can be accessed via a single graphical user interface (GUI)." Another level is a "physical facility specifically designed to organize workspace and service delivery around the integrated environment described above."[31] An information commons may be a department, a floor in a large library, or a separate building that would enable library staff and users to learn about and use a wide variety of information technology in one space. Some information commons combine the service of traditional reference sections, media departments, instructional services, research data services, and an information desk that might act as a "nerve center" for the entire operation. Information commons revolve not around printed materials but around electronic information. They represent the first major twenty-first-century development for libraries in general and ILI in particular. Many academic libraries are reorganizing along these lines, and public librarians are also beginning to consider alternative methods of information services for the future.

INSTRUCTION IN SCHOOL MEDIA CENTERS

Historical Developments

Public school media centers gradually emerged as a national movement following World War II, the launch of *Sputnik* by the Soviet Union in 1957, and federal funding and the War on Poverty in the 1960s. There had been many earlier efforts. The first school libraries in the United States were started by private academies in New England, the Boston Latin School, and a few schools in the Midwest. Between 1830 and 1876, twenty-one states passed enabling legislation to encourage the formation of school library systems, but this was ineffective at this time.[32]

Schools in the late nineteenth century had a great increase in the number of students, a lack of qualified teachers, and poor facilities. Instruction was based largely on drills, rote learning, textbooks, and examinations. These trends discouraged the foundation of school libraries at that time, and many teachers were not inclined to encourage their students to read beyond their textbooks. Existing collections were small, poor, and unsupervised. They were often kept in locked closets or cupboards for the teachers' reference and were "seldom cataloged or publicized." Funding, which was generally inadequate, was often spent for other purposes. There were classroom collections in public elementary schools. Some private academies, on the other hand, had donated collections as large as those in small city libraries. A few public libraries, such as those in Worcester, Massachusetts, or Providence, Rhode Island, did extensive outreach with the schools.[33]

The period from roughly 1896 to 1945 was marked by the formation of several organizations, the publication of the earliest school library standards, and library activities related to schools. A number of organizations grew out of the National Council of Teachers of English (NCTE), the National Education Association (NEA), and ALA beginning in this period. In 1896, ALA created a committee on cooperating with the NEA. This committee was called the School Libraries Section and it would eventually incorporate library committees of NCTE, NEA, and ALA.[34]

In 1923, NEA created a Department of Visual Instruction (DVI). In 1945, DVI became the Department of Audio-Visual Instruction (DAVI). By 1952, DAVI was sponsoring conferences independent from NEA and by 1953 publishing its own journal. In 1971, NEA-DAVI became the Association for Educational Communications and Technologies (AECT) and was independent of NEA. This organization moved into its own building in 1977. By that time, it had nine divisions and several affiliates. AECT also has a long history of cooperation with many organizations with similar interests. From 1960 on, it would collaborate with the American Association of School Librarians (AASL) on standards.[35]

ALA had the most committees of all in the early twentieth century. They had a Roundtable of Normal and High School Librarians, which started in 1913, and a School Libraries Section, starting in 1914. Their School Libraries Committee, which had worked with NEA, merged with their School Libraries Section in 1935. The AASL would not be organized as a division until 1951.[36]

The earliest school library standards created during this time were formulated in *Standard Library Organization and Equipment for Schools of Different Sizes,* which focused on high school libraries. These standards were initially created by a committee formed by the NEA and the North Central Association of Colleges and Secondary Schools in 1918 and informally named the "Certain Standards" after Charles C. Certain, chair of this committee. The "Certain Standards" were adopted and published by ALA in 1920. These standards were very influential in the development of high school libraries at that time. Issues covered included facilities, the qualifications of librarians, collection development, instruction in library use, funding, appropriations, and state supervision.[37] During this time, many high schools worked with public libraries in their areas, and some established school library collections.

In 1925, ALA and NEA published *Report of the Joint Committee on Elementary School Library Standards,* which was probably forty years ahead of its time. According to Cheryl McCarthy, it "reflected changes in education and the need for supplementary materials." These standards promoted the collection of books for recreational reading, the integration of books with other media, and improved staffing in the form of qualified librarians and supportive district supervisors. Unlike the earlier Certain Standards, this report was not embraced by school officials. By 1940, only ten states had their own standards for elementary school libraries. These libraries would not fully develop until after World War II.[38] Elementary schools often had classroom collections.

The period 1945–1980 marks a time when public school libraries at all levels finally came into their own. It started with the 1945 publication of the first school library standards for all schools K–12 by ALA, *School Libraries for Today and Tomorrow.* According to these standards, school boards were now responsible for school libraries, which were to serve as centers for reading and literacy, information, reading guidance, and instruction.[39] These goals are very similar to those of public libraries, which would have the most influence on their school counterparts in the 1960s and 1970s, as school media *programs* were promoted. In 1951, AASL was finally created as a more autonomous and independent division within ALA that could now design its own activities.[40]

After the Soviet Union launched the first satellite, *Sputnik,* in 1957, Americans became very concerned with the state of their educational system, particularly in language and science instruction. Congress passed the National Defense Education Act (NDEA) in 1958 to enable schools to buy science, mathematics, and foreign language books as well as materials other than textbooks. School libraries were not specifically mentioned in this legislation, but they were supported indirectly.[41]

The Knapp School Libraries Project examined excellent elementary and secondary school libraries in 1963–1965. It found that school libraries that meet national standards are vital in fulfilling the educational goals of their schools. This project used demonstration programs of exemplary libraries to show the value of school media centers to teachers, administrators, professors in teacher education programs, and others.[42]

As an outgrowth to both the civil rights movement and the federal War on Poverty, Congress passed the Elementary and Secondary Education Act in 1965 and funded collection development and programming in school and public libraries. Elementary school libraries were established in places where they did not exist before. At this time, federal funding for school libraries and media centers were specifically designated and consistent. This consistency encouraged states to supplement funding and to create their own standards for school libraries. Unfortunately, the Education Consolidation and Improvement Act (ECIA) passed in 1982 ended categorical funding for school libraries, and funds were available for block grants that a variety of school personnel had to compete for. Local school systems could also determine how federal funds would be spent. These developments led to many schools being unable to keep their collections current as well as to cutbacks in state funding and support.[43]

As NEA-DAVI changed to AECT, this organization worked closely with AASL to create three other sets of standards. In 1960, AASL and NEA-DAVI created *Standards of School Library Programs*.[44] During the 1950s, when many school libraries were first developing, librarians focused on their collections and other physical aspects of their libraries. According to Barbara Stripling, the emphasis was on building solid centralized collections and on using the collection to support the curriculum.[45] School librarians were influenced by their public library counterparts in the 1960s and did a lot of programming in their libraries. In addition, the 1960 standards urged librarians to use library materials in relation to classroom materials. During this time, the standards addressed the evolution from school libraries to school library *programs* with an emphasis on using and integrating books and other media,[46] fulfilling many of the goals of the *Report of the Joint Committee on Elementary School Standards* from 1925!

In 1969, AASL and NEA-DAVI created one set of standards between them, *Standards for School Media Programs*. Libraries were now considered media centers, and librarians media specialists. These standards also put more emphasis on instruction, and especially on curricular and instructional planning with teachers.[47] In 1975, AASL and AECT published *Media Programs: District and State*, which emphasized "the need for a unified media program in each school under the direction of a media specialist and supported by a district-level supervisor." The master's degree was first mentioned as a necessary qualification at this time. Librarians were urged to participate more in curriculum development.[48]

More recent standards include *Information Power: Guidelines for School Media Programs* (1988); *Information Power: Building Partnerships for Learning* (1998); and *Empowering Learners: Guidelines for School Library Programs* (2009). The first ILI standards, "Nine Information Literacy Standards for Student Learning," are also in the 1998 version of *Information Power.*[49] "Standards for the 21st Century Learner" were initially published in print and online in 2007. The 2009 *Standards for the 21st Century Learner in Action* elaborate on these more recent ILI standards from AASL. ILI has emerged since 1980 not only as the most important thing that school media specialists do, but also as an anchor for everything else in the school media setting. (ILI standards will be described in more detail in chapter 6.)

With the rise of ILI, school media specialists have contributed to this field in several ways:

- Creating several general standards to be met by school media centers, two editions of *Information Power and Empowering Learners* as well as *The Nine Information Literacy Standards for Student Learning*, and *Standards for the 21st Century Learner* to promote information literacy to elementary, middle, and high school students.
- The extensive work on students' research strategies by Kuhlthau, as well as specific conceptual frameworks created by Kuhlthau, Michael Eisenberg and Bob Berkowitz (the Big 6 and the Super 3), Alice Yucht (FLIP/IT), and others.
- The development of Webquests and cybertours—using a series of related websites to teach students how to search for information—exemplified particularly in the work of Tom March.

Contributions and Issues

School media specialists have done just about everything that academic librarians have done but on a smaller scale, reflecting the ages of their students, the size of their school, and the level of their resources and support. Both academic and school libraries have emphasized instruction over the provision of information and guidance, especially in recent decades. Librarians in both settings emphasize giving direct, formal instruction in library and information use to groups of people in the form of classes. Academic and school librarians are all concerned with the use of standards in planning and evaluating Information Literacy Instruction; learning theories; critical thinking; conceptual frameworks or best ways to teach students to plan research strategies, especially for term papers; information literacy theory and philosophy; and teaching techniques. Librarians in both settings see a strong need to tie ILI to their local curricula, and they accomplish this with varying degrees of success.

Stripling mentions three stages in the evolution of school library programs: the source approach or the location and use of sources; the pathfinder or research strategy approach; and more recently, the process approach where the learner constructs her or his own meaning after examining a variety of evidence, such as a paper trail.[50] These stages parallel many of the instructional trends in academic libraries.

Academic and school librarians were on parallel tracks for many years without necessarily networking with each other. In 1998, members of AASL and ACRL formed a Task Force on the Educational Role of Libraries and created a Blueprint for Collaboration. There is now an AASL/ACRL Interdivisional Committee on Information Literacy to share ideas with both ALA divisions on how to teach K–20 students to be information literate. Also, since networking and cooperation between school and public youth librarians have been so important and because there are so many issues, the AASL, Association of Library Services to Children (ALSC), and Young Adult Library Services Association (YALSA) formed an Interdivisional Committee on School/Public Library Cooperation.

This cooperation is a real necessity because school media centers vary widely in quality, where they exist, for several reasons—staffing, funding, and the structure of their programs.[51] School libraries and media centers can be staffed by trained librarians, teachers, or in some cases volunteers who may or may not be trained. The initial training and certification of school media specialists can vary widely by state, and continuing education opportunities would vary as well. Funding also varies widely between school districts and over time, especially with the major changes in federal legislation and funding. It will be harder to track this with electronic resources, but until recently, one could look at printed materials in a school media center and tell how much they have been funded by local, state, and federal government, and when most of this funding occurred. The structure of programs can also make a difference. School media specialists with the freedom and flexibility to set their own schedules can interact more with teachers to plan instruction directly related to what students are learning in class. In many school systems, the type, consistency, and quality of instruction can vary by school levels. In addition, schools in wealthier areas are usually much better supported than those in poorer areas. As a result, public libraries have always been "back-up" libraries and "libraries of last resort" for the schools.

In addition, public librarians also work with charter schools, private and parochial schools, and home schoolers in addition to preschoolers and families. Charter schools tend to have particular goals and areas of focus. Private and parochial schools may not have libraries at all or they may be affected by different accreditation requirements. Home schoolers tend to be more independent scholars. (How to deal with these issues is described in more detail in chapter 8.)

INSTRUCTION IN SPECIAL LIBRARIES

Medical, Social Sciences, Humanities, and Law Libraries

Special libraries and librarians (or information specialists) have differed from all other libraries and librarians in their general focus and philosophy. While school and academic librarians have emphasized instruction, and public librarians have emphasized a combination of information, instruction, and guidance, special librarians have always emphasized a direct provision of information, not usually in the form of citations, but in the form of reports and recommendations. Much instruction that does occur in special libraries is individualized in nature. However, tracer bullets, also known as pathfinders or mini-bibliographies, were created in special libraries like the MIT libraries and the Library of Congress. Information literacy is also one professional competency among approximately a dozen of the Special Library Association's *Competencies for Special Librarians of the 21st Century.*

Medical librarians have a long history of instruction, especially for medical staff, but occasionally for patients and their families as well. Most of the bibliotherapy movement of the mid-twentieth century was started and led by medical librarians. Bibliotherapy is used to help patrons locate printed and electronic materials to help them deal with clinical or developmental issues. Examples would include recovering from depression or preparing a preschooler for the upcoming birth of a new sibling.

The Medical Library Association has a Consumer and Patient Health Information Section (CAPHS) and an Educational Media and Technologies Section (EMTS). In addition, there are a number of Patient and Family Learning Centers around the country. The one at the Massachusetts General Hospital, Boston, is especially outstanding, with a variety of ILI activities.

Ron Chepsiuk describes five more medical information literacy initiatives created by cooperating medical organizations and libraries. The Humana Foundation and Libraries for the Future created the Wellness Information Zone project. They work with the Fulton County (Atlanta, Georgia) and Houston, Texas, Public Libraries, as well as health boards and community centers in Atlanta and DeKalb County, Georgia, and Louisville, Kentucky. The University of Alabama at Birmingham started a free consumer information service, Health InfoNet, that is available statewide from Alabama's public and medical libraries. In 1998, the Health Sciences and

Human Services Library at the University of Maryland, Baltimore, started to develop consumer health websites for the public. Participating libraries are now collecting information about Maryland health care providers for their databases. The Oklahoma Department of Libraries, the Oklahoma State Library, the Spanish Language Outreach Program established by Bill and Melinda Gates, and OCLC's WebJunction have worked together to provide health information to Spanish-speaking people in Oklahoma. Central Michigan University in Mount Pleasant has developed an interactive online Research Readiness Self-Assessment (RRSA) to enable health sciences students and other members of the public to assess their level of information literacy in health.[52]

Librarians from special humanities and social sciences collections in academic and in major public libraries also instruct in information use and use other forms of outreach to attract patrons, but these efforts are not always described in detail on the Web. Some research libraries and collections, like the New York Public Library (NYPL) Humanities and Social Science Library and the University of California, Los Angeles (UCLA), Chicano Studies Research Center Library have offered formal instruction to interested groups. Other research libraries, such as NYPL's Schomberg Center for Research in Black Culture, offer programming and conferences related to their subject areas, rather than formal Information Literacy Instruction. The American Association of Law Librarians has a special interest section on Research Instruction and Patron Services (RIPS).

The Business and Corporate World

Business libraries, especially in corporations, represent a very different approach to the provision of information, in comparison to other types of libraries. In the for-profit business world, information is viewed not as something free for everyone, but as a commodity that is not for all. Companies go to great lengths to protect trade secrets, such as KFC's secret sauce or the recipe for Coca-Cola. But even within companies, only certain people may have access to certain information, and this access is often on a "need to know" basis. In the business world, information is used to solve problems and for strategic planning and is often called "corporate intelligence." For the most part, the business world is considerably more competitive than cooperative.

Like lawyers and scientists, business people often look for specific bits of information rather than for overviews that provide more context. Timeliness is vital and in some cases may be more important than accuracy. Many time-strapped managers prefer mediocre information by the deadline to superb information which comes too late to be used for urgent decisions. They also want direct information.[53]

Some business information is "proprietary" or only available to the organization producing the information. Some information is not available in published forms. Some business information is "controlled," and its use is restricted to "qualified subscribers." Most business reference sources are produced by specialized publishers. Because of the need for timeliness, most of this information has been available on a subscription basis, even before the Internet was widespread.[54]

As a result, corporate librarians do very little Information Literacy Instruction for groups, and what they do is not likely to be mentioned on their Web page, if that is publicly available. Many public and academic business collections on the Web offer electronic pathfinders as their main mode of instruction, at least on the Internet. However, one public business library, the NYPL Science, Industry, and Business Library (SIBL), has an extensive schedule of classes comparable to those in many academic libraries. The sessions emphasize business and science information on the Internet.

A library partnership between Oregon State University and the Corvallis-Benton County Library promoted extensive ILI to the business community by hiring an economic development librarian who helps business people work with both libraries. This librarian works with small businesses, does bibliographic counseling by appointment, and trains public librarians, people from the Chamber of Commerce, and others.[55]

Three new fields in the corporate business world would have a large effect on any instructional or other activities in corporate libraries or information centers. They are Knowledge Management (KM), Competitive Intelligence (CI), and Information Architecture (IA). Knowledge Management attempts to take a systematic approach to the use and management of all kinds of knowledge within a firm, both explicit, in the form of databases, company policies, and other records, and implicit, in the form of employee knowledge, skills, and experience. Knowledge managers encourage the sharing of information within companies. Corporate Intelligence promotes the ethical aspects of gathering and interpreting information on a company's competitors. Information Architecture, a field that can be especially relevant to public librarians, is concerned with the building of the corporate super websites. Experts in this field investigate ways that good information can be made more readily available to their audiences by applying the principles of architecture to the design of websites and other information systems.

The Information Architecture Institute outlines the goals of this field in their online document *The 25 Theses*. The theses are strikingly similar to many of the goals of ILI. Like ILI, IA has emerged as a direct result of the third wave and the Internet. Two of the major goals of IA are to enable people to better "communicate, collaborate, and experience one another" and to allow users to "create, manage, and share" information. *The 25 Theses* states that "all people have a right to know where they are and where they are going and how to get what they need."[56] Both IA and ILI use a variety of old and new tools to accomplish their purposes, and these tools are being created and maintained by a wide variety of people who bring their own perspectives and who "all add flavor to the stew." *The 25 Theses* establishes an excellent philosophical framework for everybody designing websites, especially to instruct or to share information, and the theses apply to other aspects of ILI as well.

KM, IA, and CI all have their own professional associations, and one can take courses through them as well as at universities. Kent State University in Ohio and Dominican University in Illinois offer degrees in Knowledge Management, and Kent State also offers a degree in Information Architecture. Johns Hopkins University offers a certificate in Corporate Intelligence.

More information and perspectives on information literacy in different kinds of libraries can be found in Teaching About Information, a website designed by Donna L. Gilton, as well as in Esther S. Grassian and Joan R. Kaplowitz's *Information Literacy Instruction: Theory and Practice*. Within ALA, the Library Instruction Round Table (LIRT) is concerned with instruction in all kinds of libraries. The members meet at every ALA meeting, have a website, and publish a newsletter.[57]

ILI AS A DEPARTMENT STORE: COMPONENTS OF INSTRUCTION

Information Literacy Instruction is a system like a department store, with multiple components.[58] The ILI department store has windows of bibliographies, pathfinders, point-of-use instruction, and other indirect, asynchronous instruction in both print and electronic forms. The building design and its signage is also a part of the instructional program (and the only part that most people ever see). These principles also apply to using Information Architecture to design good websites.

The ILI basement and first floor consist of tours, orientations, and basic computer instruction on using the mouse, word processing, e-mail, and computer systems like Microsoft Office. The second floor offers more advanced and specific instruction to help people with research. This instruction is similar to much of what is presented in college and school libraries. The third floor is structured for administration and support. This as an integrated system, and all levels of instruction are important. In designing instructional programs, librarians choose from a variety of these components, which support each other. (Later chapters in this book will discuss wide choices in goals, learning theories, and teaching and evaluation techniques that can also help.)

INFORMATION ENFRANCHISEMENT AND THE THREE-LEGGED STOOL OF REFERENCE SERVICES

Multiple Roles of Public Libraries

In 1876, Samuel Swett Green, who was then the director of the Worcester (Massachusetts) Public Library, published an article in one of the first issues of *American Library Journal* (now *Library Journal*) entitled "Personal Relations between Librarians and Readers."[59] He proposed the creation of a new library service to provide information to business people, to instruct students on library use, and to guide people in their recreational reading. His concept of providing information, instruction, and guidance is referred to as "the three-legged stool" of reference services.

In the twentieth century, special libraries emerged as information centers. School media centers and academic libraries emerged as both information and educational centers. Only public libraries serve as free community information, educational, and cultural centers by providing information, instruction, and guidance. Evidence of this triple approach can be seen in the goals of many individual public libraries, in their planning documents, in the roles of public libraries cited by S. Randle England and other authors, and internationally in the *IFLA/UNESCO Public Library Manifesto*.

Major public libraries that mention their informational, cultural, and educational purposes on their websites include Boston, Detroit, Enoch Pratt in Baltimore, Houston, Miami-Dade, Milwaukee, and Queens. Sandra Nelson's *Strategic Planning for Results* has chapters on planning informational services and cultural awareness activities as well as chapters devoted to several aspects of lifelong learning, including public Internet access; early literacy; adult, teen, and family literacy; homework help; and information fluency, an aspect of ILI that promotes computer use.[60]

England cites informational, cultural, and educational roles of public libraries mentioned by others. As information centers, public libraries serve as gateways to government information and as "the people's research and development department." As cultural centers, they "give institutional form to our collective memory." As educational centers, public libraries support independent scholars and teachers, self-directed learners, public education, family literacy, and lifelong learning.[61]

The *IFLA/UNESCO Public Library Manifesto* "proclaims UNESCO's belief in the public library as a living force for education, culture, and information" and lists their specific educational, cultural, and information missions.[62] The educational missions include the following:

- Creating and strengthening reading habits in children from an early age.
- Supporting both individual and self conducted education as well as formal education at all levels.

- Providing opportunities for personal creative development.
- Facilitating the development of information and computer literacy skills.
- Supporting and participating in literacy activities and programs for all age groups, and initiating such activities if necessary.

Their cultural goals include the following:

- Stimulating the imagination and creativity of children and young people.
- Promoting awareness of cultural heritage, appreciation of the arts, scientific achievements and innovations.
- Providing access to cultural expressions of all performing arts.
- Fostering inter-cultural dialogue and favoring cultural diversity.

Their informational goals include the following:

- Supporting the oral tradition.
- Ensuring access for citizens to all sorts of community information.
- Providing adequate information services to local enterprises, associations, and interest groups.

School and college libraries are part of *formal* education, and schools are mandatory. Public libraries promote nonformal, voluntary, and supplementary education in the form of cultural programming, and they encourage the lifelong learning and independent study of its users through reference, reader's advisory, and other services. The role of public libraries in promoting several kinds of literacy has already been mentioned.

The Original Information Commons

If school and college libraries are the heart of their respective institutions, public libraries are the heart of their communities. They are still important and vital as one of the few places where all are welcome and all can gather. Public libraries' role as America's "front porch," "public square," and cultural meeting place is vital.[63] No other type of library serves quite this role. Public libraries not only welcome a broader and less well-defined audience than any other libraries, but they are also trusted to network with a variety of community agencies and organizations.

Candy Hillenbrand affirms the role of public libraries as community gathering places by mentioning the U.S. idea of public libraries as a "commons," and Hugh Mackay views public libraries as the new "village green."[64] The idea of public libraries as a "commons" is provocative for two reasons. In colonial New England, the "commons" was where everybody in town grazed their livestock. "Commons" still survive in many New England towns and cities to this day as parks and gathering places—the Boston Commons and Public Gardens being one of the most famous examples. Academic libraries and a few public libraries are now experimenting with "information commons," places where library users can gather to learn about the latest computer technologies and information search techniques. However, one can say that public libraries were our first "information commons," and some, like my hometown library, are located close to town squares, village greens, or "commons."

Hillenbrand also discusses how public libraries promote social capital, social inclusion, and community building. She cites Francois Matarasso and other experts, maintaining that public libraries should serve not only the educational but other social needs of their communities, including information on "information technology, employment, families, poverty, health, community development, promoting partnerships, democracy, and local culture." The goals of information enfranchisement would encompass all of these other goals.

Expanding on both social capital and information enfranchisement is the idea of public libraries as "third places" where people can go when they are not at home or at work. This is based on the work of Ray Oldenburg, who described "how cafes, coffee shops, bookstores, bars, hair salons, and other hangouts" promote community. People go to these places for companionship and lively conversations. Researchers like Cathryn Harris have also argued for public libraries as "third places" that can build community and promote social capital. Libraries promote social capital and information enfranchisement by providing Internet and information technology access, providing instruction to help patrons use these resources, providing other programs that promote lifelong learning and general literacy, and building connections between individuals, groups, and governments. Libraries have also been influenced by bookstores that provide cafes which also promote a lot of social capital as people meet and converse with each other.[65]

Unique Aspects of Public Library Instruction

Compared to ILI in academic libraries, public library instruction is more informal, personal, indirect, basic, and collaborative and often combined with forms of guidance. While there is overlap between instruction in public and academic libraries, no one should expect public library instruction to look just like academic instruction. Public librarians do many of the instructional activities of their school and college counterparts, but they also do a variety of instructional and other activities that nobody else does. All of these trends should be taken into account in planning instruction for individual public libraries or in creating standards for public library instruction in general.

Public Libraries as Ultimate Libraries

Not only were public libraries the *original* information commons, but they have served as "people's universities," as well as de facto school and college libraries. The public libraries of Cleveland and Atlanta/Fulton County refer to themselves as "people's universities," and NYPL has used the term "everybody's university." Several major public libraries mention lifelong learning on their websites, and others stress their informational, cultural, and educational goals.

Some public libraries have also served as de facto academic libraries under particular circumstances. For example, some of the first major public libraries, such as those in Boston, New York, and Cleveland, built extensive research collections that have been used by college students, professors, independent scholars, and others. As an undergraduate, I supplemented my excellent college library with the research collections at the Boston Public Library, which was established fifty years before my college was founded.

While some college students with information anxiety may stay away from all libraries or try to do all of their research on the Web, others try to do their academic research in local public libraries. These trends are particularly noticeable in small college towns. There are also now distance education students taking college courses online who depend on their local public libraries for their research. This necessitates interlibrary cooperation and instruction in all types of libraries.

Some public libraries cooperate with universities and other organizations to offer courses and sometimes degrees to students. In the late 1980s, public libraries in Oklahoma worked with the Oklahoma State Regents for Higher Education to promote continuing higher education for "everyone, everywhere, every day in Oklahoma." In 1994, the Palm Springs Public Library in California was offering long-distance learning programs to enable students to earn master's degrees in several fields. In 1999, Liverpool City Library in Australia was cooperating with the University of the Third Age to offer courses to people aged fifty and over that were tailored to their needs. In 2001, the Tower Hamlets Library System in East London replaced several of their traditional branches with "Idea Stores." Among their goals was to offer credit and non-credit courses, to "serve as feeders for area colleges" and vocational schools, and to develop a closer working relationship with teachers in the area.[66]

INSTRUCTION IN PUBLIC LIBRARIES: HISTORY AND BACKGROUND

Early Public Libraries and Their Activities

The first tax-supported public libraries in the United States were created in Peterborough, New Hampshire, in 1833 and in Boston, Massachusetts, in 1852 and were used as agents of self-improvement and social control.[67] The wealthy and upper-middle-class founders believed that public libraries would morally uplift the community, encourage self-improvement, and discourage social problems, such as drinking in taverns.

Public libraries were started in the nineteenth century for many of the same reasons that information literacy emerged in the late twentieth century. Some people viewed mass-produced books as a threat to moral standards, to the social order, and to classical Western learning and thought.[68] This view would be similar to the way that others would perceive the Internet at the turn of the twenty-first century.

Nineteenth-century public librarians did not formally instruct groups of students in information use, but they did several other things that were very important. Samuel Swett Green, the library director who created the concept of the "three-legged stool" of reference services, was one of the first librarians to visit schools, share public library books with them, and create reading lists that encouraged students to read classic literature from the library. He met with three educators—the superintendent of the Worcester Public Schools, a school board member who was also a library trustee, and the principal of the normal school (now Worcester State University). Then Green personally visited schools, taking illustrated travel books with him. He offered two library cards to teachers—one for their personal use and another for their classes. The results were spectacular. The public library became an important adjunct to the Worcester school system, adding history and geography to their curriculum. The library distributed reading lists to teachers and students and set aside a room just for teachers and their students that was also used for class visits to the library. Green oriented new teachers to the library, and as a result of his activities, students at the normal school also learned to incorporate the use of library books into their teaching.[69]

Other pioneers in this area were William Eaton Foster of the Providence, Public Library, Rhode Island, and Charles Francis Adams of Quincy, Massachusetts. Foster delivered public library books to the schools and met mainly with school principals and administrators who selected books to be read by students. Like Green, he distributed annotated book lists and set aside a room at the public library for student use. Adams, a school board member and a library trustee, encouraged teachers in the Quincy public schools to get library cards. His activities were part of the extensive educational innovation happening there at that time.

A number of scholars in the late nineteenth century were protesting the system of rote learning in most schools at that time, and the activities of Green, Foster, and Adams were very much in tune with this movement for change. Herbert Spencer, G. Stanley Hall, and William James criticized nineteenth-century education for not promoting or encouraging self-education or lifelong learning and for "disgusting students with books, reading, and learning." They maintained that education should be interesting, practical, relevant, and as pleasant as possible for students.[70]

This philosophy was further promoted and implemented by Johann Heinrich Pestalozzi and Johann Friedrich Herbart. Pestalozzi maintained that learning should consist not just of "the gathering of facts, but the employment of these facts to solve practical problems." In this regard, he foreshadowed many of the philosophical foundations of ILI by a century. Herbart was more interested in teaching about morals and believed that knowledge should be organized around history and literature. He also maintained that education should spark the interest of learners. In 1861, Edward Sheldon established a teachers college in Oswego, New York, that was designed to apply these philosophies. Teachers trained there were able to teach without depending on textbooks.[71] By the turn of the twentieth century, public librarians around the country were following the lead of Green, Foster, and Adams.

Library Instruction in Public Libraries: Twentieth-Century Developments

Twentieth-century public youth librarians have continued the work of Green, Foster, and Adams by visiting classes, extending outreach to teachers and students, creating or using book lists, hosting class visits to the library, and in some cases creating rooms especially for teachers and students. Public librarians have also done more formal instruction in cases where there were no school librarians, but this activity has been poorly documented.

Public librarians do not generally do a lot of publishing, and this was especially true in the past. However, a more important reason for the absence of documentation is that although public librarians have always instructed, their teaching was called everything but instruction. They would report any instruction they did as programming, outreach, school visits, or class visits to the library. For instance, class visits to the library could have included a browsing session for teachers and students, a story hour, a book talk, a basic orientation, a tour, or more extensive and intensive instruction to help students prepare for their assignments. It is not always easy to tell from reports how much more formal instruction went on. In addition, public librarians have long instructed through the creation of bibliographies, reading lists, and occasionally handbooks but have not viewed these materials as part of instruction. Poor record keeping about these activities by some library systems has not helped this situation.

If public librarians did not recognize their own instruction, neither did their peers working in other kinds of libraries. Most traditional public library instruction has always differed greatly from that found elsewhere. Public library instruction has been characterized as the following:

- Informal and individual (or one on one).
- Combined with guidance, such as reader's advisory services or bibliotherapy.
- Asynchronous or indirect, including handbooks, pathfinders, mini-bibliographies, building design, signage, and more recently websites and other electronic information.
- Very basic for the most part, with the emphasis on tours in a variety of forms; handbook information on library services, policies, and hours; information on catalog use; and very basic computer information, when offered.
- More collaborative. Public libraries often need to work with schools and other organizations to design effective instruction on doing research.

Historically, in addition to tours, orientations, reading lists, and outreach to students, public librarians have done more formal, advanced instruction upon request where school libraries were poor or nonexistent. A recent example is "the reflective learning environment," a cooperative venture between the Otterup public library and the Norafyns Gymnasium (secondary school) in Denmark described by Annette Skov. A public librarian spends twenty-seven hours a week instructing teachers and students in information use, and students are encouraged to reflect on their use of information. The public library provides databases, and students are trained to use these.[72] This instruction is one good approach for areas with no school media centers.

This program reminds me of several experiences from my own past. In 1960–1962, when I was in grades 4–6, I participated in a formal and established cooperative program between my school and the local public library. It was mainly a reading program taking place during the school year in which students were encouraged to read and to do book reports on at least ten books from the public library. Teachers would grade and keep track of these reports, sometimes using a chart that the whole class could see. At the end of the year, there would be a school assembly where students who fulfilled this requirement received a certificate and a wooden pin of a bookworm. We had no school libraries at the elementary level at that time, and Helen Cammett, the children's librarian at my local branch library, instructed all of the fourth graders in my area on the difference between fiction and nonfiction, the Dewey decimal system, and how to use the card catalog to locate books on the shelf. This was the first and almost the only library instruction I ever received. This program was happening at the same time as the academic Monteith Experiment at Wayne State University in Detroit.

In the 1970s, while academic librarians were beginning to do library orientations and "one-shot" bibliographic instruction, I started my career in library instruction as a children's librarian at the Boston Public Library. At that time, the youth librarians did school visits and programming and created mini-bibliographies and reading lists for children and young people. Librarians at the central library often did class tours of the library building.

While working at two inner-city branches, I was invited by teachers in the neighborhood to instruct their classes on information use. In one instance, I taught eighth graders how to find books in both the children's room and the adult section of a very small branch. In another case, I taught third graders from the parochial school next door how to find books using both the Dewey and Library of Congress classification systems. This instruction was conducted under the most primitive of conditions. The children's room was an old reconverted swimming pool in the basement of the library with a collection on two levels. The entire instructional session took place in the bottom of the pool. The technology used included blank sheets of typing paper, black magic markers, and the children, themselves. After the children learned about types of catalog cards, the elements of a cataloging record, and how to use tracings, they stood in a line and held up pieces of paper with first Dewey, then LC numbers on them. Other students put their classmates in first Dewey, then LC order. Then all of the students looked up titles in the catalog and found them on the shelves. Evaluation of these sessions was equally primitive. The students used the children's room to complete their assignments, and their teacher voluntarily expressed her pleasure with the sessions. After doing these presentations, I reported all of this instruction to my supervisors either as programming, along with my story hours, or as class visits to the library.

Needless to say, none of these activities appeared in the library literature or showed up in any surveys of public libraries occurring at that time. This point raises the question of whether other public librarians did this either officially, like Cammett, or in a more ad hoc manner, as I did it. Another question is how often public library instruction occurred. I believe that this activity was rare at that time, but that it did occur and that it has been underreported. However, a few descriptions of early formal public library instruction can be found in the library literature.

Dayton-Montgomery County held an instruction seminar in three sessions on using the library catalog, periodical indexes, basic reference tools, and how to approach library research problems. The Enoch Pratt Free Library designed a fifteen-page booklet that was used by tour leaders. The Tulsa City-County Library created orientation slide shows for adults and teenagers and instructed business people, as requested. The Malaga Cove

Plaza Library, in California, organized library orientations for mothers of preschoolers who participated in story hours. These orientations evolved into lectures, book talks, and other activities organized by members of the public.[73]

Leaders during this time were the Detroit Public Library and the Denver Public Library. In Detroit, Friends of the Library gave information tours to the public, which were advertised on bookmarks. Librarians gave brief instructional talks at area schools and specialized orientations for genealogists.[74]

Most important was the extensive instructional work of the Denver Public Library, which was comparable to the early academic instruction at Stephens College and Earlham College. In 1968, Denver had a library handbook, *How to Use the Library: A Guide to Denver Public Library*. Librarians there did basic instruction in catalog use and other subjects, did a workshop series on library use, instructed Spanish-speaking patrons who were in English as a Second Language (ESL) and literacy programs, conducted tours and other activities for specialized groups, and created "On Your Own," a series of different activities to promote various forms of independent learning. The workshop series consisted of four or five sessions that included an overview of library services, information on using the card catalog, a session on popular reference books, a tour of the library, and follow-up evaluation. This series was so popular that it was repeated many times.[75] All of this was occurring in 1968, the year before Evan Farber did his presentation at ALA and sparked a national BI movement in academic libraries.

Descriptions of other early public library instruction in Virginia Beach, Virginia, Ramsey, New Jersey, Oakland, California, Kitchener, Ontario (Canada), and Sheffield, England, can also be found in John Lubans's *Educating the Public Library User*.[76] More recent trends include electronic instruction with the rise of the Internet and the Internet Public Library and much activity around the world, especially in Scandinavian and English-speaking countries with long public library traditions, as well as in some developing countries. The next chapter will describe these and other contemporary trends in public library instruction.

NOTES

    1. Donna L. Gilton, "Information Literacy as a Department Store: Applications for Public Teen Librarians," *Young Adult Library Services* 6, no. 2 (2007): 39.

    2. Theresa Jehlik, "Information Literacy in the Public Library," *Nebraska Library Association Quarterly* 35, no. 4 (2004): 9–13; Alisa Koning, "Information Literacy in New Zealand Public Libraries," *Aplis* 14, no. 4 (2001): 159–63; Genevieve Hart, "Public Libraries and Information Literacy Education: Views from Mpumalanga Province," *South African Journal of Library and Information Science* 72, no. 3 (2006): 174.

3. Amy Brunvand, "The Information Commons: Librarians vs. Libertarians," *American Libraries* 32, no. 4 (2001): 42–43.

4. Paul Zurowski, *The Information Service Environment: Relationship and Priorities* (Washington, D.C.: National Commission on Libraries and Information Sciences, 1974).

5. Esther S. Grassian and Joan R. Kaplowitz, *Information Literacy Instruction: Theory and Practice*, 2nd ed. (New York: Neal-Schuman, 2009), 3–6.

6. American Library Association (ALA), Presidential Commission on Information Literacy, *Final Report* (Chicago: ALA, 1989).

7. H. Sager, "Implications for Bibliographic Instruction," in *The Impact of Emerging Technologies on Reference Service and Bibliographic Instruction*, ed. G. Pitkin (Westport, Conn.: Greenwood, 1995), 51.

8. Barbara Humes, *Understanding Information Literacy* (Washington, D.C.: National Institute on Postsecondary Education, Libraries, and Lifelong Learning, 1999), www.libraryinstruction.com/infolit.html; Robin Angeley and Jeff Purdue, "Information Literacy: An Overview," http://pandora.cii.wwu.edu/dialogue/issue6 .html; Lori Arp, "Information Literacy or Bibliographic Instruction: Semantics of Philosophy?" *RQ* 30, no. 1 (1990): 46–49; Shirley J. Behrens, "A Conceptual Analysis and Historical Overview of Information Literacy," *College and Research Libraries* 55 (July 1994): 309–22; Loanne Snavely and Natasha Cooper, "The Information Literacy Debate," *Journal of Academic Librarianship* 23 (January 1997): 9–14.

9. American Association of School Librarians (AASL) and Association for Educational Communications and Technology (AECT), "Information Literacy Standards for Student Learning," in *Information Power: Building Partnerships for Learning* (Chicago: ALS/AASL, 1998), 8–44; AASL and AECT, *Standards for the 21st-Century Learner*, www.ala.org.

10. Genevieve Hart, "Public Libraries in South Africa: Agents or Victims of Educational Change?" *South African Journal of Library and Information Science* 70, no. 2 (2004): 110–20; Hart, "Public Librarians and Information Literacy Education," 172–84.

11. En Gauge, "21st-Century Skills: Literacy in the Digital Age," www.grrec.ky .gov/SLC_grant/Engauge21st_Century_Skills.pdf.

12. Karen E. Downing, Barbara MacAdam, and Darlene P. Nichols, *Reaching a Multicultural Student Community: A Handbook for Academic Librarians* (Westport, Conn.: Greenwood, 1993).

13. A. Ben Wagner and Cynthia Tysick, "Onsite Reference and Instruction Services: Setting Up Shop Where Our Patrons Live," *Reference and User Services Quarterly* 46, no. 4 (2007): 60–65.

14. Gisela Ewert, "The Beginnings of Instruction in Library Use: Selected German Examples from the 17th to 19th Centuries," *Research Strategies* 4 (Fall 1986): 177–84.

15. Mary F. Salony, "The History of Bibliographic Instruction: Changing Trends from Books to the Electronic World," *Reference Librarian* 24, nos. 51–52 (1995): 33–36; Larry Hardesty and John Mark Tucker, "An Uncertain Crusade: The History of Library Use Instruction in a Changing Educational Environment," in *Academic Librarianship: Past, Present and Future*, ed. John Richardson Jr. and Jinnie Y. Davis (Englewood, Colo.: Libraries Unlimited, 1989): 99–102; Frances L. Hopkins, "A Century of Bibliographic Instruction: The Historical Claim to Professional and

Academic Legitimacy," *College and Research Libraries* 43, no. 3 (1982): 193–94; Michael Lorenzin, "A Brief History of Library Instruction in the United States of America," www.libraryinstruction.com/lihistory.html.

16. Salony, "The History of Bibliographic Instruction," 36–39; Hopkins, "A Century of Bibliographic Instruction," 194; Lorenzin, "A Brief History of Library Instruction in the United States of America."

17. B. Lamar Johnson, *Vitalizing the College Library* (Chicago: ALA, 1939).

18. Louis Shores, "The Library Arts College, A Possibility in 1954?" *School and Society* 41 (January 26, 1935): 110–14.

19. Harvey Branscomb, *Teaching with Books: A Study of College* (Chicago: ALA, 1940).

20. Salony, "The History of Bibliographic Instruction," 40–42; Hopkins, "A Century of Bibliographic Instruction," 195–96; Lorenzin, "A Brief History of Library Instruction in the United States of America"; Hardesty and Tucker, "An Uncertain Crusade," 104–5.

21. Hardesty and Tucker, "An Uncertain Crusade," 104–5.

22. John Lubans, *Educating the Library User* (New York: Bowker, 1974); Salony, "The History of Bibliographic Instruction," 42–43; Hardesty and Tucker, "An Uncertain Crusade," 164–65.

23. Pamela Kobelski and Mary Reichel, "Conceptual Frameworks for Bibliographic Instruction," *Journal of Academic Librarianship* 7, no. 2 (1981): 73–77; Anne K. Beaubien et al., *Learning the Library: Concepts and Methods for Effective Bibliographic Instruction* (New York: Bowker, 1982).

24. Constance A. Mellon, *Bibliographic Instruction: The Second Generation* (Littleton, Colo.: Libraries Unlimited, 1987); Cerise Oberman and Katina Strauch, eds., *Theories of Bibliographic Education: Designs for Teaching* (New York: Bowker, 1982).

25. Daniel Bell, *The Coming of the Post-Industrial Society* (New York: Basic Books, 1999); Alvin Toffler, *The Third Wave* (New York: Bantam, 1981).

26. National Commission on Excellence in Education, *A Nation at Risk: The Imperative for Educational Reform* (Washington, D.C.: U.S. Department of Education, 1983).

27. Jacqueline Mancall, Shirley Aaron, and Sue A. Walker, "Educating Students to Think," *School Library Media Quarterly* 15, no. 1 (1986): 18–27; Carol Kuhlthau, *Information Skills for an Information Society: A Review of Research* (Syracuse, New York: ERIC, 1987), ED 297 740.

28. Patricia Senn Brievik and Robert Wedgeworth, eds., *Libraries and the Search for Academic Excellence* (Metuchen, N.J.: Scarecrow, 1988).

29. Patricia Breivik and E. Gordon Gee, *Information Literacy: Revolution in the Library* (New York: American Council on Education/Macmillan, 1989).

30. ACRL, Institute for Information Literacy, *Immersion '10 Program*, www.ala.org.

31. Donald Beagle, "Conceptualizing an Information Common," *Journal of Academic Librarianship* 25, no. 2 (1999): 82–89; Russell Bailey and Barbara Tierney, "Information Commons Redux: Concept, Evolution, and Transcending the Tragedy of the Commons," *Journal of Academic Librarianship* 28, no. 5 (2002): 277, 286; Andrew Richard Albanese, "Campus Library 2.0: The Information Commons Is a Scalable, One-Stop Shopping Experience for Students and Faculty," *Library Journal* 129 (April 15, 2004): 30–33; Alison Cowgill, Joan Beam, and Lindsay Wess, "Imple-

menting an Information Commons in a University Library," *Journal of Academic Librarianship* 27, no. 6 (2001): 432–39.

32. Cheryl McCarthy, "Progress in School Library Media: Where Have We Been? Where Are We Now? And Where Are We Going? *Advances in Librarianship* 30 (2006): 271, 273–75; Dee Garrison, *Apostles of Culture: The Public Librarian and American Society, 1876–1920* (New York: Macmillan, Free Press, 1979), 53.

33. McCarthy, "Progress in School Library Media," 273–75; Garrison, *Apostles of Culture*, 53.

34. Patricia Pond, "Development of a Professional School Library Association: American Association of School Librarians," *School Media Quarterly* 5, no. 1 (1976); American Association of School Librarians, "AASL History: 1914–1951," www.ala.org.

35. Association for Educational Communications and Technology (AECT), "Association for Educational Communications and Technology in the Twentieth Century: A Brief History," www.aect.org.

36. Pond, "Development of a Professional Library Association."

37. McCarthy, "Progress in School Library Media Programs," 279.

38. McCarthy, "Progress in School Library Media Programs," 279–80.

39. McCarthy, "Progress in School Library Media Programs," 280–81.

40. McCarthy, "Progress in School Library Media Programs," 281; Pond, "Development of Professional Library Associations."

41. McCarthy, "Progress in School Library Media Programs," 278–79.

42. McCarthy, "Progress in School Library Media Programs," 282–83.

43. McCarthy, "Progress in School Library Media Programs," 281–82.

44. McCarthy, "Progress in School Library Media Programs," 282.

45. Barbara Stripling, "Quality in School Library Media Programs: Focus on Learning," *Library Trends* 44, no. 3 (1996): 631–56.

46. McCarthy, "Progress in School Library Media Programs," 282.

47. McCarthy, "Progress in School Library Media Programs," 284.

48. McCarthy, "Progress in School Library Media Programs," 284.

49. McCarthy, "Progress in School Library Media Programs," 285–89; AASL, *Empowering Learners: Guidelines for School Library Programs* (Chicago: ALA, 2009); AASL, "Standards for the 21st-Century Learner," www.ala.org; AASL, *Standards for the 21st Century Learner* (Chicago: ALA, 2009).

50. Stripling, "Quality in School Library Media Programs," 631–56.

51. Gilton, "Information Literacy as a Department Store," 41.

52. Ron Chepsiuk, "Prognosis Literacy," *American Libraries* 38, no. 11 (2007): 54–56; *Wellness Information Zone*, www.wellzone.org; *Health Infonet of Alabama*, http://healthinfonet.org; University of Maryland, Baltimore, Health Sciences and Human Services Library, "Consumer Health," http://guides.hshsl.umaryland.edu/consumerhealth.

53. Michael Lavin, *Business Information: How to Use It, How to Find It* (Phoenix, Ariz.: Oryx, 1992): 1–2.

54. Lavin, *Business Information*, 3–5.

55. John Berry, "The Valley Library," *Library Journal* 124 (June 15, 1999): 38–41.

56. Information Architecture Institute, *The 25 Theses*, http://iainstitute.org.

57. Donna L. Gilton, "Instruction in Different Types of Libraries," Teaching About Information, www.uri.edu; Grassian and Kaplowitz, *Information Literacy*

Instruction, 337–63; ALA, Library Instruction Round Table (LIRT), http://fleetwood
.baylor.edu/lirt/.

58. Gilton, "Information Literacy as a Department Store," 40.

59. Samuel Swett Green, "Personal Relations Between Librarians and Readers,"
American Library Journal 1 (October 1876): 74–81.

60. Sandra Nelson, *Strategic Planning for Results* (Chicago: ALA, 2008).

61. S. Randle England, "The Consequences of Promoting an Educational Role for
Today's Public Libraries," *Public Libraries* 46, no. 2 (2007): 55–56.

62. *IFLA/UNESCO Public Library Manifesto*, 1994, http://archive.ifla.org/VII/s8/
unesco/eng.htm.

63. England, "The Consequences of Promoting an Educational Role for Today's
Public Libraries," 56.

64. Candy Hillenbrand, "Public Libraries as Developers of Social Capital," *Aplis*
18, no. 1 (2005): 4–12.

65. Ray Oldenburg, *The Great Good Place* (New York: Marlowe, 1999); Oldenburg, *Celebrating the Third Place: Inspiring Stories About the "Great Good Places" at the
Heart of Our Communities* (New York: Da Capo, 2002); Cathryn Harris, "Libraries
with Lattes: The New Third Place," *Aplis* 20, no. 4 (2007): 145–52.

66. Sylvia G. Faibisoff and Deborah J. Willis, "Public Library Adult Learning
Center Renewal," *Public Library Quarterly* 9, no. 2 (1989): 41–42; Evan St. Lifer
and Michael Rogers, "Library Offers Master's Degrees: Palm Springs Long-Distance
Learning Benefits Students and Library," *Library Journal* 119 (September 15, 1994):
16–17; Jennifer Burrell, "Now the Hard Part: End User Education," *Aplis* 12, no. 3
(1999): 105–13; Thomas Patterson, "'Idea Stores': London's New Libraries," *Library
Journal* 126 (May 1, 2001): 48–49.

67. England, "The Consequences of Promoting an Educational Role for Today's
Public Libraries," 56–58; Linda Crismond, "Reinventing Libraries: Responding to
the Forces of Change," in *Reinvention of the Public Library for the 21st Century*, ed.
William L. Whiteside Sr. (Englewood, Colo.: Libraries Unlimited, 1998); Garrison,
Apostles of Culture, 36–50.

68. England, "The Consequences of Promoting an Educational Role for Today's
Public Libraries," 56; Thomas Augst, "American Libraries and Agencies of Culture,"
American Studies 42, no. 3 (2001): 12.

69. Garrison, *Apostles of Culture*, 55–56.

70. Garrison, *Apostles of Culture*, 51–52.

71. Garrison, *Apostles of Culture*, 52–54.

72. Annette Skov, "Information Literacy and the Role of Public Libraries," *Scandinavian Public Library Quarterly* 37, no. 3 (2004): 4–7.

73. Ruth T. Newman, "Instructing the Out-of-School Adult in Public Library
Use," in *Educating the Public Library User*, ed. John Lubans Jr. (New York: Bowker,
1974): 62–63.

74. Newman, "Instructing the Out-of-School Adult in Public Library Use," 62.

75. Newman, "Instructing the Out-of-School Adult in Public Library Use," 63–67.

76. John Lubans, ed., *Educating the Public Library User* (Chicago: ALA, 1983),
87–137.

2

Current Developments in Public Library Instruction

This chapter discusses current forms of public library instruction in the United States as well as developments abroad. It also considers the state of the literature on this topic.

FORMS OF PUBLIC LIBRARY INSTRUCTION

Experts in both ILI and public library history can debate whether public librarians instructed their patrons on information use in the past, how they did this, and how often this occurred. However, because of the third wave information revolution and the rise of the Internet, if public librarians did not instruct their patrons before, they are certainly doing it now. This instruction takes many forms:

- Outreach to teachers, parents, scholars, business people, people in institutions, unemployed people, and other groups.
- Instruction in combination with other programming and activities, such as literacy and book discussion groups.
- Information and referral services connecting people to local organizations and agencies.
- Networking with schools, institutions, and organizations.
- Reader's advisory and other services to independent and lifelong learners.
- Indirect, asynchronous instruction.
- Promotion of new technologies to the public, including computer and Internet instruction to elders and other adults.

- Electronic networking with other organizations, businesses, and especially the government to connect people to technology.

Community Outreach

Public librarians incorporate ILI activities as they reach out to diverse groups. The Multnomah County Public Library in Oregon and Providence Public Library in Rhode Island have offered extensive outreach to teachers, and Providence does outreach to parents as well. The Library of Congress has information on its website and sessions at the library instructing scholars on how to make the best use of the library's resources. The Humanities and Social Science Library of the New York Public Library (NYPL) provides instruction at the Celeste Bartos Education Center by offering classes on many subjects.

The gold standard for public library instruction to the business community is offered by the Science, Industry, and Business Library (SIBL) at NYPL. This library places tours and other orientation information on their website and offers an extensive list of classes or sessions on basic library skills, business and industry information, government information, the Internet and the World Wide Web, research skills, and science and technology information. Business and sci/tech sessions include business basics, advertising research, finding company and industry information, introduction to trademarks in business, introduction to science information, engineering research, food science, patents, and emerging technologies in science and industry.

While SIBL represents the epitome of public library ILI in business and a major source of inspiration to other librarians, activities at the Pikes Peak Library District in Colorado and at the Downtown and Business Branch of the Carnegie Library of Pittsburgh may reflect more typical activities that can be fairly easily replicated elsewhere. Terry Zarsky at the Pikes Peak Library District in Colorado Springs, Colorado, started his outreach to the business community by joining and being active in several local business organizations, such as the local Chamber of Commerce and the Small Business Development Center.[1] After establishing credibility with the business community, he conducted research by surveying his patrons, which led to his developing an orientation for the business community entitled "Minding Your Business." He organized a workshop on writing a business plan and developed bibliographies and handouts. The Downtown and Business Branch of the Carnegie Library of Pittsburgh offers workshops on topics such as basic investment, job searches, business start-up courses from SCORE, dealing with job discrimination, and enjoying humor in the workplace.[2] These workshops are in combination with book discussion groups and other general cultural programs.

Public librarians are also reaching out to people in jails and other institutions. Instruction can be incorporated into much of this outreach, which would also be integrated with reading literacy programs, book talks, and other traditional library approaches. Former prisoners also need help with finding work and housing upon their release. Families of inmates could be another audience for ILI and many other forms of library outreach. Kathleen de la Pena McCook outlines these and other important issues affecting prisoners and describes existing standards and other materials on this subject.[3]

Some public libraries are using computer and information literacy instruction to help unemployed people find new jobs. This training is essential because not everybody is computer or information literate, yet most jobs are now being advertised on the Web. It is necessary for applicants to use the Web to apply even for jobs that do not require computer skills. The Institute for Information Literacy at the Danville, Virginia, Public Library instructs unemployed patrons on how to use Microsoft Office, send attachments, search and browse the Internet, and use these skills for job hunting.[4]

Some public libraries have reached out to children and young people with ILI. Lauren Collen created a "computer camp" for middle school students that taught them how to determine their information needs, how to find information, and how to put this information into a report. This instruction enabled her students to do better assignments and to do more research on their own.[5]

Lark Birdsong, a student at the University of Washington Information School, has created the Information Literacy Initiative, now affiliated with the Center for Information and Society at the University of Washington, with the support of Michael Eisenberg, a creator of the Big 6 program.[6] Birdsong has focused on instructing children and young people "at risk," homeless women, job seekers, entrepreneurs, and people over fifty. She has networked with the Boulder and Denver public libraries in Colorado, Boulder's Small Business Development Center, the Colorado I Have a Dream program, and with the Osher Lifelong Learning Institute at the University of Denver. For her curriculum, she has drawn from the Big 6 process created by Eisenberg and Bob Berkowitz. Her curriculum is "geared toward individuals in nonacademic, nonschool environments who desire lifelong learning skills." Many of her activities can also be replicated in public libraries with or without partnerships with other organizations and agencies.

Combined ILI and Cultural Programming

Danville's Institute for Information Literacy combines hardcore ILI with more traditional library programs to encourage information and general cultural literacy and to promote lifelong learning in many respects. Their literary and cultural programming includes activities for preschoolers, storytelling, outreach, a library salon featuring lectures and performances, a series on Virginia and other regional authors, and a discussion group on world events.

Many traditional library activities such as literacy and ESL programs, book discussion groups, lectures, and performances can be combined with elements of ILI. Also, storytelling, puppet shows, and other elements of cultural programming can be used to promote information literacy.

Information and Referral (I&R) and Community Networking

Public libraries use information and referral (I&R) services to connect people with institutions that can help them. Questions can be as casual as finding a pottery class or a music camp or as vital as dealing with forms of family abuse, alcoholism, or drug abuse. Information literacy would be helpful in determining the best institutions or agencies to deal with the issue at hand. Any ILI in this context would be minimal but relevant.

Elements of ILI can also be used as public librarians network with a variety of institutions, organizations, and agencies in their communities. Librarians can share information with agencies, enabling them to work together to market ILI to many diverse groups of people.

Lifelong Independent Learning and Readers' Services

As promoters of informal education and lifelong learning, public libraries have always served independent learners through readers' advisory, bibliotherapy, and other services. These services fulfill both public libraries' mission as "the people's university" and Louis Shores's earlier concept of the "library-college." This is true student-centered learning where the "curriculum" is set by users, themselves. Formal and nonformal elements of learning can be applied here. Yet many independent learning activities are invisible, even to librarians and their patrons. Library users do not always ask extensive questions, or let librarians know of any outcomes from their research. In certain cases, users may not realize, at least initially, that they are doing research. And once a casual, informal activity is "formalized" in any way, it is no longer so casual!

Independent learners tend to be people working on a research project over a long period of time that is not school or work related. The most well-known examples in public libraries are people doing research on genealogy or local history. One retired high school French teacher was doing extensive research on African American history at an inner-city branch because he finally had the time to pursue a subject that he was passionate about. Independent learners abound at public libraries but their work may be largely invisible.

A whole other issue is reader's advisory services, which is guidance in finding, evaluating, and using popular literature. This can be in the form of service to individuals and indirect instruction in print and on the Web. There has been a Renaissance in readers' advisory services since the mid-1990s, which includes book discussion groups in and outside of libraries and other developments. Whether reader's advisory services are on a parallel track with ILI on nonfiction and literary materials or whether these worlds can come together is a matter of controversy, reflecting traditional public library goals of promoting "the best of culture" versus more popular literature. (These issues will be discussed in more depth in chapter 7 and in *Lifelong Learning in Public Libraries: Tools and Tips for Practitioners*.)

Indirect, Asynchronous Instruction

Public libraries have always instructed indirectly through the use of the following:

- Guidebook information on library services, policies, and hours.
- Written tours.
- Building design and signage.
- Point-of-use instruction to help patrons use complicated sources.

All of this asynchronous instruction has migrated to the Web, with general information on library Web pages, electronic pathfinders and webliographies, and electronic tours. The online version of building design and signage would be Information Architecture or website design, and point-of-use instruction can be found on websites as "About This Source," "?," or "Frequently Asked Questions (FAQ)" pages.

Promoting New Technologies

At this time, the most extensive ILI in public libraries consists of computer and Internet instruction. This instruction is seen, particularly in many large and mid-sized public library systems, where public librarians are making computers available to patrons such as older adults who may not otherwise have this access. By instructing patrons in the use of computers and the Internet, it is hoped that they will be computer and information literate by the time they are able to purchase their own computers and personally connect to the Internet. This computer instruction is sometimes combined with literacy, ESL classes, or workshops on job or career information. Basic computer and media literacy blend with more hardcore information literacy.

One place that does several of these activities is the Dudley Literacy Center, part of an inner-city branch of the Boston Public Library. Public libraries usually market and advertise this instruction as part of their programming, along with their more traditional cultural programming.

Computer information can be taught on three levels. The first level is teaching library users basic computer skills, including using the mouse, word processing, e-mail, and other aspects of programs like Microsoft Office. Most public libraries that instruct on computer use focus on introducing patrons who have not used a computer before, as well as people with computer anxiety. Participants are taught how to get the most out of their computers before they even begin to seriously deal with the Internet.

A second level is on teaching "Internet 1.0," which focuses mainly on how to effectively use search tools and how to evaluate websites. Many public and academic libraries instruct on Internet searches, either in person, with tutorials, or using a combination of both approaches. Some Web tutorials combine this with other elements of ILI. Good tutorials include *Bare Bones 101: A Basic Tutorial on Searching the Web* from the University of South Carolina, Beaufort; *How to Be a Webhound* from the Maricopa County Community College in Phoenix, Arizona; net.TUTOR from Ohio State University; and *Outline Advancement of Student Information Skills* (OASIS) from San Francisco State University.[7]

For the third level, Learning 2.0 was created and developed by Helene Blowers and other librarians from the Public Library of Charlotte and Mecklenburg County (PLCMC) in North Carolina to instruct librarians about wikis, blogs, and other emerging technology of Internet 2.0.[8] Librarians around the country are taking advantage of Learning 2.0 for their own professional development. Systems like Learning 2.0 can also be adopted and adapted (with permission) to teach the public about this latest technology, both directly and indirectly.

Electronic Networking

Some libraries are participating in electronic networking with other libraries, organizations, companies, and especially government agencies in order to connect everybody in an area to broadband Internet access, and public library ILI has been strongly recommended to be part of this process. Examples include Connecting Canadians and OneCommunity.

Connecting Canadians is a major initiative of the Canadian government to connect Canada's citizens to the Internet. Six programs are part of Connecting Canadians: Canada Online, Smart Communities, Canadian Content Online, Electronic Commerce, Canadian Governments Online, and Connecting Canada to the World. This initiative uses public libraries and other public agencies to assist in the implementation of the program. Connecting Canadians has been very successful in encouraging resource sharing and new services among libraries and in enabling some rural libraries to become library leaders.[9]

The program has emphasized technological access and connections over human needs, leading to an intense need for public librarians to promote information literacy to the public. Scholars such as Heidi Julien and Reegan D. Breu have urged more government support of public libraries to enable them to better instruct their patrons.[10] Public libraries must also keep up with multiple technological changes and consider the impact of this form of ILI on their more traditional lifelong learning activities.

A similar program in northern Ohio, OneCommunity connects "public and nonprofit institutions to a next-generation fiber-optic network, enabling those institutions to offer enhanced, innovative solutions, and transforming the region's image and economic future by attracting outside investment and creating business and job opportunities."[11] OneCleveland, an earlier version of this program, connected area public libraries to museums and to the Metro Health System, Cleveland's public hospital. The Cuyahoga County Public Library and the Cleveland Museum of Art cooperated in linking storytelling to museum exhibits for schoolchildren. Nurses from the Metro Health System provided health information on the Cleveland Public Library's KnowItNow24x7 live Web reference service. Many possibilities for instruction can emerge from programs and initiatives like OneCommunity. Members of the public need instruction on how to access and take full advantage of new services such as these.

PUBLIC LIBRARY INSTRUCTION OUTSIDE THE UNITED STATES

ILI has been promoted in various forms around the world, particularly in English-speaking and Scandinavian countries with strong traditions of public libraries, adult education, or both. Canada and Australia are very similar as former British colonies with indigenous populations, later European settlers and other immigrants, general survival issues because of climate and geography, and scattered patterns of settlement. Governments of both countries rely strongly on technology to tie everyone together, Canada with Connecting Canadians and Australia with Connect Australia and other initiatives.

In Canada, the creation and promotion of Connecting Canadians by the government and its initial emphasis on technology over people has led to proposals for more ILI from public libraries and for more government support for them to do this. The goal was to make Canada the world's most connected country. However, having access to the Internet and being able to effectively use it are two different phenomena. People also need more information on assessing government services. The new technology enables members of the public to read newspapers from around the world and to correspond with distant friends and relatives by e-mail. New nontraditional patrons are now using Canadian public libraries, and user expectations have risen dramatically. Training for both staff and the general public is a real issue.[12]

In Australia, the drive toward digitization is also coming from the government, leading to several programs.[13] Connect Australia is intended to improve broadband services in regional, rural, and remote areas. Other programs supported by the Australian government include a $2 billion Communications Fund to enable the government to respond to future demands for broadband, the Australian Broadband Guarantee to provide broadband to previously neglected areas, the Broadband Connect Infrastructure Program to support a few large-scale infrastructure projects, Clever Networks to deliver broadband to some regional areas, and Backing Indigenous Abilities to improve communications services in indigenous communities.

Kerrie Burgess investigated the impact of government services on the Australian public and found that there was a major disconnect between the development of these services by the government and library patrons' use of these services.[14] Burgess called for more government help for public libraries in order to better promote these services. As in Canada, there is technology to make the Internet widely available but a real need to promote ILI among the citizens.[15]

One Australian public library that has done a variety of ILI activities is the Liverpool City Library. Their activities include a library and information orientation and basic ILI for Technical and Future Education (Tafe) students; introductory Internet classes for the general public; a technology room or "information commons" where librarians teach patrons the Internet for "job seeking, computer skills development, communications, and research"; a partnership with the University of the Third Age to enable people over fifty to take courses designed for their needs; orientations for school classes; and tailored courses for other groups, such as police officers.[16]

The Library and Information Association of New Zealand Aotorea (Lianza) has a working group to promote ILI in public libraries. This group surveyed New Zealand public libraries to ascertain their instructional practices and found that most libraries provide orientations and informal help on using library resources. Larger New Zealand libraries were more likely to provide ILI, to designate staff members to implement this, and to have written policies and plans. Librarians provide ILI for children through homework centers, word processing classes, summer reading programs, and book groups. Relatively few libraries published self-help guides, formally documented their ILI activities, or designated staff specifically to do this.[17]

In the United Kingdom, the Department for Culture, Media, and Sport has defined information literacy as a core activity within three areas of emphasis: "promotion of reading and informal learning; access to digital skills and services, including those from the government; and tackling social exclusion and building community." Ronan O'Beirne describes the online information literacy tutorial for public librarians planned by the Bradford Libraries Archives and Information Services and Imperial College, London.[18]

The Tower Hamlets Library System in East London has closed and sold several traditional libraries and replaced them with "information stores," which are being marketed as "street-corner universities." The purpose of these information stores is to combine adult and recreational education with traditional library activities. Instructional activities include an on-line tour, pamphlets, brochures, and hotlines. Future plans include adult education with credit and noncredit courses, Web-based instruction, and outreach to teachers.[19]

Professionals from Norway, Sweden, Finland, Iceland, and Denmark are in the process of developing a national policy on information literacy that will be shared between these countries. Skov describes several joint projects between public libraries and elementary and secondary educators in this region.[20]

In South Africa, there is now a strong demand for public libraries to sponsor both ILI for school students and reading literacy classes for adults as a result both of major third wave technological changes and the end of apartheid. The Curriculum 2005 initiative marked a major change in the curricula of South African schools from second-wave schooling to third-wave learning. Curriculum 2005 represents a major shift from lectures and textbooks that train docile workers to resource-based and problem-based learning that train independent researchers. Students now must follow several steps to do their research and use multiple resources. This curricular change has resulted in a greatly increased use of public libraries by elementary and secondary students and a call for public libraries to provide ILI to students. Librarians from underfinanced libraries are beginning to ask for help from the government and other sources in order to implement this instruction.[21] There is also a need for public libraries to provide more literacy and adult education for older users.[22] Advocates of more information and reading literacy stress the need for partnerships between libraries and other institutions and more resources and support. ILI in many other countries around the world is also mentioned in the works of Hannelore Rader.[23]

THE LITERATURE ON PUBLIC LIBRARY INSTRUCTION

Literature specifically on public library instruction has not been extensive over the years. Formal advanced instruction in public libraries has been rare until recently, but it has also been underreported. The literature on this subject consists of the following:

- Bibliographies on BI and ILI in all libraries.
- Reviews of the research literature.
- Texts and other information on how to instruct in all kinds of libraries.

Rader estimates that 60 percent of all materials on ILI are from academic libraries, 20 percent from school media centers, and the rest from other locations.[24] Materials specifically on public library instruction are very rare. This reality is reflected in bibliographies on this subject and in reviews of the literature. A number of texts address the issue of public library instruction in various ways.

General Bibliographies on BI and ILI

A bibliography focusing on instructional activities in libraries before 1980 is Deborah Lockwood's *Library Instruction: A Bibliography*, which mentions only several general descriptions of specific instructional activities in public libraries.[25] The most extensive bibliographical work in the fields of BI and ILI have been by the Library Instruction Round Table (LIRT) and especially by Hannelore Rader. Both have issued annual bibliographies as well as several articles summarizing trends in this field over a period of twenty-five to thirty years.

In the June 2011 issue of their newsletter, LIRT lists the twenty best articles on library instruction published in the preceding year. Almost all of these articles are on academic libraries, and most of the rest are on school media centers. LIRT has also published "Top Twenty-Five of LIRT's Top Twenty Instruction Articles" as well as the pamphlet *From Chalkboard to Keyboard: 25 Years of Library Instruction Research*, both of which reflect these annual trends.[26]

The annual bibliography on BI and ILI published by the *Reference Services Review* (*RSR*), and originated by Rader, lists articles on instruction by library type. Articles, specifically on public libraries, have been especially rare, with three to five articles usually published annually—and most of these articles are general descriptions of instructional activities. In some years, there are no publications specific to public libraries. The *RSR* annual bibliographies also list instructional articles related to all kinds of libraries. Many of these trends are reflected in Rader's articles summarizing this literature over long periods, "A Silver Anniversary: 25 Years of Reviewing the Literature Related to User Instruction" and "Information Literacy 1973–2002: A Selected Literature Review."[27]

Reviews of the Research Literature

General reviews of the research literature in this field include works by Michael Eisenberg and Michael K. Brown, Sherri Edwards, Christine Bruce, and Hannelore Rader.[28] LIRT's 2002 bibliography *From Chalkboard to Keyboard* also focuses on the general research literature in this field. Several articles describe earlier research specifically on public library instruction. For example, Ruth T. Newman describes surveys conducted in the 1960s and 1970s by Kathleen Molz, Mary Lee Bundy, Edward E. Olson, and others.[29]

Jerry Carbone mentioned two early surveys of library use instruction by Olson in Indiana in 1970 and Bernard Vavreck in Pennsylvania in 1983.[30] Olson found that only 10 percent of small public libraries in Indiana were promoting extensive instruction. Vavreck later found that 70 percent of Pennsylvania's small rural libraries were committed to instructing in library use, with at least 90 percent conducting orientations for school classes, as well as library tours, which reflected a general growth of activities during this time. Other articles that Carbone found, cited, and discussed reflected ongoing activities of individuals in public libraries and other settings, such as Christopher Compton in Denver, Colorado, Margaret Hendley in Ontario, Canada, and Sheldon L. Tarakan in Port Washington, New York.[31]

The best review of the early research literature on public library instruction is the 1991 article "Library Use Instruction Research and the Public Library" by Susan Diehl and Terry L. Weech.[32] According to them, the literature at that time focused on six issues:

- Do public librarians believe that library instruction is needed?
- What are the information literacy skills of public library users?
- Do public libraries conduct ILI?
- Should public librarians emphasize providing information or giving instruction?
- How do academic library users feel about their own need for instruction?
- What do public library users think about their own research skills?

On the need for public library instruction, Diehl and Weech cite early recommendations for this from ALA, John Berry of *Library Journal*, and state task forces and committees in Ohio, Connecticut, Michigan, and Virginia. Diehl and Weech also mention surveys by Newman, Jean Brooks, Sheryl Anspaugh, Frederick Reenstjerna, and Roma Harris confirming that public librarians believe they should instruct patrons in information use.[33]

Public librarians may have felt this way because of their perceptions that their users were not skilled in using libraries. According to Diehl and Weech, this was the subject of studies by Molz, Peter Simmons, and Linda Bly.[34] Leslie Edmonds found that children at the Downers Grove Public Library in Illinois had difficulty in using the card catalog.[35] Edmonds, Paula Moore, and Kathleen Mehaffey Balcom were conducting a similar study of children using keyboard terminals at the Orchard Park Elementary School in Carmel, Indiana. A related study, not cited by Diehl and Weech because it was occurring during that time, was Gale Eaton's study of the locational skills of children using public libraries and how to instruct children on library use.[36]

Several studies throughout the 1970s and into the early 1980s confirmed that public library use instruction was rare.[37] Both Olson and Vavreck showed some exceptions. Olson found that larger libraries in Indiana did instructional activities, but not smaller ones. Vavreck found instructional activities in most of the small Pennsylvania libraries that he surveyed, but most of these were very basic and not called "user education" by librarians.[38]

Diehl and Weech mentioned the "information vs. instruction" debate in public libraries discussed in articles by Lubans, Anita Schiller, Bly, Janice R. Mustain-Wood, and Harris.[39] These authors disagreed on whether public librarians should instruct patrons on finding information, or whether they should give patrons direct information. However, even the proponents of direct information approved of instruction under some circumstances. Other experts, such as James Rice and Michael Mahaney, argued for giving library users a choice between direct information, instruction, or a combination of both.[40] All libraries seem to have been pulled more in the direction of instruction because of the emerging technologies of the last two decades.

Diehl and Weech cite several studies focusing on the self-perceived instructional needs of academic library users, including studies by Lubans, Benita J. Howell, Edward B. Reeves, and John Van Willigen.[41] Beth J. Shapiro and Philip M. Marcus noticed that academic library users were happy with the results of searches viewed as poor by librarians.[42] According to Diehl and Weech, similar research on public library users was conducted by Bundy, the Gallup organization, Elrich and Lavidge Inc., and Kirkendall and Stoffle.[43] Roma Harris and B. Gillian Michell showed that public library users are also pleased with their research and consider public libraries easy to use.[44] However, George Schanze, a library user, urged public librarians to instruct patrons in information use.[45]

Texts and Other Information on How to Instruct

Several texts have been published over the last few decades on how to plan instructional programs in public and other libraries. Most focus on instruction in all kinds of libraries but have information relevant to public libraries.

The first text focusing specifically on public library instruction was the 1983 *Educating the Public Library User*, edited by Lubans.[46] It includes several articles on subjects still very relevant to public library instruction: comparisons of library instruction in public and other settings; relationships with school media specialists; working with adult distance learners; characteristics of adult learners; and how to plan, implement, evaluate, and administer instructional programs. The book also features profiles and descriptions of early public library instructional programs in Virginia, New Jersey, California, Ontario (Canada), and the United Kingdom.

The LIRT Library Instruction Handbook published in 1990 includes chapters on planning, executing, and evaluating instructional programs in academic, public, school, and special libraries.[47] The public library chapter discusses needs assessments, program goals and objectives, program evaluation, levels and methods of instruction, instructional content and materials, program management, networking with community organizations, and library instruction for children. The chapter also includes examples of needs assessments, program evaluation forms, a public library course outline and assignment, and public library publicity, as well as an extensive bibliography.

The best current, general text on conducting ILI is *Information Literacy Instruction: Theory and Practice* by Esther S. Grassian and Joan C. Kaplowitz.[48] The book is designed to be used in all library settings and is particularly strong on learning theories, instructional techniques, and teaching diverse communities. The section specifically on public library instruction gives an excellent introduction and overview of ILI issues affecting public libraries. It covers needs assessment and community surveys, networking with other organizations and agencies, signage, pathfinders and other indirect instruction, tours and other orientations, independent learners, "instruction for one," instruction at the point of need, and introducing people to new technology.

In 2003, I created the website Teaching About Information, which includes many websites describing the theory and organization of ILI, learning theories, instructing diverse patrons, what people should know about information, how to instruct, instruction in different library settings, and cooperation between different libraries, institutions, and organizations.[49]

All of these sources address in some degree the differences between public library and other instruction, recognizing the importance of basic instruction, indirect instruction, market research via community analysis, independent lifelong learners, networking with community agencies, and ties between information and other literacies. Current periodicals about ILI include *Communications in Information Literacy, Educator's Spotlight Digest,*

Journal of Information Literacy, and *Studies in Media and Information Literacy Education* (*SIMILE*). Other journals with ILI information include *College and Research Libraries, Evidence-Based Library and Information Practice, Journal of Academic Librarianship, Portal: Libraries and the Academy, Reference and User Services Quarterly, Reference Librarian,* and *Reference Services Review.*[50]

NOTES

1. Terry Zarsky, "Instruction for the Business Community," *Colorado Libraries* 26, no. 4 (2000): 38–39.

2. Carnegie Library of Pittsburgh, *Downtown and Business Events*, www.clpgh .org/locations/downtown/programs.cfm.

3. Kathleen de la Pena McCook, "Public Libraries and People in Jail," *Reference and User Services Quarterly* 44, no. 1 (2004): 26–30.

4. Otis D. Alexander, "Library Services for the Unemployed and the Institute for Information Literacy," *Virginia Libraries* 52, no. 2 (2006): 34–35.

5. Lauren Collen, "Teaching Information Literacy in the Public Library or Why a Public Librarian Would Take on the Role of a School Librarian," *Knowledge Quest* 37, no. 1 (2008): 12–16.

6. Lark Birdsong, "Information Literacy Training for All," *Searcher* 17, no. 8 (2009): 18–54.

7. University of South Carolina Beaufort Library, *Bare Bones 101: A Basic Tutorial on Searching the Web*, www.sc.edu/beaufort/library/pages/bones/bones.shtml; Maricopa Community College Library, *How to Be a Webhound*, www.mcli.dist.maricopa .edu/webhound; Ohio State University, *net.TUTOR*, http://liblearn.osu.edu/tutor; San Francisco State University, *Outline Advancement of Student Information Skills* (OASIS), http://oasis.sfsu.edu.

8. Helene Blowers, "The C's of Our Sea Change: Plans for Training Staff, from Core Competencies to Learning 2.0," *Information Today* 27, no. 2 (2007): 10–15; Meredith Farkas, " A Roadmap to Learning 2.0," *American Libraries* 38, no. 2 (2007): 26; Kathy Ishizuka, "Come Blog with Me: NC Library Encourage Staff to Play in the 2.0 Sandbox," *School Library Journal* 52, no. 9 (2006): 22–23; Robin Hastings, "Journey to Library 2.0: One Library Trains Staff on the Social Tools Users Employ," *Library Journal* 132 (April 15, 2007): 36–37.

9. Heidi Julien and Reegan D. Breu, "Instructional Practices in Canadian Public Libraries," *Library and Information Science Research* 27, no. 3 (2005): 281–301.

10. Julien and Breu, "Instructional Practices in Canadian Public Libraries," 281–301.

11. OneCommunity, *About Us*, www.onecommunity.org; Sari Feldman and Lev Gonick, "The Dream of OneCleveland," *Library Journal* 130 (September 1, 2005): 34–36.

12. Heidi Julien and Sandra Anderson, "The Public Library in 'Connecting Canadians,'" *Canadian Journal of Information and Library Science* 27, no. 4 (2002/2003): 5–29.

13. "New Australian Government Broadband Initiative Will Boost IPSTAR Sales in Australia," www.thaicom.net/eng/press.aspx?id=174.

14. Kerrie Burgess, "Public Libraries and Egovernment," *Aplis* 19, no. 3 (2006): 118–25.

15. Angela Newton and Debbi Boden, "Information Literacy Development in Australia: Angela Newton and Debbi Boden Meet Christine Bruce, Author of *The Seven Faces of Information Literacy*," *Library and Information Update* 5, nos. 1–2 (2006): 42–43.

16. Burrell, "Now for the Hard Part," 105–13.

17. Ailsa Koning, "Information Literacy in New Zealand Public Libraries," *Aplis* 14, no. 4 (2001): 159–63.

18. Ronan O'Beirne, "Raising the Profile of Information Literacy in Public Libraries," *Library and Information Update* 5, nos. 1–2 (2006): 44–45.

19. Patterson, "'Idea Stores'," 48–49.

20. Skov, "Information Literacy and the Role of Public Libraries," 4–7.

21. Genevieve Hart, "Public Libraries in South Africa: Agents or Victims of Educational Change?" *South African Journal of Library and Information Science* 70, no. 2 (2004): 110–120.

22. Hart, "Public Librarians and Information Literacy Education," 172–84; Mary Nassimbeni, "Adult Education in South African Public Libraries: A Profile of Activities," *South African Journal of Library and Information Science* 72, no. 1 (2006): 12–26.

23. Hannelore B. Rader, "User Education and Information Literacy for the Next Decade: An International Perspective," *Reference Services Review* (Summer 1996): 71–75; Rader, "Information Literacy 1973–2002: A Selected Literature Review," *Library Trends* 51, no. 2 (2002): 247–48.

24. Rader, "Information Literacy 1973–2002," 242.

25. Deborah Lockwood, comp., *Library Instruction: A Bibliography* (Westport, Conn.: Greenwood, 1979).

26. ALA, Library Instruction Round Table (LIRT), "Top Twenty-Five of LIRT's Top Twenty Instruction Articles," http://fleetwood.baylor.edu/lirt/top25.htm; ALA, LIRT Research Committee, *From Chalkboard to Keyboard: 25 Years of Library Instruction Research* (Chicago: ALA).

27. Hannelore Rader, "A Silver Anniversary: 25 Years of Reviewing the Literature Related to User Instruction," *Reference Services Review* 28, no. 3 (2000): 290–96; Rader, "Information Literacy 1973–2002," 242–59.

28. Michael B. Eisenberg and Michael K. Brown, "Current Themes Regarding Library and Information Skills Instruction: Research Supporting and Research Lacking," *School Library Media Quarterly* 20 (Winter 1992): 103–9; Sherri Edwards, "Bibliographic Instruction Research: An Analysis of the Journal Literature from 1977 to 1991," *Research Strategies* 12 (1994): 68–78; Christine Susan Bruce, "Information Literacy Research: Dimensions of the Emerging Collective Consciousness," *Australian Academic and Research Libraries* 31, no. 2 (2000): 91–109; Rader, "A Silver Anniversary"; ALA, LIRT Research Committee, *From Chalkboard to Keyboard*.

29. Newman, "Instructing the Out-of-School Adult in Public Library Use," 59–62; Kathleen Molz, "The 'State of the Art' of Public Library Orientation," *Maryland Libraries* 34 (Winter 1968): 10–17; Mary Lee Bundy, "Metropolitan Public Library Use," *Wilson Library Bulletin* 41 (1967): 950–61; Edward E. Olson, *Survey of User Policies in Indiana Libraries and Information Centers*, Indiana Library Studies Report No. 10, Peter Hiatt, gen. ed. (Bloomington, Ind.: The Center, 1970).

30. Jerry Carbone, "Library Use Instruction in the Small and Medium Public Library: A Review of the Literature," *Reference Librarian* (1984): 149–57; Olson, *Survey of User Policies in Indiana Libraries and Information Centers*; Bernard Vavrek, "Struggle for Survival: Reference Services in the Small Public Library," *Library Journal* 108 (May 15, 1983): 966–69.

31. Christopher Compton, "Innovation in Library Instruction Applied to an Adult Education Course," in *Progress in Educating the Library User*, ed. John J. Lubans Jr. (New York: Bowker, 1978): 135–37; Margaret Hendley, "The Librarian as Teacher," *Ontario Library Review* 63 (March 1979): 45–48; Sheldon L. Tarakan, "Opening the Attic Door: Bibliographic (and Other) Instruction at Port Washington Public Library," *Book Mark* 38 (Fall 1979): 249–52.

32. Susan Diehl and Terry L. Weech, "Library Use Instruction Research and the Public Library," *Public Libraries* 30, no. 1 (1991): 33–42.

33. Newman, "Instructing the Out-of-School Adult in Public Library Use"; Jean Brooks, "User Education in Public Libraries," in *Seminar on User Education Activities: The State of the Art in Texas* (Bethesda, Md.: ERIC, 1977), ED 138 249; Sheryl Anspaugh, "Public Libraries: Teaching the User?" in *Progress in Educating the Library User* (New York: Bowker, 1978); Frederick R. Reenstjerna, "Developing Statewide Library Instruction Standards: Rationale and Preliminary Steps," in *Teaching Library Use Competence: Bridging the Gap from High School to College: Papers Presented at the Eleventh Annual Library Instruction Conference Held at Eastern Michigan University, May 7–8, 1981*, ed. Carolyn A. Kirkendall (Ann Arbor, Mich.: Pierian, 1982), 102; Roma H. Harris, "Bibliographic Instruction in Public Libraries: A Question of Philosophy," *RQ* 29 (Fall 1989): 94.

34. Molz. "The 'State of the Art' of Public Library Orientation"; Peter Simmons, "Studies in the Use of the Card Catalogue in a Public Library," *Canadian Library Journal* 31 (August 1994): 330, 335; Linda Bly, "Library Skills: An Informal Survey," *Arkansas Libraries* 42 (June 1985): 21.

35. Leslie Edmonds, "The Birth of a Research Project," *Top of the News*, 43 (Spring 1987): 323–25; Edmonds, Paula Moore, and Kathleen Mehaffey Balcom, "An Investigation of the Effectiveness of an Online Catalog in Providing Bibliographic Access to Children in a Public Library Setting," unpublished report submitted to ALA, 1988, and cited by Patricia A. Hooten, "Online Catalogs: Will They Improve Children's Access?" *Journal of Youth Services in Libraries* 2 (1989): 270.

36. Gale Eaton, "What the Public Children's Library Needs to Know About Locational Skills Instruction in Elementary Schools," *Journal of Youth Services in Libraries* 2 (Summer 1989): 357–66.

37. Molz, "The 'State of the Art' of Public Library Orientation," 10–11; Margaret Groggin et al., *The Report on the Instruction in the Use of Libraries in Colorado Presented to the Colorado Council of Library Development by (Its) Committee on Instruction in the Use of Libraries* (Denver: The Committee, 1973); Newman, "Instructing the Out-of-School Adult in Public Library Use," 61; Carla J. Stoffle, Johanna Herrick, and Suzanne Chernik, *Library Instruction Programs 1975: A Wisconsin Directory* (Madison: Wisconsin Library Association, 1975): 44; Anspaugh, "Public Library Instruction," 127–28; Reenstjerna, "Developing Statewide Library Instruction Standards," 101–2; Carolyn A. Kirkendall and Carla J. Stoffle, "Instruction," in *The Service Imperative for Libraries: Essays in Honor of Margaret E. Monroe*, ed. Gail A. Schlachter (Littleton, Colo.: Libraries Unlimited, 1982): 56.

38. Olson, *Survey of User Services Policies in Indiana Libraries and Information Centers*, 96; Vavrek, "A Struggle for Survival," 969.

39. Lubans, *Educating the Public Library User*, 8; Anita R. Schiller, "Reference Service: Instruction or Information? *Library Quarterly* 35 (January 1965): 52–60; Bly, "Library Skills," 21; Janice R. Mustain-Wood, "Library Instruction: The Public Library," *Colorado Libraries* 9 (June 1983): 34–36; Harris, "Bibliographic Instruction in Public Libraries," 95–96.

40. James R. Rice, "Library Use Instruction with Individual Users: Should Instruction Be Included in the Reference Interview?" *Reference Librarian* (Spring/Summer 1984): 81–82; Michael C. Mahaney, "Client-Centered/Situational Bibliographic Instruction: A Mouthful That Need Not Always Be Said," *Bookmark* 46 (Fall 1987): 36.

41. Lubans, "Nonuse of the Academic Library," *College and Research Libraries* 32 (September 1971): 365; Lubans, "Library Use Instruction Needs from the Library Users'/Nonusers' Point of View: A Survey Report," in *Educating the Library User*, 404–405; Benita J. Howells, Edward B. Reeves, and John Van Willigen, "Fleeting Encounters: A Role Analysis of Reference Librarian–Patron Interaction," *RQ* 16 (Winter 1976): 127.

42. Beth J. Shapiro and Philip M. Marcus, "Library Use, Library Instruction, and User Success," *Research Strategies* 5 (Spring 1987): 60–69.

43. Bundy, "Metropolitan Public Library Use," 952, 956; Gallup Organization, *The Role of Libraries in America* (Frankfurt: Kentucky Department of Libraries and Archives, 1976): 42; Elrick and Lavidge Inc., *Public Library Usage in Illinois*, Illinois State Library Report No. 1 (Springfield: Illinois State Library, 1977); Kirkendall and Stoffle, "Instruction," 57.

44. Roma H. Harris and B. Gillian Michell, "The Social Context of Reference Work: Assessing the Effect of Gender and Communication Skill on Observers' Judgments of Competence," *Library and Information Science Research* 8 (January–March 1986): 97.

45. George Schanze, "A View from a Library Phobic," *Colorado Libraries* 14 (June 1988): 23.

46. John Lubans Jr., comp. and ed., *Educating the Public Library User* (Chicago: ALA, 1983).

47. May Brottman and Mary Loe, eds., *The LIRT Library Instruction Handbook* (Englewood, Colo.: Libraries Unlimited, 1990).

48. Esther S. Grassian and Joan R. Kaplowitz, *Information Library Instruction: Theory and Practice*, 2nd ed. (New York: Neal-Schuman, 2009).

49. Donna L. Gilton, *Teaching About Information*, http://www.uri.edu/artsci/lsc/Faculty/gilton/Index.html.

50. *Communications in Information Literacy*, www.comminfolit.org/index.php/cil; *Educator's Spotlight Digest*, Syracuse, N.Y.: Syracuse University, S.O.S. for Information Literacy, 2005– ; *Journal of Information Literacy*, London: Chartered Institute of Library and Information Professionals, Information Literacy Group, 2007– ; *Studies in Media and Information Literacy Education* (*SIMILE*), Toronto: University of Toronto, 2001– ; *College and Research Libraries*, Chicago: ALA, 1939– ; *Evidence-based Library Information Practice*, Calgary: University of Alberta Learning Services, 2006– ; *Journal of Academic Librarianship*, Ann Arbor, Mich.: Mountainship Publishing, 1975– ; *Portal: Libraries and the Academy*, Baltimore, Md.: Johns Hopkins University Press, 2001– ; *Reference and User Services Quarterly*, Chicago: ALA, 1997– ; *Reference Librarian*, New York: Haworth, 1982– ; *Reference Services Review*, Ann Arbor, Mich.: Pierian, 1977– .

3

How People Grow and Learn

An understanding of educational theories about how we grow and learn is helpful for establishing sound practices in Information Literacy Instruction (ILI).[1] And do we have theories about how people grow, learn, think, feel, and mature! This chapter reviews the major schools of thought on how people grow and learn, including developmental theories, behaviorism, cognitive psychology, constructivism, and educational humanism. The developmental theories describe how people grow in their thinking and reasoning over time. Behaviorism focuses on how people act and how to measure and change this behavior. Cognitive theories are used to investigate ways in which people think. Some cognitive psychologists study information processing or "the brain as computer" and others study metacognition, which is thinking about thinking, as well as effective learning techniques.

While constructivism is viewed as the most important school within cognitive psychology, it can also be regarded as a combination of cognitive psychology and educational humanism, or humanistic approaches to education. Constructivism is described here as a separate movement influenced by these two schools of thought. Followers of constructivism use humanistic teaching techniques, such as Active Learning, that can be more easily applied to traditional classrooms. On the cognitive side, it is concerned with Discovery Learning, Guided Design, Problem-based Learning, and various research and problem-solving strategies, and there is an emphasis on learning by doing, as scientists do. ILI applications include the core ILI goals of the Big 6, the ACRL standards, and the work of Carol Kuhlthau and Alice Yucht, which would describe ILI as defining the need for information and then finding, evaluating, and properly using it.

Educational humanism includes many advocates from education, philosophy, and psychology, as well as multiple movements taking place in several countries over the last three centuries. Public libraries are part of this movement. Educational humanism has a lot in common with constructivism but goes beyond traditional classrooms in many ways, including alternative schools and informal education for people of all ages, especially the very young and adults. In the educational humanism approach, students set their own curriculum, if there is any. Students rather than teachers and other professionals determine what is to be taught and learned.

Three learning styles will be briefly described in this chapter: perceptual or learning modalities (or modality), field dependence and independence, and multiple intelligence. Scholars investigating modality observe how people learn through their senses or whether they are visual, auditory, or tactile students, who learn by doing. Field dependence and independence indicate whether people are global or analytical learners. Howard Gardner describes at least seven different forms of intelligence: verbal-linguistics, logistical-mathematical, visual-spatial, body kinesthetic, musical, intrapersonal, and interpersonal. This chapter looks at how these learning styles apply to instruction in public libraries and other settings.

HOW PEOPLE MATURE: DEVELOPMENTAL THEORIES

Developmental theories attempt to show how people change over time. Since public libraries serve people of all ages, there is much to be learned here. Developmental theories, especially the work of Jean Piaget, are often grouped with cognitive theories but differ from them in several ways. Developmental theories are used to investigate intellectual, social, and moral development, and psychologists from this school tend to believe that any change is due to maturation. Cognitive psychologists focus more on thinking and intellectual development and tend to believe that changes in people are due to their educational and life experiences. Major developmental psychologists include Erik Erikson, Jean Piaget (early work), William Perry, Mary Belenky, and Lev Vygotsky.

Erik Erikson

Erik Erikson was a high school dropout, a painter, a tutor, and one of Sigmund Freud's patients. He was trained as an analyst by Anna Freud and always thought that he was a Freudian, but he developed many ideas of his own.[2] Erikson may have been more independent because he was exposed to anthropology and ethnology and he studied Sioux and Yurok Indians in

North America as well as many other groups around the world. He was a professor at Harvard, Yale, and Berkeley, was a psychotherapist for soldiers during World War II, and studied both normal and exceptional children. Erikson maintained that people go through eight stages of life, with a major task, positive and negative outcomes, and corresponding social institution at each stage.[3] According to him, people who did not do well at one stage also had difficulty with all later stages.

In the first year of life, according to Erikson, babies learn either to trust or to mistrust. They bond with their mothers or other caregivers. Erikson believed that the virtue emerging at this time was hope, and that a corresponding social institution at this age was religion.

Toddlers between the ages of one and three must learn either autonomy or shame and doubt. During this period, they are being toilet trained and they are dealing with issues of rules, self-control, and self-esteem as they learn the magic of the word "no." Will is a virtue to this stage, and corresponding social institutions are representatives of law and order (the police, the courts).

Preschoolers between the ages of three and five are either developing initiative, curiosity, and responsibility or a sense of guilt. A sense of purpose is a virtue to be developed at this time, and the corresponding social institution for this age group is economics.

Elementary and middle school students between the ages of six and thirteen will either develop a sense of industry or a sense of inferiority. They begin more formal education between the ages of five and seven and learn the technology of society both in formal schools and (hopefully) nonformal institutions in the community, such as scouting or religious bodies. Stars, merit badges, and other forms of recognition for competence are important to children in this age group, and the corresponding social institution is the culture's technology.

Adolescents are trying to find their identity and can either ultimately determine this or have identity confusion. This phenomenon can be seen with middle and high school students who are subject to peer pressure and especially with college students who try different roles and identities. A virtue to develop during this time is faith, and the corresponding social institution is ideology.

Most young adults are choosing both careers and marriage partners and are starting their own families. They can either find intimacy or isolation. A virtue of this stage is love, and the corresponding social institution is ethics. Erikson believed that achieving intimacy was impossible without self-knowledge and awareness.

People in middle age have usually raised their own families and are often established in their careers. They can now mentor and guide the next generation both at work and in the community and can achieve either generativity or stagnation. The virtue emerging at this time is care, and the corresponding social institution for this stage is education.

Senior citizens or elders are retiring from their work, dealing with declining health, reevaluating their lives, and trying to pass on their wisdom to younger generations. In many cases, they are also actively contributing to their community and may be patriarchs and matriarchs of extended families. Elders can achieve either integrity or despair. The virtue emerging at this time is wisdom, and corresponding institutions can be any or all of the ones already mentioned above.

Erikson has been criticized for basing his conclusions on personal and subjective observations rather than general ones, for reflecting males better than females, and for not describing very well *how* people move from one stage of life to another.[4] Erikson's model was one of the first to really attempt to be universal and to deal with both Western and non-Western cultures. One can ask whether his theories stand the test of time, however. In the 1960s, when his theories were very popular, most people finished their formal education by or before their early twenties and chose one spouse and career at that time. Now people may live through several careers and marriages and pursue formal education and training over a lifetime, and in no particular order. However, Erikson still points to general concerns that adults are dealing with over time: education, relationships, work, recreation, generativity, and review of life. These are all issues that public libraries can address with ILI and other forms of lifelong learning.

Jean Piaget

Jean Piaget, a Swiss psychologist, believed that children go through four stages as they develop intellectually: sensimotor, pre-operational, concrete operations, and formal operations.[5] According to him, babies up to age two in the sensimotor stage are just beginning to explore their environment. At first, they do not realize that physical objects exist whether they can see them or not. At the end of this period, they develop the concept of object permanence and can form representations. They are also becoming aware of time, space, and causality.

Pre-operational children between the ages of two and seven have achieved object permanence but are very concrete. They do not realize that the same amount of liquid can be in containers of different sizes and shapes and still be the same. They lack the concept of conservation. Preschoolers also tend to believe that the world revolves around them. They are unable to "decenter" or to see things from other perspectives. They tend to focus on one thing at a time and have difficulty considering more than one aspect of a subject at a time. However, these characteristics change as children start formal education and move into concrete operations.

School-aged children, roughly ages seven to eleven, understand the concept of conservation. They know that one pint of a liquid will be one pint, regardless of the shape or size of its container. They can combine two or more classes into a larger group, combine several classes with each other, and deal with the null or with zero. In short, they are ready to do arithmetic and simple science. Later in this period, children can solve problems with numbers which represent real objects. They can also decenter or see things from more than one perspective. However, they are still concrete thinkers, unable to reason abstractly or to test hypotheses. Their learning is based on direct experience, and they tend to believe that there is "one right answer" to all or most problems.

According to Piaget, teens are moving from concrete operations to formal operations. They can consider and compare multiple points of view, and they realize that there are many answers to some questions and that some of these answers are better than others. Teens can think abstractly and form hypotheses. They can also deal with symbols tied to more abstract concepts. All of these characteristics contribute to critical thinking, an important aspect of information literacy, which will enable them to propose multiple solutions to problems.

Piaget's theories have been extremely influential in education, information literacy, interpretation or museum education, and many other fields. The idea of people moving from a concrete to a more formal stage of operations has been especially influential. However, later researchers have found that people move from the concrete to the formal stages of reasoning much later than Piaget thought. Piaget has also been criticized for underestimating preschoolers in some respects.[6] Other researchers have questioned whether there are really four separate stages of development, whether these stages overlaps as waves, and how people do move from one stage to another.[7] Piaget's theory of development has been applied in many different cultures, but there are still questions about how universal it really is. However, it is still a useful general framework to start with in seeing how people develop intellectually over time.

William Perry

William Perry was a counselor at Harvard University's Bureau of Study Council and did research in the 1960s on how college students learn during their undergraduate years, focusing mainly on male Harvard undergraduates.[8] He concluded that most freshmen were still in Stage 3 or the concrete operations stage as defined by Piaget. Perry observed how students went through four stages as they moved from concrete operations to more formal operations: dualism, multiplicity, relativism, and commitment to relativism.

Dualistic students are definitely concrete in their thinking. They believe that all problems are solvable, that there is one right answer to everything, that teachers and other experts know the answer, and that it is the student's responsibility to find, learn, memorize, and reproduce the answer on tests and in assignments. Dualistic students are often confused when authorities disagree with each other. College students are challenged in class to think about what they are learning, and such challenges often push them out of this stage. Interacting with more diverse classmates may also lead to a movement from dualism to multiplicity and later stages.

Students in the multiplicity stage believe that there is more than one way to solve a problem and that all ways are equally correct. They are likely to argue that everyone has a right to their opinions.

Students in the relativistic stage know that there is more than one answer to many problems, but some answers are better than others. As college students move into their majors or their professions, they may encounter criteria to help them determine which novel, poem, research procedure, or teaching method is best under a particular set of circumstances.

Perry found that some college students or graduates moved to a fourth stage—a commitment to relativism. Students would now be able to apply their ability to consider and evaluate several solutions to problems to make real-life educational, career, and personal decisions.

Women's Ways of Knowing

Researchers investigating women's development found that something was missing from Perry's observations, which had been based on a limited sample. Mary Belenky, Blythe Clinchy, Nancy Goldberger, and Jill Tarule, the four researchers who wrote *Women's Ways of Knowing* and other works, studied small groups of women from a wide variety of economic backgrounds and situations and concluded that while the women experienced many of the changes described by Perry, they were also experiencing other changes as well.[9] Gender and class had some effects on how these women moved from the concrete to the abstract in their development.

Dualistic women not only believe in one right answer to most problems, but they accept the word of all authorities in their lives—experts, parents, boyfriends, and so on. Many would silently listen to others and take in information. The researchers call this stage "received knowledge."

Women in the multiplicity stage see multiple solutions to problems and see them as equally valid, and they discover that truth is something existing not only "out there" but also within them. Since this team investigated a very diverse group of women, they found that their subjects' developmental changes were as likely to come from life experiences as from formal education. Working-class women who made this transition without initially going to college had caring teachers, professionals, friends, neighbors, and relatives in their lives.[10] In fact, some women in this situation went to college as a result of these changes, not the other way around.

Relativistic women are concerned with procedural knowledge. They believe that there is more than one answer to questions, that some answers are better than others, and that there are criteria to determine best solutions to problems. They also believe there is separated and connected knowledge. Separated knowledge is objective analysis. People using separated knowledge would determine what techniques to use to solve a problem. People using connected knowledge would see truth as "personal, particular, and grounded in firsthand experiences" and would ask, "how does this new information connect to me?"

Women committed to relativism would use "constructed knowledge" to apply procedural knowledge to their real-life decisions. While this research describes Perry's work as applying to men and Women's Ways of Knowing to women, all of this research can apply to people regardless of gender or class. These are general trends observed by all of these researchers.

Developmental Theories Criticized

Developmental theories are useful for public librarians because they show how people develop over time and sometimes over a lifetime. They do not explain everything about how people think and develop, but they provide useful background information. There are several issues and questions in the field of developmental psychology.

Do people always move from the concrete to the abstract? If so, how and when does this change happen? What does this development mean in teaching people and in their learning? When does adolescence really begin and end, and what does this mean? Several scholars, including Piaget, Perry, and researchers from Women's Ways of Knowing agree that people move from a concrete to a more abstract stage of development. Piaget believed that this happens to teens, but more recent researchers have found that this is more likely to happen to young adults in their late teens and twenties and have tracked ways in which this happens. All of these developments can affect how we instruct people at various stages of development in information use.

Do people mature with time, experience, or both? It appears that people mature both with time and with experience. Developmental theories would not show this maturation in full, but other theories and research, like cognitive theories, do show this evidence.

How universal are these theories, really? Most of these developmental theories suffer from being too centered in Western culture and too male oriented. This bias is shown in different results of research depending on gender. Almost everything described here is based on the work and observation of Westerners. However, some Western scholars have worked with much more diverse populations in their research. The early work of Erikson has already been mentioned. Herman A. Witkin's research on field dependence and independence and Howard Gardner's work on multiple intelligences will be described later in this chapter. In addition, educators, philosophers, and many scholars of color are just beginning to publish their finding on educational philosophies and learning styles within their own cultures. Other works in multicultural education can also be very useful. (Works on teaching diverse groups will be described in chapter 4.)

Are developmental theories too focused on isolated individuals? How do people develop in the context of their communities? Another researcher who wrote from a more communal Russian perspective was Lev Vygotsky, who described how people develop not only as individuals, but in the context of their communities. His work is described next.

Lev Vygotsky

Jean Piaget and Lev Vygotsky were contemporaries who both studied ways in which children develop intellectually. However, each reflected the society he came from: Piaget from the individualistic West (Switzerland) and Vygotsky from the more communal Soviet Union. Piaget described the development of people observed as individuals and believed that cognitive development makes social development possible. Lev Vygotsky believed the opposite, stating that "through others, we become ourselves."[11] According to him, children develop not only on their own but through their mastery of conceptual tools in the culture and through their interactions with peers, older children, and adults, including relatives, neighbors, and teachers. This development happens through both formal education in school and nonformal education in the home and community.

According to Vygotsky, children develop by interacting with people both more and less skilled than they are, including peers of different ages, older family members, and other people at school and in the community. When children are in a group of peers, especially those with different levels of skill, they often learn more from these peers than they would learn on their own. This same dynamic also applies to families. Vygotsky called this phenomenon the Zone of Proximal Development (ZPD). To help children and others develop, he suggested that teachers, parents, and other leaders use *scaffolding*, which is using questions, prompts, hints, suggestions, checklists, modeling, feedback, and cognitive structuring in the form of theories, categories, and rules to help students answer difficult questions and solve problems. He also maintained that instruction should be slightly ahead of what students know and can do at that time. By using scaffolding and taking advantage of Zones of Proximal Development, students can more quickly master new information that they cannot learn on their own. Scaffolding will be mentioned again as we consider constructivism in this chapter.

HOW PEOPLE ACT: BEHAVIORISM

One of the oldest theories of education that developed around the turn of the twentieth century is behaviorism, which is defined as a stimulus-response approach to learning. Behaviorists also define learning as any permanent change in behavior as a result of experience.

Behaviorism is concerned only with observable and measurable behavior, not with feelings or thinking. Behaviorists believe that all behavior is based on responses to external stimulation that rewards, encourages, ignores, or punishes the behavior.[12] The most influential behaviorist has been B.F. Skinner, whose contributions include operant conditioning, shaping, active learning, immediate feedback, programmed instruction, task analysis, and the idea that students should learn at their own pace.[13]

Operant conditioning involves influencing human behavior through reinforcement. Either positive or negative reinforcement can be used to reinforce positive behavior. Praise and other rewards can encourage positive behavior, or negative stimuli can be removed as a result. Negative behavior can be discouraged or eliminated through either punishment or "time-outs." Punishment is an unpleasant stimulant used to discourage negative behavior, and a time-out is removal from a positive stimulant until the negative behavior ceases.

The consequences to behavior of using various forms of reinforcement can be extinction, spontaneous recovery, generalization, or discrimination. Extinction is when a previously reinforced behavior decreases or ceases because it is no longer reinforced. Spontaneous recovery is the reappearance of the extinguished behavior, sometimes without reinforcement. With generalization, a person is trained to react in a particular way to a specific stimulus, so when the person is confronted with a similar one, he or she successfully behaves in a similar way. For instance, when students are introduced to one library Online Public Access Catalog (OPAC) or periodical database and use similar techniques to search similar but not identical sources, this is generalization. Discrimination is learning to notice unique aspects of seemingly similar situations, such as searching with Internet search tools and periodical databases.

Shaping is rewarding a behavior similar to the one desired. Over time, subjects must get closer to the desired behavior to be positively reinforced. Eventually, the person learns the behavior. Shaping is useful with complicated procedures or with students needing more help. Behavior modification is actively using reinforcement to encourage or discourage specific behaviors. This can be useful with autistic children and others.

Useful works about Skinner include *Walden Two* and *Beyond Freedom and Dignity* by Skinner and *What Is B.F. Skinner Really Saying?* by Robert D. Nye.[14] *Walden Two*, written by Skinner early in his career shortly after World War II, describes a utopian community based on his ideas. In the 1971 *Beyond Freedom and Dignity*, Skinner argues in favor of behavioral engineering in society as a whole to produce positive outcomes. Nye does an excellent exploration of Skinner's ideas and contributions.

Contributions of Behaviorism to Education and to ILI

Behaviorism has contributed several teaching and management techniques to the fields of education and ILI. It is definitely teacher centered and directed, with professionals determining the general curriculum as well as specific tasks of the day. There is an emphasis on changing students' behavior through modeling and imitation, shaping, other reinforcement, and if necessary, behavior modification. Other behaviorist teaching techniques are task analysis, programmed instruction, attempts at individualism, and the use of assessment and evaluation. Task analysis involves breaking down tasks into smaller steps. Mastery learning involves putting the steps into a particular order and making sure students master one step before moving to another.[15]

Programmed instruction, which was created by B.F. Skinner, is usually sequential, with steps in a certain order. This instruction can start with simple exercises where later questions build on earlier ones. Workbooks can be designed with programmed texts. Early computer-assisted instruction (CAI), a form of programmed learning, ranged from simple drill-and-practice exercises to tutorials, problem-solving activities, and simulations. All of these techniques have migrated to the Web in the form of computer tutorials.

Behaviorists individualize instruction for students in three ways. They design exercises that allow students to progress at their own pace. As instructors choose objectives for instruction, they attempt to select those that will meet specific student needs. Bloom's Taxonomy, a compendium of ranked teaching and learning objectives, is especially designed for this function. Instructors encourage active learning by urging students to investigate questions and problems. There is an emphasis on feedback, especially immediate reinforcement, so that teachers and students can tell what students are learning. Praise and other rewards are also used to promote learning.

Educational management techniques include using goals and objectives for planning and evaluation. Rubrics, outcomes, and other assessments are used to observe measurable changes in behavior. When students must actively behave in a certain way to prove that they have met a goal, this is behaviorism. Outcomes can be very tightly determined.

Behaviorism gives ILI its backbone, structure, and organization. We can see this in how activities are planned, organized, and evaluated and in some of the instructional techniques. The ACRL and AASL goals are geared to how students act and react as a result of ILI.

Positive and Negative Aspects of Behaviorism

Behaviorism has its advantages and disadvantages. Teachers using behaviorist methods assume and often make sure that all students can learn. Exercises are designed to enable students to do them at their own pace. Some students respond very well to this style of learning, and this approach can be very useful for some purposes. Behaviorists also strive to treat all users as "blank slates," which can have either a positive or a negative influence. In the debate between "nature vs. nurture," behaviorists believe that nurture, the environment, and stimulation have everything to do with how people behave.

Behaviorism can also be manipulative, controlling, impersonal, and mechanistic. Most early behaviorist research was based on animals and vulnerable people, like babies and small children. If used too rigidly, behaviorism can stifle the creativity of teachers and students. It is also not for everybody. Some people learn best in this way, while others are confused, frustrated, lost, or just plain bored. Using insights from different schools of learning and from different learning styles is important. However, behaviorist principles can be very useful as organizing tools, especially when used in moderation and in combination with cognitive, constructive, and humanistic approaches, to be described below.

HOW PEOPLE THINK: COGNITIVE THEORIES

Cognitive psychology started in the 1940s and really emerged in the 1960s and 1970s as a reaction to and criticism of behaviorism. Cognitive psychologists criticized behaviorism as too mechanistic, impersonal, and simplistic.[16] Cognitive psychologists differ from their behavioral counterparts the most in two aspects. First, while behaviorists focus only on behavior, cognitive psychologists are primarily concerned with what and how people think. To them, cognition is as important as behavior. Some cognitive psychologists are also concerned with people's feelings.

Second, to behaviorists, all people are blank slates to be affected strictly by positive and negative stimuli in their environment. Cognitive psychologists believe that people are already hardwired in their personalities, traits, and interests by the time they receive any formal education. They also believe that most people already have a base of knowledge, and when they learn something new, they are integrating this new information with what they already know. This is also a major concept of constructivism.

Cognitive psychologists can be divided into at least two groups. Some are concerned with information processing (or the brain as computer). They study how people use their brains to think. Others are concerned with metacognition and learning strategies. Metacognition is "thinking about thinking." Researchers in this area try to find better ways for people to learn.

Most researchers in education consider constructivism to be part of cognitive psychology, and for most ILI practitioners, it is the most important category of cognitive psychology. Constructivism, a blend of cognitive psychology and humanistic approaches to education, is discussed more fully in its own section of this chapter.

The Brain as Computer: Information Processing

Some cognitive psychologists compare the human brain to a computer in describing how people process information.[17] According to them, the human brain has a very short-term sensory store or register, short-term memory (STM), and long-term memory (LTM). The sensory register and STM can be compared to the short-term memory of a computer. On a computer, one must save the information on the screen before turning off the computer or it will disappear. In the case of humans, they must either transfer new information to their LTM or they will lose it. Human STM can only hold so much information for so long. Human LTM is comparable to a hard drive on a computer, storing information which will not be used right away. Information going from human STM to human LTM is similar to saving information on a computer screen to the hard drive.

Thinking About Thinking: Metacognition

Metacognition is how people think about their own thinking, especially as they develop strategies to solve problems.[18] Knowing what they know and do not know is a first step in devising an information-seeking strategy.

As people take in and learn new information, especially from books, they use several strategies to transfer information from their STM to their LTM, including rehearsal, elaboration, organization, comprehension, and affective strategies. Learners rehearse by repeating key terms aloud, taking notes, and underlining points important to them. They elaborate by connecting this new information with what they already know, and they organize it by imposing a structure on the materials that they gather. They comprehend by keeping track of their research strategies and adjusting their behavior as necessary, and they deal with their emotions by staying motivated, concentrating, and managing both their time and their anxiety.

Steps in metacognition or forming a learning plan include awareness of the search process, analysis, planning, and implementation of the plan. Researchers should be aware of what information is needed, formulate the learning plan, implement appropriate tactics, periodically monitor their progress, modify strategies when things go wrong, and realize why each step is important. They should analyze their results by asking what, when, where, why, who, and how questions. Many of these strategies are similar to information literacy and problem-solving strategies.

HOW PEOPLE SOLVE PROBLEMS: CONSTRUCTIVISM

Like cognitive psychology, constructivism is concerned with how people think, reason, and solve problems. However, it uses many humanistic teaching strategies that can be more easily adapted to traditional formal classrooms. There are many psychologists, educators, scholars, and movements with feet in both constructivism and humanism, but other forms of educational humanism take constructivism to its ultimate conclusions.

Constructivism is defined as learning by combining new knowledge with knowledge that is already with the user.[19] It is cognitive not only in considering how people integrate new information, but also in investigating many ways in which they can find information and solve problems. In this regard, constructivism is an application of metacognition. Constructivist educators use Problem-based Learning (PBL), Resource-based Learning (RBL), Discovery Learning, Guided Design, and independent learning in classrooms and other settings with an emphasis on critical thinking. Constructivist principles work especially well with science, mathematics, and other hands-on subjects, reflecting how most scientists learn. Library applications of constructivism are the core ILI goals of determining information needs and then finding, evaluating, and using information represented by the Big 6, the ACRL standards, the work of Alice Yucht and especially Carol Kuhlthau, and the creation of pathfinders and similar materials.

Constructivism is also promoted with the use of humanistic methods that can be applied in the traditional formal classroom with an emphasis on exploring and doing. Compared to behaviorism, there is a definite shift, with the student being the center of attention. Teachers still set the curriculum and plan most activities but with much more input from students. Teachers are no longer directors or "sages on stages" but are now facilitators or "guides from the side." The focus is now on students' needs and activities that will lead to self-discovery, problem solving, independent learning, or doing library and other research. There is an emphasis on many modes of learning, particularly active learning, and a shift from teaching as presentation to student learning. Activities are more self-directed and there is more emphasis on direct experience than on texts. Constructivism is now a dominant theory in formal education, traditional ILI, and some aspects of museum education or "interpretation," especially in science and children's museums.

Constructivism has a very interesting family tree. If we consider Jerome Bruner and David Ausubel to be the fathers of this school of thought, Jean Piaget and Lev Vygotsky are the psychological grandfathers. Educational forebears include Johann Pestalozzi, John Dewey, Maria Montessori, Paulo Freire, and bell hooks.

Jerome Bruner created Discovery Learning and Inquiry Learning. In Discovery Learning, students are provided with data and questions and expected to discover particular principles.[20] In Inquiry Learning, students must develop strategies to manipulate and process information. Inquiry Learning is related to both metacognition and ILI. The focus is not as much on the end product as on how students process the information. An ILI analogy to Inquiry Learning would be paper trails or diaries that students keep as they work on their research projects.

David Ausubel takes a more conservative approach to constructivism. He argues in favor of using expository or didactic teaching and reception learning as well as active learning.[21] In other words, teachers should introduce a concept with an overview or lecture first, then have students do active learning.

Jean Piaget laid the groundwork for constructivism later in his career by investigating schemes and adaptation.[22] He believed that people have schemes or intellectual ideas. As they learn new information, they either assimilate it by adding it to what they already know or they accommodate. By assimilating or accommodating, they may have to rearrange or discard some of their old knowledge to make way for the new. Disequilibrium is the discrepancy between a scheme and new information until this is resolved.

Lev Vygotsky's contribution to constructivism was scaffolding, which involves providing structure and prompts to help people learn and then withdrawing these as they master the new information.[23] Scaffolding helps students to traverse their Zones of Proxial Development. He also viewed play and social events as important in children's learning.

As educators in the nineteenth and early twentieth centuries, Johann Pestalozzi, Maria Montessori, and John Dewey all promoted active learning through manipulation of materials and by doing. Many of their classroom methods are precursors to those now used in constructivist classrooms. Constructivist ideas can also be found in the more recent work of Paulo Freire and bell hooks.[24] According to them, education should be not only for "banking" but something that can be applied to real life. Freire was concerned with promoting general literacy among oppressed people in a third world country. Pestalozzi and Montessori also worked with poor people in a variety of situations, and Dewey was very concerned with how education is tied to citizenship.

HOW PEOPLE FEEL: EDUCATIONAL HUMANISM

Educational humanism encompasses the contributions of humanist psychologists like Abraham Maslow, Carl Rogers, and Albert Bandura as well as multiple movements and phenomena, such as open, alternative, or free schools and classrooms, preschool education, adult education and lifelong learning, interpretation and other forms of nonformal education, home schooling and "deschooling." Public libraries are another important manifestation of educational humanism since they promote the nonformal education of people of all ages. They were created to supplement formal education provided by public school systems.

Educational humanism differs from constructivism in a number of ways, but mainly in degree. The biggest difference is that within educational humanism, students are freer to develop their own curriculum, if there is any. They determine what to learn and how and when to learn it. While teachers, librarians, and other professionals are involved to varying degrees, learning is driven by learners, not professionals.

In the first half of the twentieth century, educational humanism in the form of Montessori and progressive schools was very influential. Open classrooms and free schools in the United States and Great Britain in the 1960s and 1970s were another manifestation of educational humanism, which does not tend to dominate formal public education for long for three reasons. It does not work for all students or all situations. It can be difficult to account for, never mind manage. However, the main reason that educational humanism does not dominate public schools may be curricular. Who should determine what people learn in formal education and for what purposes? Many would say that teachers, librarians, and other professionals should determine what students should learn from their schooling, and that the purpose is to train students for work and for citizenship. Within educational humanism, however, learners are royalty and pursue their own educational goals.

Lifelong learners can informally educate themselves through self-teaching or consulting with experts, take advantage of institutions promoting nonformal learning, such as religious organizations, museums, camps, clubs, or public libraries, or pursue more formal education. As with constructivism, education in a humanistic context is often nonformal, with an emphasis on many modes of learning. The various manifestations of educational humanism can be grouped in the following way:

- Alternative schools and classrooms that can be progressive, open, free or pursue other philosophies.
- Nursery schools, kindergartens, day care centers, Montessori schools, preschool story hours and family literacy activities in libraries, and other programs for preschoolers.
- Adult education, lifelong learning as a movement, free-choice learning, the concept of andragogy, and public libraries as "people's universities" or Louis Shores's concept of the "library-college."
- Aspects of "interpretation" in museums and other informal settings, nonformal teaching and learning activities in religious and other organizations, and public library services to people throughout the life cycle.

Public libraries are a part of educational humanism in general. All of their traditional activities, cultural programs, literacy programs, reader's advisory services, community outreach, and networking are relevant when considering this school of educational thought. They all promote people's independent learning. These should be considered part of public library instruction.

Advocates for this point of view include the humanistic psychologists Abraham Maslow, Carl Rogers, and Albert Bandura.[25] Maslow discussed a hierarchy of needs and maintained that students' "higher order needs" could not be fulfilled without filling basic needs, such as for food or for security. Rogers wrote an excellent text on how to establish and run a school on humanistic principles. Bandura has created the concept of efficacy by combining humanism with behaviorism. In other words, how can people teach themselves to behave? His concept of efficacy, which is a combination of competence and confidence, is also a goal of ILI. These psychologists wrote for formal educators, but their principles apply just as well, if not better, in more informal settings.

Other modern and contemporary educators with links to this school of thought include Malcolm Knowles, A.S. Neill, Herbert Kohl, Freire, hooks, Nicholas Longworth, John H. Falk, Lynn D. Dierking, John Holt, and Ivan Illich.[26] Knowles was a major advocate of both adult education and the teaching method of andragogy, which draws on these humanistic principles. Neill ran Summerhill, one of the most famous "free schools" in Great Britain in the 1960s and 1970s. Kohl has written much on teaching in open, humanistic classrooms. Longworth describes how the movement of lifelong learning has evolved internationally, especially in Europe. Falk and Dierking have written *Lessons Without Limits*, which discusses lifelong "free-choice learning" in museums and other settings. They are also major writers in the field of interpretation or museum education. John Holt, who wrote about how children learn and fail, eventually became a proponent of the home schooling movement, and Illich wrote about "de-schooling society." Several of these educators have been involved in aspects of constructivism as well as in educational humanism, and some movements, like interpretation, have feet in both camps.

Postmodern aspects of humanistic education and some aspects of constructivism may emerge from the needs and characteristics of the Millennial Generation, gaming theories, the emergence of social networking and Internet 2.0, and the design of computer learning centers and information commons. It will be interesting to see what develops over time.

Traditional ILI is built largely on behaviorism, cognitive psychology, and constructivism and ends with constructivism. Although public librarians can certainly use aspects of behaviorism to plan, structure, and evaluate their instruction, much of what they do begins with constructivism and draws on educational humanism. Public libraries serve people of all ages, so public librarians can also draw on developmental psychology.

HOW PEOPLE LEARN: MODALITIES, FIELD DEPENDENCE AND INDEPENDENCE, AND MULTIPLE INTELLIGENCES

Perceptual Modalities

Modality is defined as "any of the sensory channels through which an individual receives and retains information."[27] Most researchers studying perceptual modalities have concluded that most learners are auditory, visual, or tactile and kinesthetic and that visual learners may either be visual/verbal or visual/nonverbal. Some researchers have discovered interactive, haptic, olfactory, and gustatory learners who learn through interactions with others, gestures, smell, and taste.[28] However, auditory, visual, and tactile learners have been studied the most.

Auditory people learn mainly by hearing. They respond very positively to lectures, discussions, audiotapes, the radio, and "talking heads" on television. In some cases, they may not take notes but may be able to remember a lecture just from listening to it. Auditory learners spell words by sounding them out and indicate they understand by saying "I hear you" or something similar. They will often learn how to operate computer programs through verbal instruction and talking to others, and if they have a problem, they can successfully consult with a computer guru over the telephone. Auditory learners respond well to well-designed lectures, discussions, and activities such as role-playing.

Visual individuals learn by seeing. Those who are visual/verbal learn especially by reading and respond well to written materials, such as textbooks and notes, as well as to charts, graphs, outlines, other organizers, and demonstrations. Visual/nonverbal learners respond to pictures, graphics, films, other media, and demonstrations, and some also respond well to charts, outlines, and other written materials. Visual learners in both groups take careful notes in order to concentrate, organize, and remember. They may also doodle during lectures and meetings and will sometime create their own charts to better understand a concept. They spell words by visualizing them and indicate their understanding by saying "I see" or something similar. Visual learners often depend on illustrated instructions to learn how to use a computer.

Tactile and kinesthetic individuals learn by doing. Most are very bored by lectures but respond well to activities in and out of class to enable them to apply what is being discussed in the lesson. Tactile learners take notes in class, not to remember but to have something to do. Some may knit or do something else while listening to presentations. Tactile learners spell words by physically tracing the letters, and when they understand something, they will say "I got it!" Tactile and kinesthetic learners learn about computers by diving in and experimenting right away. If one approach does not work, they try another. They respond best when lectures are supplemented not just by visuals but by relevant activities, and many thrive in classrooms using Discovery Learning.

It is not unusual for learners to have one learning style (such as a visual one) supplemented by a secondary style (such as auditory or tactile). If they do not understand something using one style, they may use their secondary style. It is also possible that some learners use different modalities to learn different things. For instance, most students would use the tactile method of "learning by doing" to master a musical instrument, computer applications, or methods of conducting scientific research, regardless of their usual learning styles.

Instructors can teach to perceptual modalities in several ways. They may combine lectures with good visuals and with activities to keep all of these learners engaged. If they will be teaching a group several times, they may also want to find out the predominant learning styles in the group and teach to those. Students with different learning styles can be accommodated with supplementary approaches.[29]

Field Dependence and Independence

This theory developed from the early, extensive research of Herman A. Witkin and Solomon Asch. During World War II, they investigated ways people react when they are getting different visual and gravitational cues. At first, individuals were put into tilting or rotating rooms. Later, they were given rod and frame tests where they were shown a tilted frame in a dark room and asked to adjust a rod to a vertical position. Subjects who always knew where they were in the first test or who could easily do the second task were described as field independent. Those having difficulty with such tasks were described as field dependent or sensitive. Later, Witkin developed an Embedded Figure Test that required people to find small shapes within a puzzle. Field independent people could do this very easily, while field dependent or sensitive people had more difficulty. Witkin discovered that people vary widely in their degree of field sensitivity and that they are quite consistent in this trait across many tests of orientation perception.[30]

Field dependent or sensitive individuals cannot see the trees for the forest. They have difficulty picking out shapes from a puzzle or finding camouflage or embedded figures. They are global, holistic learners who perceive a field as a unified whole. To them, context dominates. For instance, when learning that Abraham Lincoln was assassinated, they want to know what led to this event, what else was going on at the time, and what happened as a result. How did one thing affect another?

Field dependent learners learn skills (e.g., dancing) all at once without always knowing how they did these skills. They excel in summarizing information and respond well to cognitive and humanistic educational techniques. They sometimes depend on teachers or textbooks to give them context and may be lost with poorly organized instruction. They are influenced by others, such as teachers, parents, and peers, and in some cases, their view of themselves comes from others. Field dependent individuals are people oriented and have strong interpersonal and social skills. They prefer people to things and the personal to the abstract, and they enjoy careers in the humanities, social sciences, and arts. They are also more drawn to qualitative research.

Field independent people, on the other hand, cannot see the forest for the trees. They have no problem picking out shapes from a puzzle or finding camouflaged or embedded figures. They are analytical students who learn through task analysis or breaking a subject or process into steps or sometimes mastery learning. To them, detailed pieces of information are more important than summaries, and context does not matter as much to them. Field independent learners respond well to behaviorist and discovery teaching techniques.

Field independent individuals have a strong sense of identity from the beginning and are not as influenced by other people as their more field dependent peers. When learning from poorly organized materials, these learners can create their own order. Field independent people are oriented more to the impersonal or abstract than to the more personal, and they are object or idea oriented. They tend to be good at mathematics, science, and quantitative research.[31]

For teachers, the lesson to draw from variations in field dependency is to provide context for field dependent learners and research and learning steps for more field independent ones. Let learners know what will be covered and preview, view, and review. Also have research steps that can be covered one at a time. These teaching methods will accommodate both styles of learning.

In his research, Witkin "looked for unifying constructs to incorporate findings from different areas of psychology," such as psychoanalysis, the study of individual differences, and experimental cognitive psychology. In education, his theories have been applied to the ways teachers teach and students learn, to their interaction with each other, and to ways of counseling students in their career decisions. Witkin also studied a wide variety of societies around the world later in his career.[32]

Multiple Intelligences

Howard Gardner defines intelligence as the "ability to solve problems or to create products that are valued within one or more cultural settings."[33] Gardner described and criticized traditional IQ tests that were created in 1900 by Albert Binet for giving a one-dimensional view of intelligence for "uniform schools" with uniform or core curricula. He also criticized Western education for being "Westist, testist, and bestist"—for emphasizing the West to the neglect of the rest of the world, for focusing on written tests that measure language and mathematical ability only, and for basing all answers on one approach.

Gardner describes at least seven kinds of intelligence that schools should account for: among them are the verbal-linguistic intelligence of writers and orators; the logistical-mathematical intelligence of mathematicians and scientists; the visual-spatial intelligence of artists, engineers, and some scientists; the body-kinesthetic intelligence of dancers, athletes, actors, typists, and pianists; and the musical intelligence of musicians, composers, and listeners. Gardner also discusses at length two more personal kinds of intelligence: intrapersonal, or the ability to understand oneself, and interpersonal, the ability to understand and to get along with others.

Gardner defines each type of intelligence, describes how each one develops as a child grows, discusses biological aspects of it, and in some cases describes how the intelligence is applied in different cultures. He maintains that linguistic and musical intelligence usually emerges very early, that Piaget's theory of cognitive stages is a good description of how mathematicians develop, and that Erikson and Vygotsky describe the emergence of the personal intelligences, which depend more on what is going on in society. Gardner also describes high intelligence and achievement in each of these areas, multiple intelligences in exceptional people, and how different intelligences relate to each other. He concludes that educators should take all of these forms of intelligence into account as they plan their curricula, instruction, and assessment. Like Erikson and Witkin, Gardner has also studied a wide diversity of people from around the world, and his theory is more universal than some others. (Other aspects of reaching and teaching diverse people will be discussed in the next two chapters.)

NOTES

1. Jack Snowman, Rick McCowan, and Robert Biehler, *Psychology Applied to Teaching*, 12th ed. (Boston: Houghton Mifflin, 2009), 23–68, 219–359, 370–430; Esther S. Grassian and Joan R. Kaplowitz, *Information Literacy Instruction: Theory and Practice*, 2nd ed. (New York: Neal-Schuman, 2009), 27–64; Funderstanding, About Learning, www.funderstanding.com/about_learning.cfm.

2. Erik Erikson, *Childhood and Society* (New York: Norton, 1963, reissued, 1993), 247–74; Erikson, *Identity: Youth and Crisis* (New York: Norton, 1968); Snowman, McCowan, and Biehler, *Psychology Applied to Teaching*, 25–34; Myron H. Dembo, *Applying Educational Psychology in the Classroom* (New York: Longman, 1988), 84–88; Robert Hogan, "Erik Erikson," in *Personality Theory: The Personological Tradition* (Englewood Cliffs, N.J.: Prentice-Hall, 1976), 164–86.

3. Richard Stevens, *Erik Erikson: An Introduction* (New York: St. Martin's, 1983); Lawrence Jacob Friedman, *Identity's Architect: A Biography of Erik H. Erikson* (New York: Scribner, 1999).

4. Snowman, McCowan, and Biehler, *Psychology Applied to Teaching*, 32–33.

5. Snowman, McCowan, and Biehler, *Psychology Applied to Teaching*, 34–46, 52–53, 54–55; W. Huitt and J. Hummel, "Piaget's Theory of Cognitive Development," *Educational Psychology Interactive* (Valdosta, Ga.: Valdosta State University), www.edpsycinteractive.org/topics/cogsys/piaget.html; Dembo, *Applying Educational Psychology in the Classroom*, 52–62.

6. Snowman, McCowan, and Biehler, *Psychology Applied to Teaching*, 42–44.

7. Snowman, McCowan, and Biehler, *Psychology Applied to Teaching*, 42–43.

8. William G. Perry, *Forms of Intellectual and Ethical Development in the College Years: A Scheme* (New York: Holt, Rinehart and Winston), 57–200; Perry, "Cognitive and Ethical Growth: The Making of Meaning," in *The Modern American College*, ed. Arthur W. Chickering and associates (San Francisco: Jossey-Bass, 1981), 76–116; Peter Jarvis, John Holford, and Colin Griffin, *The Theory and Practice of Learning* (London: Kogan Page, 1988), 69–73; Rebecca Jackson, "Cognitive Development: The Missing Link in Teaching Information Literacy Skills," *Reference and User Services Quarterly* 46, no. 4 (2007): 28–32.

9. Mary F. Belenky, Blythe M. Clinchy, Nancy R. Goldberger, and Jill M. Tarule, *Women's Ways of Knowing: The Development of Self, Voice, and Mind* (New York: Basic Books, 1986), 10th anniversary ed., 1997; Goldberger, Tarule, Clinchy, and Belenky, eds., *Knowledge, Difference, and Power: Essays Inspired by Women's Ways of Knowing* (New York: Basic Books, 1996); William J. Rapaport, *William Perry's*

Scheme of Intellectual Development: A Journey Along the 9 "Perry Positions" (as Modified by Belenky et al.), www.cse.buffalo.edu/%7Erapaport/perry.positions.html; Jarvis, Holdford, and Griffin, *The Theory and Practice of Learning*, 69–73.

10. Belenky, Clinchy, Goldberger, and Tarule, *Women's Ways of Knowing*, 160–63.

11. Snowman, McCowan, and Biehler, *Psychology Applied to Teaching*, 46–52, 53–54.

12. Snowman, McCowan, and Biehler, *Psychology Applied to Teaching*, 219–44, 370–73,407–8; Grassian and Kaplowitz, *Information Literacy Instruction*, 28–30; C. George Boeree, "Behaviorism," http://webspace.ship.edu/cgboer/beh.html; Jarvis, Holford, and Griffin, *The Theory and Practice of Learning*, 21–28; Dembo, *Applying Educational Psychology in the Classroom*, 279–321.

13. Bouree, "Behaviorism"; Daniel W. Bjork, *B.F. Skinner: A Life* (Washington, D.C.: American Psychological Association, 1997); Richard I. Evans, *B.F. Skinner: The Man and His Ideas* (New York: Dutton, 1968).

14. B.F. Skinner, *Walden Two* (Indianapolis, Ind.: Hackett, 2005); Skinner, *Beyond Freedom and Dignity* (Indianapolis, Ind.: Hackett, 2002); Robert D. Nye, *What Is B.F. Skinner Really Saying?* (Englewood Cliffs, N.J.: Prentice-Hall, 1979).

15. Grassian and Kaplowitz, *Information Literacy Instruction*, 28–30.

16. Snowman, McCowan, and Biehler, *Psychology Applied to Teaching*, 245–73, 322–60, 373–86, 411–28; Grassian and Kaplowitz, *Information Literacy Instruction*, 30–36; Dembo, *Applying Educational Psychology in the Classroom*, 323–62.

17. Snowman, McCowan, and Biehler, *Psychology Applied to Teaching*, 245–58.

18. Dembo, *Applying Educational Psychology in the Classroom*, 323–28; Snowman, McCowan, and Biehler, *Psychology Applied to Teaching*, 258–67; Dembo, *Applying Educational Psychology in the Classroom*, 329–59.

19. Jerome Bruner, *Towards a Theory of Instruction* (Cambridge, Mass.: Belknap, 1967); Bruner, *In Search of Mind: Essays in Autobiography* (New York: Harper and Row, 1983); David Ausubel, *The Psychology of Meaningful Verbal Learning* (New York: Grune and Stratton, 1963); Ausubel, *Educational Psychology: A Cognitive View* (New York: Holt, Rinehart and Winston, 1968); Jacqueline Grennon Brooks and Martin G. Brooks, *In Search of Understanding: The Case for Constructivist Classrooms* (Alexandria, Va.: Association for Supervision and Curriculum Development, 1999); Concept to Classroom, *Constructivism as a Paradigm for Teaching and Learning*, www.thirteen.org/edonline/concept2class/constructivism/index.html; Snowman, McCowan, and Biehler, *Psychology Applied to Teaching*, 322–48.

20. Bruner, *Towards a Theory of Instruction*; Bruner, *In Search of Mind*.

21. Ausubel, *The Psychology of Meaningful Verbal Learning*; Ausubel, *Educational Psychology*.

22. Snowman, McCowan, and Biehler, *Psychology Applied to Teaching*, 34–36.

23. Snowman, McCowan, and Biehler, *Psychology Applied to Teaching*, 50–51.

24. Gerald L. Gutek, "Froebel, Friedrich (1782–1852)," in *Encyclopedia of Education*, 2nd ed. (New York: Thomson/Gale, 2003), vol. 3, 903–6; Gutek, "Pestalozzi, Johann (1746–1827)," in *Encyclopedia of Education*, vol. 5, 1874–76; Timothy David Selden, "Montessori, Maria (1870–1952)," in *Encyclopedia of Education*, vol. 5, 1675–80; Jonas F. Soltis, "Dewey, John (1859–1952)," in *Encyclopedia of Education*, vol. 2, 577–82; Peter McLaren and Noah De Lissousky, "Paulo Freire (1921–1997)," in *Encyclopedia of Education*, vol. 3, 900–3; Paulo Freire, *Pedagogy of the Oppressed*

(New York: Continuum, 2000); bell hooks, *Teaching to Transgress: Education as the Practice of Freedom* (New York: Routledge, 1994).

25. Snowman, McCowan, and Biehler, *Psychology Applied to Teaching*, 386–93, 428–30; Grassian and Kaplowitz, *Information Literacy Instruction*, 36–39; Carl Rogers, *Freedom to Learn* (New York: Merrill, 1994); Abraham Maslow, "A Theory of Human Motivation," in *Motivation and Personality* (New York: Harper and Row, 1970), 35–58; Dembo, *Applying Educational Psychology in the Classroom*, 387–425.

26. Gutek, "Pestalozzi, Johann (1746–1827)"; Selden, "Montessori, Maria (1870–1952)"; Sevan G. Terzian, "Rousseau, Jean Jacques (1712–1778)," in *Encyclopedia of Education*, vol. 6, 2079–81; Malcolm Knowles, *The Adult Learner: The Definitive Classic in Adult Education and Human Resource Development* (Amsterdam: Elsevier, 2005); Knowles, *The Modern Practice of Adult Education: From Pedagogy to Andragogy* (Chicago: Follett, 1980); Alexander Sutherland Neill, *Summerhill School: A New View of Childhood* (New York: St. Martin's, 1993); Herbert Kohl, *The Discipline of Hope: Learning from a Lifetime of Teaching* (New York: New Press, 1998); Kohl, *36 Children* (New York: New American Library, 1988); Kohl, *The Open Classroom: A Practical Guide to a New Way of Teaching* (New York: New York Review, 1970); Paulo Freire, *Pedagogy of the Oppressed*; Norman Longworth, *Lifelong Learning in Action: Transforming Education in the 21st Century* (London: Kogan Page, 2003); Longworth, *Making Lifelong Learning Work: Learning Cities for a Learning Century* (London: Kogan Page, 1999); John H. Falk and Lynn D. Dierking, *Lessons Without Limit: How Free-Choice Learning Is Transforming Education* (Lanham, Md.: Rowman & Littlefield, 2002); John Holt, *How Children Learn* (Reading, Mass.: Addison-Wesley, 1995); Holt, *How Children Fail* (Reading, Mass.: Addison-Wesley, 1995); Holt, *Freedom and Beyond* (Portsmouth, N.H.: Boynton/Cook, 1995); Holt, *Instead of Education: Ways to Help People Do Things Better*, 2nd ed. (Talent, Ore.: Sentient, 2003); Holt and Pat Farenga, *Teach Your Own: The John Holt Book of Homeschooling* (Da Capo, 2003); Ivan Illich, *Deschooling Society* (New York: Marion Boyars, 2000).

27. Walter Burke Barbe and Raymond H. Swassing, *Teaching Through Modality Strengths: Concepts and Practices* (Columbus, Ohio: Zaner-Bloser, 1988), 1–3.

28. Stephen Rayner and Richard J. Riding, "Towards a Categorization of Cognitive Styles and Learning Styles," *Educational Psychology* 17, nos. 1–2 (1997): 5–27.

29. Barbe and Swassing, *Teaching Through Modality Strengths*; Colin Rose, *Accelerated Learning* (New York: Dell, 1985), 145–57; Rose, "Learning Styles," in *Accelerated Learning*, http://chaminade.org/inspire/learnstl.htm; Marlene LeFever, *Learning Styles: Reaching Everyone God Gave You to Teach* (Colorado Springs, Colo.: David C. Cook, 1995), 99–107; University of Illinois, Illinois Online Network (ION), "Learning Styles and the Online Environment," www.ion.uillinois.edu/resources/tutorials/id/learningstyles.asp.

30. David R. Goodenough, "History of the Field Dependence Construct," in *Field Dependence in Psychological Theory, Research, and Application: Two Symposia in Memory of Herman A. Witkin*, ed. Mario Bertini, Luigi Pizzamiglio, and Seymour Wapner (Hillside, N.J.: Lawrence Erlbaum, 1986), 5–13.

31. *Field Dependence in Psychological Theory, Research, and Application*; H.A. Witkin, C.A. Moore, D.R. Goodenough, and P.W. Cox, "Field-Dependent and Field Independent Cognitive Styles and Their Educational Implications," *Review of Educational Research* 47, no. 1 (1977): 1–64; Bertini, "Some Implications of Field Dependence

for Education," in Bertini, Pizzamiglio, and Wapner, *Field Dependence in Psychological Theory, Research, and Application*, 93–106; Dembo, *Applying Educational Psychology in the Classroom*, 69–70.

32. Seymour Wapner, "Introductory Remarks," in Bertini, Pizzamiglio, and Wapner, *Field Dependence in Psychological Theory, Research, and Application*, 1–4.

33. Howard Gardner, *Frames of Mind: The Theory of Multiple Intelligences*, x; Gardner, "In a Nutshell," in *Multiple Intelligence: The Theory in Practice* (New York: Basic Books, 1993), 5–12; Gardner and Joseph Walter, "A Rounded Version," in *Multiple Intelligence*, 13–34; Gardner and Walter, "Questions and Answers About Multiple Intelligence Theory," in *Multiple Intelligence*, 35–48; Katherine Holmes, "Use ALL Your Smarts: Multiple Intelligences for Diverse Library Users," http://lesley.edu/faculty/kholmes/presentations/MI.html; *Multiple Intelligences for Adult Literacy and Education*, http://literacyworks.org/mi/home.html; *Walter McKenzie's One and Only Surfaquarium: I Think . . . Therefore MI: Multiple Intelligences in Education*, http://surfaquarium.com/MI/index.htm.

4

Teaching Diverse Groups

The United States is a very diverse country. "In 2000, 18 percent (almost one of five) of Americans spoke a language at home other than English," according to James Banks.[1] The U.S. immigration rate is now the highest it has been since the last major wave of immigration in 1880–1924.[2] One hundred years ago, most immigrants came from southern, central, and eastern Europe. Now they are coming from around the world, with many from Asian and Latin American countries.

This immigration is also leading to a dramatic increase in racial minorities in the United States. Almost one out of three Americans (30.6 percent) was a person of color in 2005, and in 2006 white people made up 70 percent of the workforce. Caucasians are expected to make up 65.5 percent of the workforce by 2014.[3] Forty-two percent of public school students are also from racial minorities, and this proportion is expected to rise to 45.5 percent or almost half by 2014.[4] Most cities and a growing number of suburbs are "majority minority" areas, and several states—Hawaii, California, and New York—are showing similar shifts. Moreover, one out of five people in the United States has an impairment or disability that interferes with their daily lives, and one in ten has a serious one.[5] As people age, this percentage climbs dramatically.

All of the groups described in this chapter and the next have defining characteristics, such as another country of origin, an ethnic identity, or an impairment or disability. Group members are defined both by other group members and by "outsiders," and membership in these groups, except for international students and some immigrants, is not generally voluntary. One can also belong to more than one group, as an immigrant who is also a person of color with a disability, for instance. All of these groups have been discriminated against in many ways by the mainstream culture, and often they have developed alternative cultures with institutions, leaders, and advocates as well as alternative materials, techniques, technologies, and ways of learning and living.

All of these groups vary widely and can be divided in various ways: international students by country of origin, level of education, and field of study; immigrants by country of origin, length of time in the new country, generation, and wave of immigration; racial minorities by tribes or countries of origin, religion, social class, and level of education; people with disabilities by type and degree of disability, age of onset, and best ways to access and use information.

International students and immigrants are alike in that they come from different countries and experience culture shock as they come to the United States. These two groups also differ in a number of ways. International students are usually college students with at least a secondary school education and some exposure to libraries. Library development in home countries can vary widely. Most international students need to find out how U.S. libraries differ from those at home, and how to make the best use of these libraries. Most use academic libraries.

According to the Immigration Act of 1965, most legal immigrants must have a skill that is desired in the United States. However, this act also provides for refugees.[6] Even though current immigrants are better trained and educated than many of their counterparts a century ago, they can still vary widely on how literate they are in their own language and how well they read, speak, and understand English. Some may have used public, academic, or national libraries at home, but others may have no library experience at all and view libraries as being only for the elite. While some immigrants stay in the United States for only brief periods of time, many are here permanently. They usually seek both to keep up with developments in their home countries and to learn in the new. Most immigrants use public or school libraries, although some (and their children) also use academic libraries.

Insights on international students and immigrants come from anthropology and other social sciences, studies by academic librarians, and comparative librarianship. A very useful explanation of the experiences of both new immigrants and international students comes from the culture shock theories of E.T. Hall, Wilma Longstreet, and Patty Lane. Academic librarians have studied problems that international students face in using libraries and have designed Information Literacy Instruction (ILI) to help students adjust. Public librarians work with community agencies to design collections and cultural, literacy, and other programming for diverse groups. They also do outreach. Leading libraries serving immigrant and ethnic groups include the Queens Library in New York, Brooklyn Public Library,

Cleveland Public Library, Chicago Public Library, Los Angeles Public Library, Los Angeles County Public Library, and Seattle Public Library. Other cities have also created outreach and services for immigrants. The Hartford, Public Library, Connecticut, has "The American Place," while the San Antonio Public Library in Texas has created "New Immigrants Centers" at six of their branches.[7] School librarians have explored creative ways to design curriculum and acquire materials for new immigrants in their libraries, often on a relative shoestring. Sources on comparative and international librarianship can also be very useful, especially materials on international children's and young adult literature.

Insights on multiculturalism, cultural diversity, and interactions among *people of different ethnic groups* come from many sources: ethnic studies, multicultural education, writings by professionals who work with diverse groups, community experts, scholars, professionals, leaders, media, libraries, museums, and other resources from local, regional, national, and international (or diasporic) ethnic communities. Solutions to issues include cultural competence, ethnic collections, programming, community outreach, networking, and related instruction. (Insights on people with disabilities and the best ways to teach them will be described in chapter 5.)

Two approaches to instruction that try to be universal are multicultural education and Universal Design (UD). Multicultural education is designed to reach users of all nationalities and ethnicities. Universal Design, which includes Universal Design of Learning (UDL), Universal Design of Instruction (UDI), and Universal Design of Information Literacy (UDIL), is designed to reach all people whether or not they have a disability. Universal Design started out as a concept in architecture to design buildings to be accessible to everybody. Principles of Universal Design have migrated to UDL (used on the K–12 level), UDI (used in higher education), and UDIL (Universal Design applied to ILI). Multicultural education as well as the acknowledgement of different learning styles, such as perceptual modality, field dependence and independence, and multiple intelligences, will be described in this chapter. Universal Design will be described in chapter 5. These approaches are best for most situations when there are multiple small groups of people to be served all at once and librarians do not know characteristics of specific groups.

However, there are times when librarians need to focus more on particular groups. Some circumstances that may call for this focus include minorities that are majorities or at least large groups in an area, substantial minorities with many needs, groups that need more attention than usual, and situations when library staff and the group in question do not connect very well.

Academic and especially public libraries have used both foreign-language and English-language programming, guides, and activities to reach a diverse public. Original languages and cultures can be bridges to a new experience for immigrants and international students. English-language materials and programs reach all people who want to learn about diverse groups. A combination of approaches is often necessary.

Some ethnic materials can be quite useful and are often a real necessity in areas with large populations from particular groups. These materials can provide insight for librarians working with diverse groups and can sometimes be useful for the public as well. It is important that ethnic materials be authentic, accurate, and able to cross cultures so that all can benefit.

In terms of what is covered in ILI sessions and related programs, two types of materials will be mentioned—materials *about* the group in question, and survival and other more general information needed *for* group members. Materials about groups of people should come from both mainstream and more ethnic sources.

LIBRARY INSTRUCTION FOR
INTERNATIONAL STUDENTS AND IMMIGRANTS

Culture Shock

Culture shock can be defined as "feelings of uncertainty and discomfort experienced . . . in a different culture."[8] Three groups of people who are likely to experience culture shock are those traveling or living abroad, those encountering very different cultures without leaving their countries, and expatriates who have returned home. There are four phases in culture shock: euphoria, anxiety, adjustment, and readjustment. People new to a culture often experience it as exotic and a lot of fun. After being in this culture for awhile, they realize that rules that worked at home no longer work in the new environment and they experience considerable frustration. Eventually, many adjust and can see positive and negative aspects of both their own culture and the new one. Upon returning to their home country, sojourners and ex-patriots go through culture shock all over again as they readjust to home.[9] Cultures clash when individuals from different cultures encounter each other and offend each other, without necessarily understanding why. The most theoretical works on culture shock and culture clash have been by social scientists and educators, such as E.T. Hall, Wilma Longstreet, and Patty Lane.

Hall wrote four books between 1959 and 1981 focusing on how people in different cultures view and use time and space.[10] He also discussed whether cultures were "high or low context," hierarchical or equalitarian, and collective or individual.[11] Many year later, Lane elaborated on the characteristics of cultures. She defined high context cultures as holistic ones where many things are implied rather than explained. Low context cultures function by breaking things down into separate parts and much more is explained in instruction, legislation, regulations, and even commercials. In hierarchical societies, which are organized by age, class, sex, ethnicity, or other categories, some groups have more status than others and are addressed and treated accordingly. Some societies are much more equalitarian, at least in principle. In collective societies, one's status and fate rest on one's family, tribe, ethnicity, or community. How well or poorly one does reflects back on one's community. This structure gives individuals social support but may make it difficult for them to do anything very unusual. On the other hand, people in more individualistic societies rise and fall more on their own efforts. They are also more likely to be socially isolated.[12]

Longstreet described in detail the five ways in which culture clash can occur.[13] She calls these "aspects of ethnicity," and they include:

- Verbal communication—ethnic issues in learning and judging speech, grammatical structures of languages and dialects, denotations and connotations (dictionary definitions of words and how they are really used by specific people), and discussion modes or conversational etiquette.
- Nonverbal communication—how people use space in conversation and in general (proxemics), and the frequency, quality, and location of touch (haptics).
- Orientation modes—use of space and time: body, postures, attention modes, design of architectural spaces, and the use of time.
- Social value patterns—written and unwritten rules of social behavior.
- Intellectual modes—learning and teaching styles valued by a culture.

Research by Academic Librarians

Many of these issues would become very salient as academic librarians interacted with international students at the reference desk and concluded that separate orientations were necessary in the 1980s. They published articles on the culture shock experienced by their international students and what to do about that. In 1995, Alan Natowitz summarized articles published between 1987 and 1993 and concluded that international students had language, cultural, and technological barriers interfering with their library use.[14] Students speaking English as a second language had half the reading comprehension of their U.S. classmates and less oral comprehension. Culture clash also occurred because of differences between libraries in the home country and those in the new country.

Several studies in the 1990s focused more on how international students use information. Mary Beth Allen asked students how they use online catalogs in the United States and computers in their home countries.[15] Lucinda Zoe and Diane Di Martino investigated how international students used electronic databases.[16] M.X. Liu and B. Redfern investigated "successful information seeking behavior in the library" by multicultural students.[17] All of these researchers concluded that there were cultural and language barriers to using libraries, and they recommended that library staff be more culturally aware and sensitive.

In 2000, Diane DiMartino and Lucinda Zoe further addressed issues mentioned by Natowitz, including cultural differences, learning styles, and multiple intelligences.[18] They focused particularly on language and technological issues faced by students, with an emphasis on how they were dealing with new technologies that emerged in the 1990s. In 2009, Charity K. Martin, Charlene Maxey-Harris, Jolie Ogg Graybill, and Elizabeth K. Rodacker Borgen did similar research on international students and found that they were using library resources as much as or more than their U.S. counterparts and that they were more comfortable using computers.[19] These developments may have been due to the increasing use of computers around the world, particularly by students from more affluent countries. In addition, computer programs like Google have pages geared to many countries, and computer pages can be translated into many languages.

However, while international students could find and use resources, it was discovered that all students needed more help on how to interpret these resources. Pamela Jackson surveyed international students and found that they were unfamiliar with interlibrary loan, consulting with librarians, and online or virtual reference services.[20] However, both Jackson and the team of Yan Liao, Mary Finn, and Jun Lu were discovering that international students were becoming as comfortable with computers and library resources as any of their U.S. counterparts.[21]

Some academic librarians have used public library marketing techniques to reach international students. In addition to tours, orientations, handbooks, Web pages, instructional sessions, and consultations, some librarians, such as those at the University of Tennessee, do book exhibits on international themes, do virtual outreach with diversity resource guides and subject guides on language resources in the library, meet students at their events, and do outreach and pursue partnerships with appropriate departments, such as the International Student Office.[22]

Comparative and International Librarianship

It is also possible to draw insights from the field of comparative and international librarianship to help both international students and recent immigrants. This literature describes library traditions, history, and trends as well as developments in publishing and other related industries. In this literature, we find that libraries reflect political, economic, social, and other trends in their country. More recent information describes the impact of computers, the Internet, and the information industry on people in many countries.

The literature on comparative librarianship and international librarianship reflects how these fields are treated within our profession. These fields go in and out of style, and much of the literature is old. Comparative librarianship investigates the state of librarianship in many countries and regions and compares library development in one country with that in others. International librarianship is more concerned with how librarians from different countries interact with each other, with a lot of attention paid to activities of librarians from developed Western countries in developing countries.

One helpful publication on comparative librarianship is *Global Library and Information Science: A Textbook for Students and Educators* by Ismail Abdullahi. This book gives information on current developments in public and academic libraries in most countries. Another helpful book is *Libraries: Global Reach—Local Touch*, edited by Kathleen de la Pena McCook and Kate Lippincott. Current books on international librarianship include *Global Librarianship*, edited by Martin Alan Resselman and Irwin Weintraub; *International Librarianship: Cooperation and Collaboration* by Frances Laverne Caroll and John Frederick Harvey; and *International Librarianship: A Basic Guide to Global Knowledge Access* by Robert D. Stueart.[23]

To find current information on a country, consult a library science database and type the name of the country. You can find information in *Library Literature and Information Science; Library, Information Science and Technology Abstracts (LISTA)*; and *Library and Information Science Abstracts (LISA)*, which is very international in scope. Another possibility is to look in education or general databases and combine the subject term "libraries" with the name of the country. For information on international children's literature, consult *Bookbird*, a scholarly professional periodical on this subject; *International Companion Encyclopedia of Children's Literature*, edited by Peter Hunt and Sheila Ray; and *Global Perspectives on Children's Literature* by Evelyn B. Freeman and Barbara Lehman, as well as other sources.[24]

Two reference tools with background on libraries in many countries are the *World Encyclopedia of Library and Information Services* and the original, historic *Encyclopedia of Library and Information Science*. Two older books with useful historical information are *World Librarianship: A Comparative Study* by Richard Krzys and Gaston Litton and *The World of Children's Literature* by Anne Pellowski.[25] Krzys also gives a good theoretical foundation for this field. Knowing about international and comparative librarianship can be useful for librarians working with international students and recent immigrants. They can use their knowledge about library traditions and current trends to prepare orientations for their patrons.

From Immigrant to Ethnic Communities

Immigrant groups are concerned both about their own cultures and about their new society, but they change in how they express these concerns over time. With some religious and political exceptions, recent immigrants—Generation 1.0—are still interested in news and other developments from home, so some materials from home countries and in original languages are still relevant and desired. The free databases *Paperboy* and *AJR Newslink* enable immigrants and others to look up newspapers from around the world.[26] Recent immigrants also need survival information on how to learn or improve their English, how to find employment, how to get a green card or become a citizen, and other issues.

Young people from Generation 1.5 can remember leaving the home country as young children but do much of their growing up here. Their needs often differ from relatives in both Generations 1.0 and 2.0. Immigrants' children born in this country—Generation 2.0—are often bilingual, bicultural, and conflicted. They feel both internal and external pressures to assimilate and may be ambivalent about their countries of origin. Third generation—Generation 3.0—children are usually assimilated Americans who are monolingual in English.[27] In looking for information on "the old country," they are looking for their genealogical or cultural roots.

While most international students can read English better than they can speak or comprehend it, students from Generation 1.5 are in the opposite situation. They speak English fluently and understand it well orally, but they may have more difficulty reading and writing it. Most international students are visual or "eye learners" who learned English largely through reading and the study of grammar. Generation 1.5 students learn English orally, largely by immersion. They are "ear learners."[28]

Materials on and by immigrant groups change over time. Early immigrants may initially use materials from their home countries and languages, but once they have been in their new country for awhile, they form their own organizations and media and often start language or cultural schools for their children. Some groups have started colleges, and there are ethnic studies departments at universities. Ethnic media go from being in original languages to being bilingual to eventually becoming English-language. They usually are concerned with the local, regional, national, and international or diasporic community but eventually become more locally and nationally oriented. It is important to collect materials and information from these groups, to work with their organizations, agencies, and leaders, and to advertise in their local media.

Solutions

Academic librarians have worked with international students by studying their interactions at the reference desk and their use of catalogs, databases, and other library materials. They have used this research to design instructional programs for their students. Public libraries have served their immigrant populations through outreach and networking to community agencies, developing collections, and executing cultural and literacy programs, including ESL and citizenship classes. Sometimes they work with other agencies to present programs in foreign languages. They also do cultural programs in English on diverse groups for the entire community.

Two books from the 1990s on serving immigrants in school libraries are *Serving Linguistically and Culturally Diverse Students* by Melvina Azar Dame and *Multicultural Aspects of Library Media Programs* by Kathy Howard Latrobe and Mildred Knight Laughlin.[29] Dame includes a chapter on "Library Literacy Activities That Teach and Reinforce Language," especially for ESL students. She also presents many creative collection development ideas, especially for financially strapped libraries. The text by Latrobe and Laughlin is similar to more general multicultural education textbooks but focuses on school media applications. It has chapters on specific needs and characteristics of children from various groups. Since those texts were published, much more has been done on multicultural education, and through Internet searches, librarians can easily seek out more current information.

Public librarians may want to combine their traditional programming for immigrants with some ILI. Some libraries have designed handbooks in various languages for specific groups. Public librarians can also create tours, orientations, tutorials, Web pages, pathfinders, and instructional sessions. They can work with parents and community leaders to combine ILI with outreach, networking, and programming. ILI can be part of literacy, ESL, and citizenship classes as well.

LIBRARY INSTRUCTION FOR ETHNIC AND RACIAL GROUPS

Insights from Related Fields

Insights on teaching ethnically diverse people and teaching about these groups come from many sources: cultural competence, multicultural education, earlier Library Information Science (LIS) literature, educators who teach diverse students, and ethnic scholars, professionals, leaders, media, organizations, and institutions.

Cultural competence is a major concept that originated in the health field and social work. According to the National Center for Cultural Competence, organizations that practice cultural competence "have a defined set of values and principles, and demonstrate behaviors, attitudes, policies, and structures that enable them to work effectively cross-culturally."[30] Culturally competent professionals learn as much as they can about the cultures of their clientele, use this knowledge to serve them, and conduct regular self-assessments. These organizations "adapt to diversity and the cultural contents of the communities they serve." They work closely with their consumers, stakeholders and communities, and incorporate cultural competence and diversity into their policies, administration, practice, and service. In other words, culturally competent organizations fight institutional racism by how they plan and manage their services.

LIS literature on this subject emerged mostly from health sciences librarianship.[31] However, a major article by Patricia Montiel Overall discusses implications of cultural competence in all library settings.[32] Much of her article refers to library planning and administration, but her comments on how information and literacy should be defined could have revolutionary implications for ILI, especially in a public library setting. Overall defines information as "anything that informs, builds, develops and enriches thinking and human integrative thought" and includes "diverse forms of information, such as pictures, drawings, music, dance, media, text, symbols, signs, and aural traditions, which convey meaning to humans." She defines literacy as "a social construct developed in multiple ways for social as well as educational purposes." Literacy can include not only reading but "music, storytelling, drama, sign language, media, technology, and personal use and forms of communication such as diaries." The implications of Overall's definitions for viewing, creating, and conducting ILI are provocative and will require more thought from all librarians.

Overall describes how cultural competency has evolved in the fields of health, psychology, social work, education, and LIS. She ends by describing how librarians can become culturally competent in their cognitive, interpersonal, and environmental domains. Within their cognitive domain, librarians can be aware of their own cultures and then build cultural knowledge through their informal interactions with community members as well as more formal instruction.

Within their interpersonal domains, librarians can build information competence by learning to listen to and appreciate people from diverse cultures, by developing "an ethic of caring," by continuing to work closely with members of the community, and by reflecting on both the "espoused values and practiced values" in the library community. Aspects of the environmental domain would include community-based research; understanding how community members search for, use, share, hold, and ignore information; what access community members have to books, computers, newspapers, and other media; the role of language in the development of literacy; and the library environment itself.

The field of *multicultural education* offers many insights and ideas to librarians instructing diverse populations, including philosophy, information on multiple groups, teaching ideas and techniques, curriculum development ideas, and thoughts on how schools should be redesigned to accommodate more diverse learners.

A first source to consult about this field is *An Introduction to Multicultural Education* by James A. Banks, a founder of this movement. He discusses goals, misconceptions, dimensions of the field, and many other important subjects. The goals of multicultural education are to "provide all students with the skills, attitudes, and knowledge needed to function" within mainstream, local, and other cultures, "to reduce the pain of discrimination," and to help students acquire the academic skills needed to function in a global, flat, technological world.[33]

Dimensions of multicultural education include content integration, knowledge construction, prejudice reduction, equity pedagogy, and an empowering school culture and social structure. Content integration, according to Banks, is the use of examples, data, and information from diverse cultures to illustrate "key concepts, principles, generalizations, and theories" in a subject area or discipline. Knowledge construction looks at how scholars, professionals, and other people create, evaluate, and use knowledge and how this can be influenced by the "racial, ethnic, gender, and social-class positions of individuals and groups." The impact of worldview on knowledge construction can be a very interesting approach to take in ILI.

Prejudice can often be reduced by integrating and using images and examples from diverse groups and involving students in active and cooperative learning. Equity pedagogy, according to Banks, is "using teaching techniques that are responsive to the learning and teaching characteristics of diverse groups" and drawing on students' cultural strengths. Creating an empowering school often means "restructuring the culture and organization of the school so that students from diverse . . . groups will experience educational equality and empowerment." Multicultural education is an educator's version of cultural competency. This field is concerned with attitudes and actions of the school staff; the formalized curriculum; learning, teaching, and cultural characteristics favored by the schools; language and dialects of the school; instructional materials; assessment and testing procedures; the school culture's "hidden curriculum"; and the counseling program.

Banks has published many books and articles on this subject. Other excellent texts on multicultural education are *Comprehensive Multicultural Education: Theory and Practice* by Christine I. Bennett and *Multicultural Education of Children and Adolescents* by M. Lee Manning and Leroy G. Baruth.[34] Multicultural content can also be found in more general books on teaching and educational psychology, such as *Psychology Applied to Teaching* by Jack Snowman, Rick McCowan, and Robert Biehler.[35] On the college and university level, Jossey-Bass has published the series New Directions for Teaching and Learning with several volumes on teaching diverse students.

LIS materials with useful information on multicultural teaching include the chapter "Teaching in a Diverse World: Knowledge, Respect, and Inclusion," in *Information Literacy: Theory and Practice* by Esther S. Grassian and

Joan R. Kaplowitz; *Teaching the New Library to Today's Users*, edited by Trudi E. Jacobson and Helene C. Williams; and Karen Downing's essay "Instruction in a Multicultural Setting: Teaching and Learning with Students of Color," in *Teaching the New Library to Today's Users*, on teaching in a multicultural environment. Earlier, Downing, Barbara MacAdam, and Darlene Nichols published *Reaching a Multicultural Student Community* on how to effectively work with culturally diverse students using many marketing techniques in an academic setting that public librarians have always used. An earlier book with useful ideas is *Reaching and Teaching Diverse Library User Groups*, edited by Teresa B. Mensching.[36]

Helpful articles include Donna L. Gilton's "Culture Shock in the Library: Implications for Information Literacy Instruction" and "A World of Difference: Preparing for Information Literacy Instruction for Diverse Groups," and several articles by Patrick Andrew Hall, including "The Role of Affectivity in Instructing People of Color." *The Family-Centered Library Handbook* by Sandra Feinberg, Barbara Jordan, Kathleen Deerr, Marcellina Byrne, and Lisa G. Kropp has an excellent chapter on literacy programs for culturally diverse families that ends with a great resource list.[37]

Another place to look for insights and ideas would be the work of other *educators who have worked with diverse communities*, including Gilton, Lisa Delpit, Deborah Meier, and Herbert Kohl.[38] Educators working with African Americans include Gloria Ladson-Billings, Janice E. Hale, Michele Foster, Barbara Sizemore, and Joyce E. King. There is a Commission on Research in Black Education in the American Education Research Association, and related periodicals are the *Journal of Negro Education* and *Journal of Blacks in Higher Education*. Educators writing about Latino/Latina students include Sonia Nieto, Antonia Darder, Rodolfo D. Torres, Henry Guierrez, Eugene E. Garcia, Enrique Murillo Jr., and Victoria-Maria MacDonald. An educational periodical is the *Hispanic Outlook in Higher Education*, and a relevant organization is Aspira.[39]

Books on Asian American education have been published by Li-Rong Lilly Cheng, Don T. Nahanishi, Tina Tamano Nishida, Clara C. Park, and Marilyn Mei-Young Chi. Distributors of educational materials include Asia for Kids, the Asian American Curriculum Project, Shen's Books and Supplies, South Asia Children's Books and Software, and the Multicultural Distribution Center.[40]

Educators of Native Americans include Jon Reyhner, Gregory Cajete, Marylou Schultz, Miriam Kroeger, Vine Deloria, Linda Miller Cleary, Thomas D. Peacock, and Hap Gilliland, who has also served as president of the Council for Indian Education. Four educational periodicals about Native Americans are *Journal of American Indian Education*, *Tribal College Journal*, *Canadian Journal of Native Education*, and *Winds of Change*, which also publishes an annual college guide especially for Native American young people.[41] In addition, individual tribes are creating their own schools and colleges, museums, and resources.

Other community resources include people and their organizations, their media, sources of materials, and educational resources. People and organizations include local ethnic leaders and gatekeepers and their institutions. Media include television and radio programs and stations, periodicals that range from the popular to the scholarly, newspapers, the Internet, and social networking sites. Other sources of materials would include existing bibliographies and pathfinders, review sources, ethnic and other publishers, book stores, distributors, and ethnic book awards. Some librarians also attend specialized book fairs in the United States and abroad, such as the one in Guadalajara, Mexico, and a few make buying trips abroad. There are also bookstores and distributors in the United States.

Other educational sources would be museums, ethnic studies programs, educational organizations, and designated Historically Black Colleges and Universities (HBCUs), Hispanic-Serving Institutions (HSIs), and Tribal Colleges (TCs) as appropriate. Ethnic caucuses and similar groups within ALA and specialized libraries are also educational sources of materials. There are three kinds of specialized library collections: ethnic studies collections at universities, other specialized ethnic collections in public or academic libraries not tied to ethnic studies programs, and national libraries abroad. You can use all of these resources to build collections and services for your clientele and then tell them about these things through ILI and other means. More information on how to find these resources can be found in *Multicultural and Ethnic Children's Literature in the United States* and the Teaching About Information website, both by Gilton.[42]

Learning Styles and Modes of Learning Valued by Different Cultures

One of the major controversies in multicultural instruction is whether people from different cultures have unique learning styles, how to find this out, and what to do about it. One approach would be to consult textbooks on multicultural education, check chapters on the groups most relevant to you, and ask, "Does this information apply to my audiences?"

Another approach is to teach to the learning styles described in chapter 3. We can reach most people most of the time by considering their perceptual modalities and their degrees of field dependence or independence, and their multiple intelligences. This can be done by combining good presentations and discussions (for aural learners) with good charts and graphics (for visual learners) and interesting activities (for kinesthetic learners). ILI instructors can also preview, view, and review all information for field dependent learners and break the presentation into steps for field independent learners. One can also teach to as many multiple intelligences as possible.

Bennett describes several ways to discover students' learning styles with the use of simple tests. A Hidden Figures Test can be used to test for field dependence/independence. The Edmonds Learning Style Identification Exercise (ELISE) can be used to discover students' perceptual modes or whether they are aural, visual, or kinesthetic learners.[43]

In spite of these attempts to account for all forms of learning, questions still remains. Do diverse groups have unique learning styles not yet discovered by mainstream educational researchers? Or is focusing on this a new way of stereotyping people? There is informal evidence that specific learning techniques are valued in different societies, such as memorization, recitation, rhetoric and debate, questioning, modeling and imitation, experiential learning (or learning by doing), and finding data. It is best to ask if any of these styles apply to your students, whether these styles are changing, and if so, how. Are there generational differences in your population? This is useful to know and can be incorporated into instruction, but one must really know one's audience for this to work.

TEACHING METHODS USEFUL FOR DIVERSE STUDENTS

Several teaching methods have been found to be especially effective with diverse students, including mastery learning, experiential learning, and cooperative and other active learning. With mastery learning, students learn step by step and do not move to a new step until they master the one they are working on. This method ensures that students really master what they are studying as they learn. Experiential learning is learning by doing or through projects. Internships and volunteer work are also part of this. With cooperative learning, students learn and work together in teams. Cooperative learning was created to promote better interaction between all students in newly integrated schools. By using these methods and combining them with teaching by modality, planning for field dependence and independence, and taking multiple intelligences into account, we are approaching Universal Design of Learning or Universal Design of Instruction. (More will be discussed about these teaching techniques as we consider instructing students with disabilities in chapter 5.)

Characteristics of Good Multicultural Teachers

Both Karen Downing and Ladson-Billings have produced helpful research on teaching multicultural populations as well as on the characteristics of good multicultural teachers.[44] According to their research, good multicultural teachers from all backgrounds have five characteristics: they know themselves, they are passionate about learning, they are student-centered, they are prepared to teach, and they care.

Good multicultural teachers know their own cultures and their own strengths and weaknesses. They know exactly how they feel about other people. They believe that knowledge can be "recreated, recycled, and shared." They are student centered. They respect students and try to connect to each one, and they believe that all students can learn and succeed. They also respect the varied opinions of diverse students.

Good multicultural teachers are prepared to teach. They set the tone for the class from the beginning and use their skills to motivate students and help them learn. These teachers use a variety of techniques and media. If one approach does not work, they move to another. They also use resources and information from diverse communities as needed. They help students to develop their skills and believe that it is their mission to bring knowledge out of students that is already there but buried. Good multicultural teachers are constructivists. They encourage both a community of learners and collaborative learning. Most of all, good multicultural teachers show students that they care about them.

Some Teaching Possibilities

In addition to other subjects mentioned in this book that can be covered in ILI sessions, there is a lot that can be taught about diverse people to everybody. Here are a few ideas:

Ethnic Studies

- Teach about information resources from diverse groups to everybody. Use materials from mainstream, multicultural, and some ethnic sources and compare.
- Promote critical thinking. Two tutorials from California State University, Long Beach, *Information Competence for Black Studies* and *Information Competence for the Field of Chicano and Latino Studies*, show faculty how they can incorporate ILI into their respective disciplines, with an emphasis on teaching critical thinking.[45]
- Use *Ethnic Newswatch* to compare mainstream, Black, Latino/Latina, and Native American treatment of Hurricane Katrina.
- Compare the use of controlled vocabulary on the same subject in indexes in different subjects or in databases over time.[46]
- Compare alternative and mainstream indexes.[47]

Survival and General Information

- Find, evaluate, and use resources to deal with personal or community issues.
- Choose a college. Include specialized information for specific audiences as well as more general materials on this subject. Examples would be

information on HBCUs, HSIs, or TCs, as appropriate; specialized sources on financial aid; and specialized guides to college.
- Find career and employment information. There is a real need to instruct people not bound for four-year colleges or without access to computers.
- Find genealogical information. Combine the use of general and specialized sources, depending on your audience.
- Find information on how to start a business or write a business plan.
- Find instruction for parents, caregivers, or community leaders.
- Other sessions for individuals, classes, groups, clubs, families, and other groups, some combined with literacy programs, book discussions, or cultural programs with refreshments.

Preparing to Teach

To summarize, in preparing to teach diverse groups:

- "Form partnerships and work closely with related agencies.
- Be aware of the general information needs of users as well as what they should know to effectively use your library.
- Know the characteristics of your groups.
- Be aware of the particular needs of your groups.
- Be aware of how people develop in general (see chapter 2).
- Be aware of different learning styles and multiple intelligences within different cultures.
- Tailor learning approaches for specific groups.
- Keep verbal communication at the reference desk as simple as possible.
- Apply all of your learning and teaching principles to your indirect instruction.[48]

NOTES

1. James A. Banks, *An Introduction to Multicultural Education* (Boston: Pearson, 2008), 13.
2. Banks, *An Introduction to Multicultural Education*, 93.
3. Banks, *An Introduction to Multicultural Education*, 91, 93.
4. Banks, *An Introduction to Multicultural Education*, 13.
5. Peter Hernon and Philip Calvert, *Improving the Quality of Library Service for Students with Disabilities* (Westport, Conn.: Libraries Unlimited, 2006), 1.
6. Donna L. Gilton, *Multicultural and Ethnic Children's Literature in the United States* (Lanham, Md.: Scarecrow, 2007), 53.
7. Loriene Roy, "Circle of Community: The Freezing over Moon Month or Gash-kadino-Giizis," *American Libraries* 38, no. 10 (2007): 6.

8. Audrey Shalinsky, "Culture Shock," *Encyclopedia of Anthropology*, 2nd ed., vol. 2, ed. H. James Birx (Thousand Oaks, Calif.: Sage, 2006), 682–83.

9. Donna Louise Gilton, "Culture Shock in the Library: Implications for Information Literacy Instruction," *Research Strategies* 20, no. 4 (2007): 424–25.

10. E.T. Hall, *The Silent Language* (Garden City, N.Y.: Doubleday, 1959); Hall, *The Hidden Dimension* (Garden City, N.Y.: Doubleday, 1961); Hall, *The Dance of Life: The Other Dimension of Time* (Garden City, N.Y.: Doubleday, 1973); Hall, *Beyond Culture* (Garden City, N. Y.: Anchor, 1981).

11. Gilton, "Culture Shock in the Library," 426.

12. Patty Lane, *A Beginner's Guide to Crossing Cultures: Making Friends in a Multicultural World* (Downer's Grove, Ill.: Intervarsity, 2002); Gilton, "Culture Shock in the Library," 427–28.

13. Wilma Longstreet, *Aspects of Ethnicity: Understanding Differences in Pluralistic Classrooms* (New York: Teachers College Press, 1978); Gilton, "Culture Shock in the Library," 426–27.

14. Allen Natowitz, "International Students in U.S. Academic Libraries: Recent Concerns and Trends," *Research Strategies* 13 (Winter 1995): 4–16; Gilton, "Culture Shock in the Library," 425.

15. Mary Beth Allen, "International Students in Academic Libraries: A User Survey," *College and Research Libraries* 54 (July, 1993): 323.

16. Lucinda Zoe and Diane DiMartino, "Cultural Diversity and End-User Searching: An Analysis by Gender and Language Background," *Research Strategies* 17, no. 4 (2000): 291–305.

17. M.X. Liu and B. Redfern, "Information-Seeking Behavior of Multicultural Students: A Case Study at San Francisco State University," *College and Research Libraries* 58, no. 4 (1997): 348–54.

18. Diane DiMartino and Lucinda Zoe, "International Students and the Library: New Tools, New Users, and New Instruction," in *Teaching the New Library to Today's Users: Reaching International, Minority, Senior Citizens, Gay/Lesbian, First Generation, At-Risk Graduate and Returning Students, and Distance Learners*, ed. Trudi E. Jacobson and Helene C. Williams (New York: Neal-Schuman, 2000), 17–43.

19. Charity K. Martin, Charlene Maxey-Harris, Jolie Ogg Graybill, and Elizabeth K. Rodacker-Borgens, "Closing the Gap: Investigating the Search Skills of International and U.S. Students: An Exploratory Study." *Library Philosophy and Practice* (October 2009): 1–17.

20. Pamela Jackson, "Incoming International Students and the Library: A Survey," *Reference Services Review* 33, no. 2 (2005): 197–209.

21. Yan Liao, Mary Finn, and Jun Lu, "Information-Seeking Behavior of International Graduate Students vs. American Graduate Students: A User Study at Virginia Tech 2005," *College and Research Libraries* 68, no. 1 (2007): 23.

22. Maud C. Mundava and LaVerne Gray, "Meeting Them Where They Are: Marketing to International Student Populations in U.S. Academic Libraries," *Technical Services Quarterly* 25, no. 3 (2008): 35–48.

23. Ismail Abdullahi, ed., *Global Library and Information Science: A Textbook for Students and Educators* (Munich: K. G. Saur, 2009); Kathleen de la Pena McCook and Kate Lippincott, eds., *Libraries: Global Reach—Local Touch* (Chicago: ALA, 1998); Martin Kesselman and Irwin Weintraub, eds., *Global Librarianship* (New York: Marcel

Dekker, 2004); Frances Laverne Carroll and John Frederick Harvey, *International Librarianship: Cooperation and Collaboration* (Lanham, Md.: Scarecrow, 2001); Robert D. Stueart, *International Librarianship: A Basic Guide to Global Knowledge Access* (Lanham, Md.: Scarecrow, 2007).

24. *Library Literature and Information Science* (Bronx, N.Y.: H.W. Wilson); *Library, Information Science and Technology Abstracts* (*LISTA*) (Ipswich, Mass.: EBSCO); *Library and Information Science Abstracts* (Bethesda, Md.: Cambridge Scientific Abstracts); Peter Hunt and Sheila Ray, eds., *International Companion Encyclopedia of Children's Literature* (New York: Routledge, 1996); Evelyn P. Freeman and Barbara A. Lehman, *Global Perspectives in Children's Literature* (Boston: Allyn and Bacon, 2001).

25. *World Encyclopedia of Library and Information Services* (Chicago: ALA, 1993); *Encyclopedia of Library and Information Sciences* (New York: Marcel Dekker, 1968–2003); Richard Krzys and Gaston Litton, *World Librarianship: A Comparative Study* (New York: Marcel Dekker, 1983); Anne Pellowski, *The World of Children's Literature* (New York: Bowker, 1968).

26. *Paperboy*, www.thepaperboy.com; *American Journalism Review Newslink*, www.ajr.org.

27. Gilton, *Multicultural and Ethnic Children's Literature in the United States*, 13.

28. Catherine Haras, Edward M. Lopez, and Kristine Ferry, "Latino Students and the Library: A Case Study," *Journal of Academic Librarianship* 34, no. 5 (2008): 425–33; Curt Asher and Emerson Case, "A Generation in Transition: A Study of the Usage and Attitudes Toward Public Libraries by Generation 1.5 Composition Students," *Reference and User Services Library Quarterly* 47, no. 3 (2008): 274–79.

29. Melvina Azar Dame, *Serving Linguistically and Culturally Diverse Students* (New York: Neal-Schuman, 1993); Kathy Howard Latrobe and Mildred Knight Laughlin, *Multicultural Aspects of Library Media Programs* (Englewood, Colo.: Libraries Unlimited, 1992).

30. National Center for Cultural Competence, *Conceptual Frameworks/Models/ Guiding Values and Principles*, http://nccc.georgetown.edu/foundations/frameworks .html.

31. Nancy Ottman Press and Mary Diggs-Hebson, "Providing Health Information to Community Members Where They Are: Characteristics of the Culturally Competent Librarian," *Library Trends* 53, no. 3 (2005): 397–410; Misa Mi, "Cultural Competence for Libraries and Librarians in Health Care Institutions," *Journal of Hospital Librarianship* 5, no. 2 (2005): 15–31.

32. Patricia Montiel Overall, "Cultural Competence: A Conceptual Framework for Library and Information Science Professionals," *Library Quarterly* 79, no. 2 (2009): 181–83.

33. Banks, *An Introduction to Multicultural Education*, 2–5, 30–38.

34. Christine I. Bennett, *Comprehensive Multicultural Education: Theory and Practice*, 6th ed. (Boston: Pearson, 2007); M. Lee Manning and Leroy G. Baruth, *Multicultural Education of Children and Adolescents*, 4th ed. (Boston: Pearson, 2004).

35. Jack Snowman, Rick McCowan, and Robert Biehler, *Psychology Applied to Teaching* (Boston: Houghton Mifflin, 2009), 139–77.

36. Esther S. Grassian and Joan R. Kaplowitz, "Teaching in a Diverse World: Knowledge, Respect, and Inclusion," in *Information Literacy Instruction: Theory and Practice*, 2nd ed. (New York: Neal-Schuman, 2009), 247–66; Jacobson and Wil-

liams, *Teaching the New Library to Today's User*; Karen Downing, "Instruction in a Multicultural Setting: Teaching and Learning with Students of Color," in Jacobson and Williams, *Teaching the New Library to Today's User*, 47–70; Downing, Barbara MacAdam, and Darlene Nichols, *Reaching a Multicultural Student Community* (Westport, Conn,: Greenwood, 1993); Teresa B. Mensching, ed., *Reaching and Teaching Diverse Library User Groups* (Ann Arbor, Mich.: Pierian, 1988).

37. Gilton, "Culture Shock in the Library," 424–32; Gilton, "A World of Difference; Preparing for Information Literacy Instruction for Diverse Groups," *MultiCultural Review* 3, no. 3 (1994): 54–62; Patrick Andrew Hall, "The Role of Affectivity in Instructing People of Color: Some Implications for Bibliographic Instruction," *Library Trends* 39, no. 3 (1991): 316–26; Hall, "Peanuts: A Note on Intercultural Communication," *Journal of Academic Librarianship* 18, no. 4 (1992): 211–13; Hall, "Developing Research Skills in African American Students: A Case Note," *Journal of Academic Librarianship* 29, no. 3 (2003): 182–88; Sandra Feinberg, Barbara Jordan, Kathleen Deerr, Marcellina Byrne, and Lisa G. Kropp, "Culturally Diverse Families," in *The Family-Centered Library Handbook*, 239–52.

38. Gilton, *Multicultural and Ethnic Children's Literature in the United States*, 99; Lisa Delpit, *Other People's Children: Cultural Conflict in the Classroom* (New York: New Press, 1995); Deborah Meier, *The Power of Their Ideas: Lessons for America from a Small School in Harlem* (Boston: Beacon Press, 1995); Herbert Kohl, *The Discipline of Hope: Learning from a Lifetime of Teaching* (New York: New Press, 2003).

39. Gilton, *Multicultural and Ethnic Children's Literature in the United States*, 113–14, 121.

40. Gilton, *Multicultural and Ethnic Children's Literature in the United States*, 129–30.

41. Gilton, *Multicultural and Ethnic Children's Literature in the United States*, 125–26.

42. Gilton, *Multicultural and Ethnic Children's Literature in the United States*, 112–32, 153–68; Gilton, "Who People Are: Diverse Users, Students, and Researchers," *Teaching About Information*, www.uri.edu/artsci/lsc/Faculty/gilton/People-CoverPage.htm.

43. Bennett, *Comprehensive Multicultural Education*, 199–213.

44. Downing, "Instruction in a Multicultural Setting," 50–51; Gloria Ladson-Billings, *The Dreamkeeper: Successful Teachers of African American Students* (San Francisco: Jossey Bass, 1994), 30–101.

45. *Information Competence for Black Studies*, www.csulb.edu/~ttravis/BlackStudies/information.html; *Information Competence for the Field of Chicano and Latino Studies*, www.csulb.edu/~sluevano/chls/intro.html; *Ethnic Newswatch*, Stamford, Conn.: Softline Information.

46. Downing, "Instructing in a Multicultural Setting," 56.

47. Downing, "Instructing in a Multicultural Setting," 56–57.

48. Gilton, "Culture Shock in the Library," 430–31; Gilton, "A World of Difference," 58–61.

5

Teaching People with Disabilities: Ten Steps

There are many issues related to people with disabilities (PWD). Defining disabilities and handicaps and differentiating between these terms is a major philosophical issue in itself. Useful insights on serving this population come from group members, relevant organizations, and professionals in special education, student disability services, and related fields. Solutions to problems include group activism, legislation, such as the Americans with Disabilities Act (ADA), special education, supportive student services, accessible websites, adaptive or assistive technology (AT), and Universal Design (UD) in architecture, Universal Design of Learning (UDL), Universal Design of Instruction (UDI), and Universal Design of Information Literacy (UDIL). This chapter discusses all of these developments in more detail, outlining ten steps to use in preparing to teach people with disabilities:

1. Know the issues.
2. Know the laws and the history of services, family activism, and organizations.
3. Know about developments in education and LIS.
4. Know whether your library is ADA compliant.
5. Know whether your website is accessible to all.
6. Learn about adaptive or assistive technology.
7. Plan services to people with disabilities in general.
8. Teach your staff.
9. Plan your instruction.
10. Know the needs of specific groups.

KNOW THE ISSUES

One out of five Americans (21 percent) has a disability, and one out of ten has a serious one.[1] A disability is defined as "a condition or disease that substantially limits a person's ability to perform one or more major life activities," according to Rhea Joyce Rubin.[2] Experts agree that impairments and disabilities result from natural causes, illnesses, or accidents. Handicaps, on the other hand, are a reflection of how society reacts to and treats people with disabilities.[3] This would include architectural, social, political, educational, and other barriers and discrimination imposed by society, and this starts with the attitudes of able-bodied people toward the disabled. People with disabilities and the professionals and families who work with them discourage the use of the word "handicapped" for this reason.

Also, since individuals are more important than their disabilities, they are usually referred to as "people with disabilities," or using more specific terms such as "students with hearing loss." While it may be possible for public librarians to instruct some groups with specialized needs when requested, these services should be carefully planned. Librarians need to know about related legislation, especially the Americans with Disabilities Act (ADA), developments in education and Library Information Science LIS, Universal Design, website accessibility, adaptive or assistive technology (AT), and how to plan services in general for and especially with people with disabilities and their supporters. Library staff would need to be trained on their service and instruction. From there, libraries can plan their instruction. This chapter describes steps to accomplish each of these. The last section provides sources for people with hearing loss, vision loss, or other physical disabilities, and for people with learning disabilities, attention deficit disorder, autism spectrum disorders, mental retardation, mental illness, and traumatic brain injury (TBI).

KNOW THE LAWS AND THE HISTORY OF SERVICES, FAMILY ACTIVISM, AND ORGANIZATIONS

The history of special education, the laws affecting people with disabilities, and the role of families, organizations, and institutions are all linked, interrelated, and intertwined. This history can be covered in four historical periods marked by important legislation and court cases: the years before the 1954 *Brown vs. Board of Education* decision from the Supreme Court; the years between *Brown vs. Board of Education* and civil rights legislation concerning people with disabilities in the 1970s (1954–1973); the years between this legislation and the ADA (1973–1990); and the years since then.

Before Brown vs. Board of Education (1954)

Before 1954, a few disabled children from wealthy families were taught by members of religious organizations or other tutors. Some early humanist educators developed kinesthetic and other learning techniques for children with special needs. Jean-Marc-Gaspard Itard taught the "Wild Boy of Aveyron" and deaf children. One of his students, Edouard Seguin, also taught deaf children. Maria Montessori later built on the techniques of both Itard and Seguin.

Founders of early specialized schools and institutions in the late nineteenth and early twentieth centuries were Samuel Gridley Howe, Thomas Hopkins Gallaudet, and Laurent Clerc. Howe started the first school specifically for children with disabilities and taught Laura Bridgeman, a student who was blind and deaf. Gallaudet founded the first school for deaf children in the United States. Clerc, a French teacher of deaf children who was deaf himself, came to the United States with Gallaudet to teach at his school. Gallaudet University, the only university in the world specifically for students with hearing loss, is named for Thomas Gallaudet, and the university has a Clerc Center, which provides information on deafness for the general public.

Helen Keller, who was blind and deaf, reflected all of these early trends. She first had a private tutor, Anne Sullivan Macy, who also had visual impairments and who guided Keller for much of their lives. Keller was an early student at the Perkins School for the Blind, one of the first institutions established to educate students with visual disabilities.[4] Around this time, the first public school special education classes were started in Boston, Chicago, New York City, Philadelphia, and Providence.[5]

The Civil Rights Era (1954–1973)

In 1954, parents of disabled children had few choices about the education of their children, including no education at all, institutions away from home, specialized day schools, and a few isolated special education classrooms. The 1954 Supreme Court decision in *Brown vs. Board of Education* not only struck down the "separate but equal" system affecting children of color but also stated that if public schools educate any children in their area, they must educate all of them. As with the struggle for racial integration, it would take many more years, struggles, court cases, and legislation to bring about positive change, but all developments in this field since then can be traced back to this decision. In 1965, the Elementary and Secondary Education Act provided funding to states to assist them in creating and improving programs and services to children with special needs.[6]

In this period, some teachers, professionals, and parents would question whether a separate education for children with disabilities was truly an equal one, and others were concerned about "the stigmatizing effect of labels." One researcher studied the "six hour retarded child," in other words, children classified as retarded in school but functioning normally at home and in their communities. New ideas in this field were those of normalization, mainstreaming, inclusion, and deinstitutionalization. Normalization is based on the belief that "people with disabilities should live lives as close to normal as possible." Mainstreaming is "the participation of children with disability in the general education classroom" and inclusion is "the placement of children with special needs in general classrooms with supports for the child."[7]

The late 1960s and 1970s was a period of deinstitutionalization. First people with mental disorders and then people with mental retardation were released from institutions and placed in group homes and day programs in the community. For the most part, only the most severely disabled people remained in institutions.

During this period, parents were forming organizations like the Association of Retarded Children, then the Association of Retarded Citizens, now ARC. Many were dissatisfied with the state of their children's education and some asked why their children could not be educated in regular public schools. Several parents of color sued school systems for using suspicious tests to overly assign their children to special education. Landmark cases included the *Pennsylvania Association for Retarded Children vs. the Commonwealth of Pennsylvania* in 1972 and *Mills vs. Board of Education* in Washington, D.C. Cases concerning students of color included *Diana vs. State of California* and *Larry P. vs. Riles*.[8]

In addition, the civil rights movement of the 1960s had other ripple effects on all people of color, women in general, and people with disabilities, who were also organizing their own movement in the 1970s. By 1973, Congress passed the Rehabilitation Act, the first civil rights bill created specifically to protect people with disabilities. Most of this bill concerned job training and employment. All programs that received federal funding had to be accessible to people with disabilities. Section 504 of this act protects students not covered by later legislation, but local school systems must pay for these programs.[9]

Coming of Age: From Civil Rights to the ADA (1973–1990)

The Education for All Handicapped Children Act, passed in 1974, increased funds for special education and made states responsible for creating full opportunities for students with disabilities. The Education of the Handicapped Act, passed in 1975, has been the basis for all subsequent special education practice. Major changes included the incorporation of educating students with disabilities "in the least restrictive environment" and creating

Individualized Education Plans (IEPs) for each K–12 student with special needs.[10] IEPs are designed by teachers, parents, concerned professionals, and students themselves, especially as they grow older. IEPs are learning plans for students to undertake in the next year when they are evaluated and revised for the year to follow. IEPs are also used for adults in sheltered workshops and similar settings.[11]

In 1986, special education was expanded to include services to infants and young children, and Individualized Family Services Plans (IFSPs) were added. These are IEPs for very young children and their families designed to prepare the children for school. In 1990, the Individuals with Disabilities Act (IDEA) was passed as an updated version of the Education of the Handicapped Act. Children with autism and traumatic brain injury were added to those receiving services. Extra help in the form of Individualized Transition Plans (ITPs) was provided to help high school students make the transition to work or to college.

The Americans with Disabilities Act (ADA) was passed in 1990, in time for the first students who benefitted from the legislation of the 1970s to enter the workforce.[12] Title I is about employment of people with disabilities, Title II concerns public services, and Title III concerns public accommodations and services provided by private entities.

Title II is the most stringent part of ADA and affects public schools, public universities, and public libraries, as well as all federal, state, and local government services. All new construction must be accessible to all, and older buildings covered under the ADA must be remodeled to be accessible. ADA also promoted the use of assistive or adaptable technology (AT) and communication aids. All programming also must be accessible to all, and people from all groups should be represented on advisory boards. All of these services are to be free to the public.

Developments Since 1990

IDEA was updated in 1997,[13] and the No Child Left Behind (NCLB) Act was passed in 2001. This act attempts to improve educational outcomes for all students and is concerned with accountability for results, school safety, parental choice, teacher quality, scientifically based methods of teaching, and local flexibility. The Individuals with Disabilities Act was passed in 2004 with these seven principles:

- "Zero rejection" that entitles all students with disabilities to a free public education, regardless of the nature and severity of their disability.
- Free and appropriate public education that includes specialized instruction, related services, and supplementary aids and services.
- Student IEPs that include all of these elements.

- Students educated in the "least restrictive environment."
- Nondiscriminatory evaluation.
- Parent and family right to confidentiality.
- Procedural safeguards.[14]

IDEA operates in tandem with NCLB. All students, including those with disabilities, must achieve at a certain level to earn a high school diploma, and students with disabilities are expected to learn as quickly as their able-bodied peers.[15] As a result, academic courses have been stressed more for all students and vocational courses less. These courses are more demanding, which is great for students who can meet the challenges. The number of students with disabilities who are attending college is now increasing. However, there is real concern over how to best educate students with severe disabilities.

One implication of all of these developments is that with exceptional students receiving more mainstreamed academic education, librarians can expect to see many more people with disabilities among their clientele, and orientation and instruction to them will become increasingly important. Because of IFSPs, families with young children with special needs are more likely to participate in family literacy and other programs for the young. Exceptional K–12 students may get instructional and other services either as part of a general class or as part of a heterogeneous or homogeneous special education group. High school students preparing their ITPs may need more specialized instruction on college and career information. Adults from group homes and day programs also use public libraries individually and in groups, with and without other supervision. ILI possibilities here are almost endless.

The Role of Families, Organizations, and Institutions

Families with exceptional children are often the first and last line of defense, especially for individuals unable to fend and fight for themselves. But they are not enough. They need institutions and other services, and they often form associations that lead to these services.

The parents of John F. Kennedy, along with other members of the Kennedy family, have had a pioneering role. At a time when most wealthy families would have institutionalized or hidden their disabled children, Joseph and Rose Kennedy mainstreamed their daughter Rosemary into a very close-knit, loving, and competitive family. This arrangement worked well when Rosemary was a child and a teen. However, serious problems arose later, and Rosemary was handicapped by social discrimination that severely limited her options. Sadly, Rosemary was not able to benefit from the multiple educational, social, and living options that we have today.

However, these options would not exist if her family and many less prominent families after them did not lay the groundwork for this development.

In the 1950s, the Kennedy family started a foundation and a hospital, the Kennedy Memorial Hospital, for young children with developmental disabilities. As president of the United States, John F. Kennedy established the Presidential Commission on Mental Retardation and supported the use of federal funds to educate teachers of children with disabilities.[16] His sister, Eunice Kennedy Shriver, started the Special Olympics in her backyard, and it grew into an international movement. Another sister, Jean Kennedy Smith, is a founder of VSA, Very Special Arts: The International Organization on Arts and Disability.

Examples of general organizations related to people with disabilities are the National Council on Disabilities, National Organization on Disabilities, DisabilityInfo.gov, National Easter Seal Society, and National Information Center for Children and Youth with Disabilities.[17] Organizations based at colleges include the Arch Learning Community at Dean College and Disabilities, Opportunities, Internet Working and Technology (DO-IT) at the University of Washington. There is an Association on Higher Education and Disability in Washington, D.C., as well as a website on University Centers for Excellence in Developmental Disabilities Education, Research, and Service.[18]

KNOW ABOUT DEVELOPMENTS IN EDUCATION AND LIS

This section will describe special education for K–12 students, student support services at colleges and universities, and LIS publications, organizations, institutions, and services.

Special Education: Birth Through Grade 12

Special education begins at birth and is mandatory for exceptional children at ages three through twenty-one. Children under the age of three get their services within an IFSP that determines intervention strategies for them and their families. When they turn three, the focus shifts from the family to the child, who must now have his or her own IEP.[19] IFSPs ensure that very young children with disabilities, developmental delays, or other issues receive help early in life to prevent later problems. IFSP statements include information on the child and family, a listing of major outcomes, evaluation procedures, specific intervention strategies to be used, and procedures to help the child make the transition to preschool.[20]

Public school students age three through twenty-one who qualify must submit an IEP with their teachers, parents, and other professionals every year. The information here is similar to that in the IFSP except that it takes into account students' interactions with all classmates and performances on district-wide tests. Teens age fourteen through twenty-one making the transition to college or work must fill out an ITP that describes the transition services needed, annual goals of each service, statements on education and related services, and interagency responsibilities and linkages.[21]

Since students vary so much, both in what disabilities they have and how severe these are, there is a wide range of options to enable them to be educated "in the least restrictive environment." They are from the least to the most restrictive integration into general classrooms with help from teaching consultants, visits in general classrooms from itinerant teachers, students spending some time in a "resource room" with a special education teacher and the rest of their time in a general classroom, students spending all or most of their time in a separate special class, students attending specialized day schools, or students at residential schools. As a rule, the more severe or numerous the disabilities, the more restrictive the environment.[22] Early intervention makes it possible for some children with fairly severe disabilities to be more integrated into general classrooms and to go to college later. In addition, special education includes the use of AT as appropriate and help from other professionals, such as social workers or physical therapists.

Textbooks on special education include *Special Education: Contemporary Perspectives for School Professionals* by Marilyn Friend, *Exceptional Lives: Special Education in Today's Schools* by Ann Turnbull, Rud Turnbull, and Michael C. Wehmeyer, *Exceptional Children and Youth: An Introduction to Special Education* by Nancy Hunt and Kathleen Marshall, and *Pathways for Exceptional Children: Schools, Home, and Culture* by Paul S. Kaplan.[23] These texts give useful information on how exceptional people are educated, precise descriptions of various disabilities, and good teaching tips. The more recent texts also promote UD and UDL.

Disabled Student Services: Higher Education

As students with disabilities make the transition from high school to college, they are much more on their own. They will no longer design an IEP every year. Many universities offer Disabled Student Services, and students' participation in this is entirely voluntary. Most of these services act as a bridge between students and their professors and ensure that students have whatever accommodations they need to learn more effectively in the classroom. These accommodations can range from where students sit in class to needed AT to time students may need to do tests or assignments. All of these details are worked out with students and their professors at the beginning of the term or semester. Some Disabled Student Services publish teaching tips for professors and provide instruction to teachers and librarians.

A relevant text is *Emerging Scholars: Students with Disabilities: A Handbook for Faculty and Administrators in Rhode Island Public Institutions of Higher Education* produced by Disability Services for Students at the University of Rhode Island. This handbook has teaching tips for professors, cites relevant laws, and briefly describes the work of disability services offices. The website Disability Services for Students supplements the handbook.[24] *Improving the Quality of Library Services for Students with Disabilities*, edited by Peter Hernon and Philip Calvert, also describes many of these services at colleges in the United States and abroad, as well as library initiatives. It also lists relevant laws, associations, organizations, and government agencies.[25]

Library Services: All Ages

Library services to people with disabilities also follow legislation. Books on this subject were published in the 1970s as civil rights laws affecting this population were enacted. Significant LIS information was also published shortly before and after the passage of ADA in 1990.

The newest and most useful LIS texts are *Improving Library Services to People with Disabilities* by Courtney Deines-Jones, *Improving the Quality of Library Services for Students with Disabilities* edited by Hernon and Calvert, and *Planning for Library Services to People with Disabilities* by Rhea Joyce Rubin.[26] Older titles that still have good ideas are *Preparing Staff to Serve Patrons with Disabilities* by Deines-Jones and Connie Van Fleet, *Meeting the Needs of People with Disabilities: A Guide for Librarians, Educators, and Other Service Professionals* by Ruth Velleman, and *Library and Information Services for Handicapped Individuals* by Kieth C. Wright and Judith F. Davie.[27] However, librarians would be advised to consult these sources after looking at more recent ones in LIS, special education, and related fields. Much has changed in legislation, teaching techniques, and related technologies since 1990.

The National Library Service for the Blind and Physically Handicapped (NLS) at the Library of Congress (LC) has published bibliographies on accessibility, AT, library and information services for blind and physically disabled people, and more information on physical disabilities that is all available on the Internet. NLS publishes circulars with current information on topics of interest to people with disabilities and those who serve them. These are updated frequently and include service tips. NLS also publishes lists of new publications, directories, fact sheets about NLS, and subject headings. In addition, LC publishes a Web page, Accessibility Home.[28]

The International Federation of Library Associations (IFLA) has a Libraries Services to People with Special Needs Section. Within ALA is the Association of Specialized and Cooperative Library Agencies (ASCLA), which has forums for librarians serving people with visual or physical disabilities as well as a separate one for those serving patrons with hearing loss. In the

United Kingdom, there is the Consortium for Libraries in Higher Education Networking to Improve Library Access for Disabled Users in South and Southwest England (CLAUD)[29]

Some of these organizations have created standards for library services to the disabled. There is the *IFLA Checklist: Access to Libraries for Persons with Disabilities*. ALA has published *Library Services for People with Disabilities* as well as *Library Services for People with Disabilities Policy*, which is on the Web. ASCLA has published *Revised Standards and Guidelines of Service for the Library of Congress Network of Libraries for the Blind and Physically Handicapped*. The Canadian Library Association has published *Canadian Guidelines on Information Services for People with Disabilities*.[30] There are also more specific guidelines for particular groups.

Public library services to disabled people fall into three groups: outreach centers, special needs centers, and mainstreaming. Examples of library services to disabled people include the Accessibility Center at the Phoenix Public Library, the ADA/Special Services Web page at the Seattle Public Library, the Child's Place for Children with Special Needs at the Brooklyn Public Library, the Disability Resource Center at the Montgomery County (Maryland) Public Libraries, Disability Services at the Pima County Public Library, the Ohio Library for the Blind and Physically Handicapped at Cleveland Public Library, Resources for People with Disabilities from the Berkeley Public Library, California, and Special Needs Services at the San Antonio Public Library.[31]

KNOW WHETHER YOUR LIBRARY IS ADA COMPLIANT

ADA compliance is the foundation upon which everything else rests. It is an important first step especially for serving people with physical disabilities. There are several ways of achieving this compliance. A good place to start is with Deines-Jones's "Low Cost/No Cost Ways to Improve Service Right Now."[32] After identifying barriers to library use and discussing ways to involve the community, Deines-Jones focuses on how to immediately improve the library facility with an emphasis on movement through the library, making space more inviting, and making it easier for people to see, to hear, and to find items. Then she addresses how librarians can improve service to people with disabilities in general as well as to those with specific disabilities.

Two helpful books published shortly after ADA was passed are *How Libraries Must Comply with the Americans with Disabilities Act*, edited by Donald D. Foos and Nancy C. Pack, and *The Americans with Disabilities Act: Its Impact on Libraries: The Library's Response in "Doable" Steps*, edited by Joanne L. Crispen.[33] Both summarize the ADA and outline steps libraries must take to be in compliance. Both also recommend forming committees consisting of people with disabilities as well as professionals who work with them.

Steps to planning recommended by Ruth O'Donnell include gathering information about ADA and your library, appointing an ADA coordinator, doing a self-evaluation, planning for compliance, implementing plans, and evaluating and continuing services.[34] The most current and thorough of all of the guidelines is *Checklist of Library Building Design* by William W. Sannwald.[35] Other sources on this subject would include *Accessibility: A Selective Bibliography* from NLS and the United States Access Board.[36]

Universal Design is defined as "the design of products and environments to be usable by all people, to the greatest extent possible without the need for adaptation or specialized design."[37] In the late 1980s, educators from the Center for Applied Special Technology developed Universal Design for Learning (UDL) based on the idea that "universally designed curricula make it possible for students to have full access to course content despite physical limitations, behavioral problems, or language barriers."[38] Universal Design for Instruction (UDI) takes this same principle to the college level, and UDL is applied at K–12 levels. ALA's Library Services for People with Disabilities Policy applies UD principles to library policy, resources, and services.[39] Websites on UD and UDL include those from the Center for Universal Design at North Carolina State University and the Center for Applied Technology.[40]

KNOW WHETHER YOUR WEBSITE IS ACCESSIBLE TO ALL

Having an accessible website is as important as having an accessible building. A good place to start is Web Accessibility in Mind (WebAIM). According to their guidelines, a website must be simple, consistent, clear, multi-modal, or able to provide content in multiple media, error tolerant, and attention focusing to be accessible. It is assumed that by making websites accessible to people with disabilities, they will be accessible to everybody (a principle behind Universal Design as well). Similar principles can be found in the *Web Content Accessible Guidelines* created by the Web Content Accessibility Working Group of the Worldwide Web Consortium (W3C).[41]

An organization doing research on this subject is the Archimedes Hawaii Project. Courses and webinars on designing accessible websites can be found on EASI: Equal Access to Software and Information. *Resources on Accessible Web Design*, produced by DO IT at the University of Washington, is an excellent webliography on this subject.[42]

LEARN ABOUT ADAPTIVE OR
ASSISTIVE TECHNOLOGY (AT)

Adaptive or assistive technology (AT) can range from the simple to the complex, from low-tech to high-tech, from free or inexpensive to exorbitantly expensive, and it can be online or offline. AT takes many forms. It can be an extension of what a person or a device would do anyway. For example, we use silverware or chopsticks as an extension of our fingers as we eat. Another example is our ability to adjust font sizes on our computers. AT can be in the form of a simple tool (like a magnifying glass) to help with an activity (such as reading). It can be in the form of adaptable furniture or elements added to existing technology. AT can be portable elements to be used with other technology, such as thumb drives for computers. Along with technology in general, AT is constantly changing. Keeping up with all of this is a serious challenge. It is vital that librarians work with an advisory committee consisting of people and supporters from various disabled communities to ascertain equipment that is the most needed, especially as needs change over time.

Five kinds of sources have information on AT: introductory information, portals, training resources, product directories, and product demonstration centers. A good example of an introductory essay is *What Are Assistive Devices, Technologies, and Related Services?* by the Independence Through Enhancement of Medicare and Medicaid (ITEM) Coalition. A portal is a website that connects people to a variety of websites on a particular subject. Some portals represent organizations that do several separate functions. AT portals include Abilities!, Closing the Gap, the Family Center on Technology and Disability, and the Web page Overview of Adaptive Technology from the Texas School of the Blind and Visually Impaired. Abilities! is an organization in the state of New York that provides training on how to use AT as well as a demonstration center, and this organization performs several other major functions. Closing the Gap has a website that lists and advertises their periodical, annual directory, annual conference, and webinars. Overview of Adaptive Technology includes links to other information about AT, particularly for people with visual disabilities. The Family Center on Technology and Disability provides links to a variety of resources. A website that focuses more on training people to work with AT is the Center for Accessible Technology, which offers workshops and other learning opportunities to children and adults with disabilities, school systems, businesses, and other organizations.[43]

Websites acting as product directories include the Assistive Technology Web page from the American Foundation for the Blind, Assistivetech.net from the Georgia Institute of Technology, and especially Abledata from the U.S. Department of Education. Abledata is a thorough list of products, publications, professional literature, information centers, conferences, directories, relevant U.S. and international companies, and other links.

In addition, NLS has published a circular, *Assistive Technology Products for Information Access.*

There are also regional product demonstration centers that enable people with disabilities and their supporters to test new adaptive equipment. Examples include the Massachusetts Initiative to Maximize Assistive Technology in Consumer's Hands (MATCH) and the New England Assistive Technology (NEAT) Center at Oak Hill in Connecticut. A Web page that lists other technology demonstration centers around the country is the Technology Resources page from Christian Parents Special Needs and the Alliance for Technology Access.[44]

PLAN SERVICES TO PEOPLE WITH DISABILITIES IN GENERAL

These services would be an outgrowth either of your general library planning or of planning for ADA. An excellent source that can be used with Sandra Nelson's *Strategic Planning for Results* is Rhea Joyce Rubin's *Planning for Library Services to People with Disabilities.* Another useful source is Shelley Quezada's "Nothing About Me Without Me: Planning for Library Services for People with Disabilities," which describes how Rubin's planning model was used in Massachusetts libraries.[45] Rubin mentions making sure that the library is ADA compliant and the website accessible as first steps in this process. She also urges librarians to investigate programs, technology, and special services already at the library, as well as staff qualifications and experience.

The next step is scanning the community, and Rubin gives excellent suggestions on how to find the number of people with various disabilities in a service area and what ages most of them are. She describes how to survey library users and nonusers, how to work with a planning committee, and how to analyze the library's current long-range plan. Librarians and their committees can then compare research results and feedback and use this information to determine new areas of need. Then they can set and finalize goals and objectives, draft the new plan, and plan for evaluation. In doing this procedure, librarians can plan for collection development, outreach, programming, and instruction. Librarians can plan general orientations but also design specific instruction for particular audiences as needed.

TEACH YOUR STAFF

Library staff should know five things in addition to general ILI techniques to effectively teach people with disabilities:

- Facts and myths about different disabilities, including "how it feels" or "what it is like."
- General etiquette.
- Customer service tips.
- Assistive technology and how to use it.
- UDL, UDI, UDIL, and other teaching tips.

Training sessions for librarians can be led by knowledgeable librarians, professionals from related fields, individuals with disabilities, or a combination. Trainers would need to be knowledgeable about all of these issues.

Factual information on various disabilities as well as materials on "how it feels" or "what it is like" can be obtained in a number of ways. One is the use of adult and children's books on the topic. Some of the best of these sources are autobiographies and other works by individuals with disabilities or their families. In addition, the website In My Own Words offers writings by people with disabilities.[46] There is also information on Australian and English Internet sites that can be used in training librarians, including a Disability Awareness Kit from Open Road and an article on the same subject for librarians.[47] Some of these materials include simulations.

A knowledge of both general etiquette and customer service tips is very useful in this context. ALA has published a series of fifteen tip sheets called "Library Accessibility—What You Need to Know.[48] These tip sheets have information on working with people with developmental disabilities, learning disabilities, physical disabilities, autism spectrum disorders, mental illness, people who are deaf or hard of hearing, and people with multiple disabilities. Other subjects covered are service animals, children with disabilities, volunteers and staff with disabilities, AT, and what library trustees need to know. Each tip sheet includes several points of etiquette, service tips, resources, and other information. Tip sheets can also be found in Rubin's *Planning for Library Services to People with Disabilities*. Additional information can be found in *Improving Library Services to People with Disabilities* and *Preparing Staff to Serve Patrons with Disabilities*, both by Deines-Jones, and in *Emerging Scholars* from the University of Rhode Island and *Library and Information Services for Handicapped Individuals* by Wright and Davies.

Here are a few points on protocol:

- General rules of etiquette and the Golden Rule still apply. Be as polite and sensitive as possible.
- People first, disability second. Use terminology such as "people with _____." Focus as much as possible on specific individual needs.

- Speak directly to the person, even when they are accompanied by an interpreter or an aide.
- Respect personal space, including wheelchairs.
- Respect working animals. They are allowed in libraries. Do not pet or interact with them.
- Do not assume. Find out as much as possible before offering help. Listen carefully first.

Sources of more specific service tips will be described at the end of this chapter.

General teaching tips to start with can be found in the article "Training Rewards and Challenges of Serving Library Users with Disabilities" by Cynthia Holt and Wanda Hole, as well as in *Emerging Scholars*.[49] They discuss the need of librarians to be aware of etiquette and protocol when working with people with disabilities. They mention personality traits that good teachers should have, how they should prepare for instruction, and how they can get students connected and involved in the classroom. *Emerging Scholars* puts more stress on classroom teaching, focusing on supporting materials that students should have, how teachers should lecture using a multisensory approach, other class activities, how to give assignments, and how to relate to students. By incorporating techniques that take modality and field dependence/independence into account, teachers using these methods are using aspects of UDL, UDI, or UDIL.

PLAN YOUR INSTRUCTION

Two things to consider in planning instructional sessions are what to teach and how to teach it. Most people with disabilities would be interested in the same subjects that concern everybody else. However, they may be especially interested in certain subjects. Where an ILI session for people with disabilities might really differ from that of other groups would be an emphasis on how to use old and new assistive technologies to access, use, and create information.

One general methodology that would work for a group of very diverse students is the use of a wide variety of media, presentation and teaching techniques, assignments, and even evaluations. If one methodology or medium does not work well for a class, the teacher can always use something else. This is where UDL, UDI, and UDIL come in.[50]

UDL has three principles—multiple means of representation, multiple means of expression, and multiple means of engagement. In multiple means of representation, course materials are presented in multiple formats. Multiple means of expression allow students multiple opportunities to express what they are learning. Multiple means of engagement are the many methodologies that teachers use in the classroom, such as lecturing, active learning, and collaborative learning.

Ted Chodock and Elizabeth Dolinger describe nine UDL principles that can be applied to ILI and can be called UDIL.[51] They are the following:

- *Equitable Use*—useful and accessible instruction for all. Some UDIL applications: Web-based course guides, pathfinders, printed communications with simple fonts.
- *Flexibility in Use*—a choice of instruction for diverse students with a wide range of ability and talents. Some UDIL applications: varied teaching methods to take modality and field dependence/independence into account.
- *Simple and Intuitive Instruction*—clear and predictable instruction with no unnecessary information. Use of constructivism to build on what students already know. Some UDIL applications: subjects chosen by students, teaching only skills related to the assignment, minimizing library jargon.
- *Perceptible Information*—information designed to be communicated to all, regardless of students' sensory abilities or other circumstances. Some UDIL applications: accessible websites, information in multiple formats.
- *Tolerance for Error*—planning for students with different abilities and levels of preparation. Some UDIL applications: student practice, supervised seat work.
- *Low Physical Effort*—minimal physical effort to focus more on learning. Some UDIL applications: citation-making software, printicons, and other computer shortcuts.
- *Size and Space for Approach and Use*—classrooms and other spaces designed for maximum student use. Some UDIL applications: classrooms with space for group work and quiet study, information commons that incorporate instruction.
- *A Community of Users*—promotion of interactions between students, classmates, and teachers. Some UDIL applications: student teams, collaboration with teachers, chat rooms in classroom management systems, such as Blackboard and Sakai, and social networking tools like Facebook to promote collaboration.
- *Institutional Climate*—welcoming and inclusive instruction with high expectations for all. Some UDIL applications: IEPs, collaboration with teachers on class goals and understandings ahead of time.

All of these methods should work most of the time with most people, especially in any kind of heterogeneous groups.

KNOW THE NEEDS OF SPECIFIC GROUPS

At times, library instruction will be directed toward homogeneous groups with specific learning styles, goals, and issues. This section summarizes characteristics and needs of nine specific groups of people with disabilities. It also provides information on general characteristics, service tips, guidelines and standards, library programs, library resources and organizations, other relevant organizations, resources, and websites.

The Deaf Community/People with Hearing Loss

Hearing loss can affect one or two ears and vary from slight to profound. Deafness is defined as a hearing loss so severe that people have difficulty processing linguistic information with or without amplification. There are several points of differentiation: whether the person is partially or totally deaf, when hearing loss occurred, and how deaf people prefer to communicate. Having hearing or deaf parents may be another factor. It is more difficult for children who are born deaf or become so before learning to talk to communicate using speech. Children with hearing loss are taught to communicate through lip reading and speech, sign language, a combination of the two, and through other methods.

Sign language is a language in its own right. Like all languages, it is both a means of communication and a way of thinking. As a means of communication, it varies from country to country and can be communicated with "accents" in certain areas or among certain groups. Unlike other languages, sign language is expressed through gestures rather than speech.

Sign language is also a way of thinking. It touches on culture: some people are deaf and proud of it. In fact, many do not view themselves as disabled. Librarians and other leaders of the deaf community, such as Alice Lougee Hagemeyer, have promoted deaf awareness by celebrating National Deaf History Month, compiling pathfinders and bibliographies, promoting deaf studies, and writing about famous deaf people, who include Thomas Edison, Ludwig van Beethoven, Laurent Clerc, Frederick Barnard, Laura Bridgeman, Helen Keller, and others.

Hagemeyer created *The Legacy and Leadership of the Deaf Community: A Resource Guide for Librarians and Library Programs* as well as *Deaf Awareness: Handbook for Public Libraries* and *Celebrate Deaf Legacy: National Deaf History Month Kit*. She is a founder of Friends of Libraries for Deaf Action (FOLDA), which created *The Red Notebook*, another source of information for librarians.[52]

An important first place to go for information on people who are deaf or hard of hearing is the Laurent Clerc National Deaf Education Center of Gallaudet University through their Web pages Info to Go. The Gallaudet

University Library has Web pages on Deaf Research Help, Frequently Asked Questions—Deaf-Related and Deaf Research Guides. The Rochester Institute of Technology offers the Web page Deaf Studies Internet Resources.[53]

Specific points of etiquette, serving, and teaching people with hearing loss can be found in *Communicating in the Library with People Who Are Deaf and Hard of Hearing*, created by the Gallaudet University Library; *Communication Tips with People Who Are Deaf or Hard of Hearing*, by the organization Michigan Deaf and Hard of Hearing People; and the University of Rhode Island's *Emerging Scholars*.[54] More information on serving people with hearing disabilities and the deaf community can be found in *Improving Library Services to People with Disabilities* by Deines-Jones and a special issue of *Library Trends* that includes an article on instructing this population.[55] Guidelines and standards include *Guidelines for Library Services to Deaf People* by IFLA and *Guidelines for Library and Information Services to the American Deaf Community* by ALA-ASCLA.[56]

Institutions serving deaf and hard of hearing people include Gallaudet University and its Clerc Center, the Postsecondary Education Programs Network (PEPNet), and a number of public libraries around the country. While Gallaudet is the world's only university that is totally dedicated to serving students with hearing loss, colleges and universities in PEPNet serve mostly hearing students but do extensive outreach to the deaf community and other students with hearing loss. PEPNet has four regional centers, and several of them have programs, collections, and websites with very valuable information for instructional librarians.[57] The four regional centers are the Rochester Institute of Technology (RIT) for the Northeast; California State University at Northridge (CSUN) for the West; University of Tennessee for the South; and St. Paul College, a community and technical college in Minnesota, for the Midwest.

RIT has the National Technical Institute for the Deaf (NTID), which is one of its eight colleges. It is the "first and largest technological college for students who are deaf and hard of hearing." Students can earn an associate's degree here and transfer to other programs at RIT. The university also maintains a Deaf Studies Archives and a page of Web links. CSUN has a National Center on Deafness, which offers a wide range of supportive services to students from the deaf community and those who are hard of hearing. The PEPNet Resource Center is housed at CSUN, which also produces an excellent page of Web links.

Among public libraries, San Francisco Public Library has a Deaf Services Center, and the District of Columbia Public Library offers varied library services for the deaf and hard of hearing. The Pinellas Public Library Cooperative in Florida has a Deaf Literacy Center, which offers a variety of programming and resources, and the Hennepin County Library in Minnesota has a Deaf and Hard of Hearing Collection.[58]

Other organizations serving the deaf community are the National Institute on Deafness and Other Communications Disorders, the Alexander Graham Bell Association for the Deaf, the American Deafness and Rehabilitation Association, and Deafsign. Michigan State University has an American Sign Language Browser, and another website is Self-Help for Hard of Hearing People in America, by the Hearing Loss Association of America. Resources for people with deafness or blindness include the NLS reference circular *DB-LINK* by the National Consortium on Deaf-Blindness, and the resources of the American Association of the Deaf-Blind.[59]

People with Visual Difficulties

People with visual difficulties can be categorized in several ways. One is by amount of vision.[60] People with low vision can read print but depend on magnifying glasses and other aids. A few read Braille print. People who are functionally blind use Braille and other assistive technologies to read but can use functional vision for other tasks. People who are totally blind must learn through tactile and auditory means and usually read Braille or use other technology. It also matters when individuals lost their sight. Children born blind or who lose their sight early are more likely to be taught how to read Braille. People who lose their sight later in life use more auditory means to access information. Those who lose their sight especially because of diabetes do not have the feelings in their fingertips to be able to read Braille.

A number of books have been written about people with visual disabilities. One is Gerald Jahoda's 1993 *How Do I Do This When I Can't See What I'm Doing?: Information Processing for the Visually Disabled*, a guide for people adjusting to losing their sight. He gives good tips about everyday living but emphasizes how to find, store, and use information in that context. He also gives advice on computer use, although some of the information may now be out of date. Kevin Carey has published two articles on recent changes in technology and how these are affecting visually impaired people (or VIPs in England). All three works have insights for librarians.[61]

Etiquette tips can be found on the American Foundation for the Blind website as well as in *Emerging Scholars, Improving Library Services* by Deines-Jones, and *Planning for Library Service to People with Disabilities* by Rubin. The American Foundation for the Blind also offers a free self-paced course on instructing adults with visual impairments.[62] Standards and guidelines include *Libraries for the Blind in the Information Age: Guidelines for Development* from IFLA and *Revised Standards and Guidelines of Service for the Library of Congress Network of Libraries for the Blind and the Physically Handicapped* from ALA-ASCLA.[63]

Library resources and organizations include the National Library Service for the Blind and Physically Handicapped, Bookshare, and InfoEyes Information Service. Bookshare provides downloadable books in DAISY and Braille format; a sign-up fee is required for this service. InfoEyes Information Service is a virtual reference service from the Perkins Braille and Talking Book Library.[64] Relevant organizations include the American Foundation for the Blind, National Federation of the Blind, and American Printing House for the Blind.

People with Physical Disabilities

Etiquette, service, and teaching tips for instructing people with physical disabilities can be found in *Improving Library Services to People with Disabilities* by Deines-Jones and *Planning for Library Services to People with Disabilities* by Rubin. Several more etiquette sources and other information can be found in *Physical Handicaps: A Selective Bibliography* published by NLS, which also published the circular *Physical Disabilities: Information and Advocacy Organizations 2000.*[65]

People with Learning Disabilities

In the 1990s, learning disabilities were grouped together with mental retardation, traumatic brain injury, and attention deficit disorder—in short, most physiological conditions affecting the brain. More recently, learning disabilities have been a separate category, although some sources put this with attention deficit disorder and traumatic brain injury. About 30 percent of people with learning disabilities also have attention deficit disorder. All of this matters because it affects where and how you can find information on people who suffer from all of these disorders.

Learning disabilities are defined as "a disorder in one or more of the basic psychological processes involved in understanding or using language, spoken or written." An indication of a learning disability is when students have trouble learning subjects in school but otherwise show definite signs of intelligence. Excluded from this definition are learning problems that result from other causes, such as "visual, hearing, or mobility disabilities, mental retardation, mental illness or socio-economic disadvantages." Examples of learning disabilities are dyslexia (difficulty in understanding written words), dysgraphia (writing difficulties), dyscalculia (difficulties with mathematics), auditory and visual processing disorders (difficulty in understanding language in spite of normal hearing or vision), and other nonverbal learning disabilities.[66]

Teaching tips can be found in many places, including LIS publications by Deines-Jones and Rubin, articles by Sandy Guild, Virginia Ross, and Lynn

Akins, and special education textbooks by Paul S. Kaplan, Ann Turnbull, Rud Turnbull, and Michael L. Wehmeyer. Exemplary library programs for students with learning disabilities can be found at Landmark College in Putney, Vermont, and Beacon College in Leesburg, Florida. Landmark College also has a National Institute for Research and Training that does more research on this issue.[67]

Relevant organizations and websites include the National Center for Learning Disabilities, Learning Disabilities Association of America, Learning Disabilities Worldwide, Learning Disabilities Association, Perspectives Network, Misunderstood Minds, LD Resources, and LD Online. More organizations can be found through *Learning Disabilities: National Organizations and Resources*, a circular from NLS, and National Organizations, a Web page from LD Online.[68]

People with Attention Deficit Disorder

People with Attention Deficit Disorder (ADD) or Attention Deficit Hyperactivity Disorder (ADHD) exhibit a pattern of inattention or hyperactivity. According to Turnbull, Turnbull, and Wehmeyer, these characteristics must be persistently frequent and severe, "interfere with the person's ability to function," be manifested in the person before they are seven years old, "persist for at least six months," be present in at least two settings, and not be attributable to another disability.[69]

Organizations and websites specifically for people with Attention Deficit Disorder include Attention!: Children and Adults with Attention Deficit Disorders (CHADD). More organizations can be found in *Learning Disabilities: National Organizations and Resources*, a circular by NLS.[70]

People with Autism Spectrum Disorders

Five disorders are part of the autism spectrum: autism, Rett's disorder, childhood disintegrative disorder, other pervasive developmental disorders, and Asperger's syndrome. The two most common disorders are autism and Asperger's syndrome.[71]

Symptoms for autism include atypical language development with delayed language and echolalia, atypical social development, repetitive behavior, problem behavior particularly in young children, a need for a predictable environment, sensory and movement disorders, and differences in intellectual functioning. It is estimated that 70 percent of children with autism are also mentally retarded, but some are savants with a talent for dates, numbers, music, or art, and others have normal intelligence if they can be reached early and effectively. Working with autistic children is a long-term process.

Older children, teens, and adults with Asperger's syndrome have significant challenges in their social and emotional functioning but do well in their language and intellectual functioning. Some people diagnosed as autistic as young children are rediagnosed with Asperger's as they grow up, especially if they can get help as children.

More information on teaching people with autism spectrum disorders can be found in "The Equal Opportunity Disorder," an article by Debra Lau Whelan, and in *Emerging Scholars*, special education texts like *Exceptional Lives*, and on the excellent website Libraries and Autism: We're Connected. Relevant organizations and websites include Autism Society of America, Autism Speaks, and Online Asperger's Syndrome Information and Support (OASIS).[72]

People with Mental Retardation

People with mental retardation suffer limitations in both their intellectual functioning and adaptive behavior. They have cognitive problems with short-term memory and difficulty in using generalizations. They can also be very dependent on others, but this dependence can be reduced with training. People with mental retardation are also challenged in their conceptual, social, and practical skills.[73] Yet they strive to live as normally as possible and have most of the same interests that others do. In some cases, keeping up with siblings and other peers who are their age or slightly younger can be both a challenge and a struggle.

Educational techniques useful with this population can be found in special education texts, such as *Pathways for Exceptional Children* and *Exceptional Lives*. In the 1990s, Dennis Norlin investigated the information needs of people with mental retardation and found that these individuals had sophisticated interests and learned not so much to solve problems as to joyfully pursue those interests.[74] Materials available to them at that time included children's literature (too childish); high-interest, low-vocabulary books (too geared to teens); and reading materials for new adult readers (too dull). At that time, adults with mental retardation preferred magazines and media. There may be more and better material available to them now. Some picture books are now being written for an older audience, and graphic novels have become very popular. Some adult books come with many photographs and illustrations. Books like the Time/Life books may be good for this audience.

Other general information on providing library services to people with mental retardation and other developmental disorders include "We're Not Stupid, You Know: Library Services for Adults with Mental Retardation" by Norlin, *Information Services for People with Developmental Disabilities* edited by Linda Lucas Walling and Marilyn M. Irwin, *Library Services for People with Mental Retardation*, and standards from ALA-ASCLA.[75]

Public library programming specifically for people with mental retardation and other developmental disabilities include services to exceptional children offered by the Public Library of Cincinnati and Hamilton County, Ohio. Librarians visit schools, hospitals, and other facilities serving children with special needs, bring collections to these locations, and do programming there. This library also collects materials about and for children with special needs and for parents and professionals.[76]

Programming in other settings include the College Learning Experience Activities Resources (CLEAR) at the Johnson County Community College in Kansas and the Next Chapter Book Club. CLEAR provides noncredit continuing education classes for adults with developmental disabilities or severe learning disabilities. Students must be motivated to attend. Classes are offered in basic skills and other subjects. The Next Chapter Book Club gives teens and adults with developmental disorders a chance to read books and socialize with friends. A few of these book clubs meet in libraries, but most meet at bookstores, cafes, and other community settings.[77] Related organizations include the ARC of the United States, National Association of Councils on Developmental Disabilities, and National Down Syndrome Society.[78]

People with Mental Illness

Many mental illnesses, especially the severe ones, are based on physiological problems. The most common disorders among adults are depression, bipolar disorder, and anxiety disorder. According to Turnbull, Turnbull, and Wehmeyer, the most common mental disorders among children and teens are anxiety disorders, mood disorders, oppositional defiant behavior, other conduct disorders, and schizophrenia. Anxiety disorders would include separation anxiety, generalized anxiety disorders, phobias, panic disorders, and obsessive-compulsive disorders.[79]

In working with people with mental illnesses, service tips may be more important than teaching tips. In her article "Library Psychiatry: Is There a Place for the Mentally Ill in Your Library?" Jennifer Murray outlines policies and procedures that libraries should have in place as they serve people with mental illnesses. She also describes at some length how to respond to patrons' questions "not based on reality" and how to have "difficult conversations," as necessary. Murray urges law librarians to work with public libraries, social work organizations, and social service agencies in their area.[80]

In *Emerging Scholars*, many of the teaching tips for students with mental health disabilities are similar to those for people with learning disabilities and with Attention Deficit Disorder. Turnbull, Turnbull, and Wehmeyer take a different approach to instructing this population. They emphasize mastery learning for students in the early grades, service learning in the middle grades, and conflict resolution in the upper grades. They also promote family and school partnerships. ASCLA has published *Guidelines for Library Services for People with Mental Illness*, and relevant organizations are the National Institute for Mental Health and Mental Health America.[81]

Traumatic Brain Injury

According to Turnbull, Turnbull, and Wehmeyer, traumatic brain injury is "an acquired injury to the brain caused by an external physical force resulting in total or partial functional disability, psychosocial impairment or both, that adversely affects a child's educational performance." These injuries are acquired since birth and caused by external forces, so birth injuries and strokes do not count in this regard. Depending on what area of the brain is damaged and how badly, people with traumatic brain injury may have characteristics similar to those of people with learning disabilities, communication disorders, behavioral disorders, mental retardation, physical disabilities, and other health impairments.[82]

The best teaching methods depend on the individual and his or her strengths and weaknesses. Many of the techniques for working with autistic students apply here: multiple techniques and media, schedules, prompts to aid memory, and frequent student responses and feedback. More information on working with this population can be found in information on working with other groups with neurological issues. Traumatic brain injury is also covered in the NLS bibliography *Learning Disabilities: National Organizations and Resources*.[83]

NOTES

1. Peter Hernon and Philip Calvert, eds., *Improving the Quality of Library Services for Students with Disabilities* (Westport, Conn.: Libraries Unlimited, 2006); Rhea Joyce Rubin, *Planning for Library Services to People with Disabilities* (Chicago: ALA. ASCLA, 2001), 2–3.

2. Rubin, *Planning for Library Services to People with Disabilities*, 2–3.

3. Rubin, *Planning for Library Services to People with Disabilities*, 2–3; Nancy Hunt and Kathleen Marshall, *Exceptional Children and Youth: An Introduction to Special Education* (Boston: Houghton Mifflin, 2006), 3–5; Courtney Deines-Jones, *Improving Library Services to People with Disabilities* (Oxford: Chandos, 2007), 2–3.

4. Hunt and Marshall, *Exceptional Children and Youth*, 7–8; Marilyn Friend, *Special Education: Contemporary Perspectives for School Professionals*, 2nd ed. (Boston: Pearson, 2008), 5–8.

5. Friend, *Special Education*, 6–7.

6. Friend, *Special Education*, 8–9.

7. Hunt and Marshall, *Exceptional Children and Youth*, 8–9.

8. Friend, *Special Education*, 9.

9. Helen R. Adams, "Access for Students with Disabilities," *School Library Media Activities Monthly* 25, no. 10 (2009): 54; Ann Turnball, Rud Turnball, and Michael L. Wehmeyer, *Exceptional Lives: Special Education in Today's Schools* (Upper Saddle River, N.J.: Pearson, 2007), 22; Hunt and Marshall, *Exceptional Children and Youth*, 17–18.

10. Friend, *Special Education*, 10–11; Hunt and Marshall, *Exceptional Children and Youth*, 12–13.

11. Hunt and Marshall, *Exceptional Children and Youth*, 25–30.

12. Friend, *Special Education*, 11; Hunt and Marshall, *Exceptional Children and Youth*, 12–18; Donald L. Foos and Nancy C. Pack, eds., *How Libraries Must Comply with the Americans with Disabilities Act* (Phoenix, Ariz.: Oryx, 1992), 8–31; Joanne L. Crispen, ed., *The Americans with Disabilities Act: Its Impact on Libraries: The Library's Response in "Doable" Steps* (Chicago: ALA, ASCLA, 1993), 1–8; Americans with Disabilities Act Home Page, www.ada.gov.

13. Friend, *Special Education*, 11; Hunt and Marshall, *Exceptional Children and Youth*, 12–18.

14. Friend, *Special Education*, 12–14.

15. Friend, *Special Education*, 27–28; Hunt and Marshall, *Exceptional Children and Youth*, 519–523.

16. Hunt and Marshall, *Exceptional Children and Youth*, 7–11.

17. National Council on Disability, www.ncd.gov; National Organizations on Disabilities, http://nod.org; Disability Info.gov www.disability.gov; National Easter Seal Society, http://easterseals.com; National Information Center for Children and Youth with Disabilities, www.icdri.org.

18. Dean College, Arch Learning Community, www.dean.edu; University of Washington, Disabilities, Opportunities, Internet Working and Technology (DO-IT), www.washington.edu/doit/; Association on Higher Education and Disability (AHEAD), www.ahead.org; University Centers for Excellence in Developmental Disabilities Education, Research, and Service (UCEDD), www.workworld.org.

19. Feinberg, Jordan, Deerr, Byrne, and Kropp, *The Family Centered Library Handbook*, 268–69.

20. Hunt and Marshall, *Exceptional Children and Youth*, 24–26.

21. Hunt and Marshall, *Exceptional Children and Youth*, 24–30.

22. Hunt and Marshall, *Exceptional Children and Youth*, 10.

23. Friend, *Special Education*; Ann Turnbull, Rud Turnbull, and Michael L. Wehmeyer, *Exceptional Lives: Special Education in Today's Schools* (Columbus, Ohio: Pearson, 2007); Nancy Hunt and Kathleen Marshall, *Exceptional Children and Youth: An Introduction to Special Education* (Boston: Houghton Mifflin, 2006); Paul S. Kaplan, *Pathways for Exceptional Children: School, Home, and Culture* (Minneapolis/St. Paul: West, 1996).

24. *Emerging Scholars: Students with Disabilities: A Handbook for Faculty and Administrators in Rhode Island Public Institutions of Higher Education* (Kingston: University of Rhode Island, 2004); University of Rhode Island, Office of Student Life, *Disability Services for Students*, www.uri.edu/disability/dss.

25. Hernon and Calvert, *Improving the Quality of Library Services to People with Disabilities*, 1.

26. Courtney Deines-Jones, *Improving Library Services to People with Disabilities* (Oxford: Chandos, 2007); Hernon and Calvert, *Improving the Quality of Library Services for Students with Disabilities*; Rhea Joyce Rubin, *Planning for Library Services to People with Disabilities* (Chicago: ALA, Association of Specialized and Cooperative Library Agencies, 2001).

27. Courtney Deines-Jones and Connie Van Fleet, *Preparing Staff to Serve Patrons with Disabilities* (New York: Neal-Schuman, 1985); Ruth A. Velleman, *Meeting the Needs of People with Disabilities: A Guide for Librarians, Educators, and Other Service Professionals* (Phoenix, Ariz.: Oryx, 1990); Kieth C. Wright and Judith F. Davie, *Library and Information Services for Handicapped Individuals* (Englewood, Colo.: Libraries Unlimited, 1989).

28. National Library for the Blind and Physically Handicapped (NLS), *NLS: That All May Read*, www.loc.gov/nls/reference/index.html; Library of Congress, "Accessibility Home," www.loc.gov/access.

29. International Federation of Library Associations (ILFA), Libraries Services to People with Special Needs Section, www.ifla.org/en/lsn; ALA, Association of Specialized and Cooperative Library Agencies (ASCLA), www.ala.org/ala/mgrps/divs/ascla/ascla.cfm; Consortium for Libraries in Higher Education Networking to Improve Library Access for Disabled Users in South and Southwest England (CLAUD), www.bris.ac.uk/claud/welcome.html.

30. B. Irvall and G.S. Nielson, *IFLA Checklist: Access to Libraries for Persons with Disabilities*, IFLA Professional Reports, No. 89, www.ifla.org; ALA, ASCLA, *Library Services for People with Disabilities Policy*, www.ala.org/ala/mgrps/divs/ascla/asclaissues/library services.cfm; ALA, ASCLA, *Revised Standards and Guidelines of Service for the Library of Congress Network of Libraries for the Blind and Physically Handicapped* (Chicago: ALA, 2005); Canadian Library Association, *Canadian Guidelines on Library and Information Services for People with Disabilities*, www.cla.ca.

31. Phoenix Public Library, Accessibility Center, www.phoenixpubliclibrary .org; San Antonio Public Library, Special Needs Services, http://guides.mysapl.org; Cleveland Public Library, Ohio Library for the Blind and Physically Disabled, http://cpl.org; Brooklyn Public Library, The Child's Place for Children with Special Needs, www.brooklynpubliclibrary.org; Montgomery County Public Libraries, Disability Resource Center, http://montgomerycountymd.libguides.com/disabilityservices; Berkeley Public Library, Resources for People with Disabilities, www.berkeleypublic library.org; Seattle Public Library, ADA Special Services, www.spl.org; Pima County Public Library, Disability Services, www.library.pima.gov/services/disability/.

32. Deines-Jones, "Low Cost/No Cost Ways to Improve Service Right Now," in *Improving Services to People with Disabilities* (Oxford: Chandos, 2007), 123–47.

33. Donald D. Foos and Nancy C. Pack, eds., *How Libraries Must Comply with the Americans with Disabilities Act* (Phoenix, Ariz.: Oryx, 1992); Joanne L. Cooper, ed., *The Americans with Disabilities Act: It's Impact on Libraries: The Library's Responses in "Doable" Steps* (Chicago: ALA, ASCLA, 1993).

34. Ruth O'Donnell, "Planning to Implement the ADA in the Library," in Foos *How Libraries Must Comply with the Americans with Disabilities Act*, 32–69.

35. William Sannwald, *Checklist of Building Design Considerations* (Chicago: ALA, 2009).

36. NLS Reference Bibliographies, *Accessibility: A Selective Bibliography*, www.loc.gov/nls/reference/bibliographies/accessibility.html; United States Access Board, www.access-board.gov.

37. Ted Chodock and Elizabeth Dolinger, "Applying Universal Design to Information Literacy: Teaching Students Who Learn Differently at Landmark College," *Reference and User Services Quarterly* 49, no. 1 (2009): 26; Bettye R. Connell et al., "The Principles of Universal Design: Version=0," North Carolina State University, Center for Universal Design, www.design.ncsu.edu/cud/about_ud/udprinciplestext.htm.

38. Chodock and Dolinger, "Applying Universal Design to Information Literacy"; Center for Applied Special Technology (CAST), "About UDL," http://cast.org/research/udl/index.html.

39. ALA, ASCLA, *Library Services for People with Disabilities Policy.*

40. North Carolina State University, College of Design, Center for Universal Design, www.design.ncsu.edu/cud/; CAST, Universal Design for Learning (UDL), www.cast.org.

41. Web Accessibility in Mind (WebAIM), *Evaluating Cognitive Web Accessibility*, www.webaim.org/articles/evaluatingcognitive/#principles; World Wide Web Consortium (W3C), Web Content Accessibility Working Group, *Web Content Accessibility Guidelines*, www.w3.org/TR/WAI-WEBCONTENT/#loc.

42. University of Hawaii, Archimedes Hawaii Project, http://archimedes.hawaii.edu; EASI: Equal Access to Software and Information, http://people.rit.edu/easi; University of Washington, Disabilities, Opportunities, Internet Working, and Technology (DO IT), *Resources on Accessible Web Design*, www.washington.edu/doit/Resources/web-design.html.

43. Independence Through Enhancement of Medicare and Medicaid (ITEM), *What Are Assistive Devices, Technologies, and Related Services?* www.itemcoalition.org/what_are_at.html; Abilities! www.abilitiesonline.org/Programs.aspx; Closing the Gap, www.closingthegap.com/about_us.lasso; Family Center on Technology and Disability, www.fctd.info/; Texas School for the Blind and the Visually Impaired, *Overview of Assistive Technology*, www.tsbvi.edu/resources/21-technology/1004-overview-of-assistive-technology; Center for Accessible Technology, www.cforat.org.

44. American Foundation for the Blind (AFB), *Applied Technology*, www.afb.org; Georgia Institute of Technology, Center for Assistive Technology and Environmental Access, Assistive tech.net: National Public Website on Assistive Technology, http://assistivetech.net; U.S. Department of Education, National Institute on Disability and Rehabilitation Research, Abledata, www.abledata.com; NLS, *Assistive Technology Products for Information Access*, comp. Carol Strauss (Washington, D.C.: 2000), www.loc.gov/nls/reference/circulars/assistive.html; Massachusetts Initiative to Maximize Assistive Technology in Consumers' Hands (MATCH), www.massmatch.org; New England Assistive Technology (NEAT), NEAT Center at Oak Hill, www.neatmarketplace.org; Christian Parents Special Kids/Alliance for Technology Access, *Technology Resource*, www.cp-sk.org/cpsktechnologyaccesscenters.htm.

45. Sandra Nelson, *Strategic Planning for Results* (Chicago: ALA, 2008); Rubin, *Planning for Library Services to People with Disabilities*; Shelley Quezada, "Nothing

About Me Without Me: Planning for Library Services for People with Disabilities," *Public Libraries* 42, no. 1 (2003): 42–46.

46. George Washington University, Center for Excellence in Developmental Disabilities, *In My Own Words*, www.gucchdgeorgetown.net/ucedd/words.html.

47. *Disability Awareness Kit: A Training Resource for Public Library Customer Service Staff*, www.openroad.net.au/access/dakit; Aly Peacock, "Disability Awareness for Libraries: How Have the Open Rose Group Used Their Training Packages in Four Member Institutions?" *Focus* no. 37 (Spring 2006): 24–27, www.sconul.ac.uk/public ations/newsletter/37/8.pdf.

48. *Library Accessibility: What You Need to Know*, www.ala.org/ala/mgrps/divs/ascla/asclaprotools/accessibilitytipsheets/; Rubin, *Planning for Library Services to People with Disabilities*, 74–80; Deines-Jones, *Improving Library Services to People with Disabilities*, 135–39; Deines-Jones and Connie Van Fleet, *Preparing Staff to Serve Patrons with Disabilities* (New York: Neal-Schuman, 1995); *Emerging Scholars*; URI, Office of Student Life, *Disability Services for Students*; Wright and Davie, *Library and Information Services for Handicapped Individuals*.

49. Cynthia Holt and Wanda Hole, "Training Rewards and Challenges of Serving Library Users with Disabilities," *Public Libraries* (January/February 2003): 37; *Emerging Scholars*, 12–14; URI, Office of Student Life, *Disability Services*.

50. Choddock and Dolinger, "Applying Universal Design to Information Literacy," 26.

51. Choddock and Dolinger, "Applying Universal Design to Information Literacy," 27, 28–30.

52. Alice Hagemeyer, *The Legacy and Leadership of the Deaf Community* (Chicago: ALA, ASCLA, 1991); Hagemeyer, *Deaf Awareness: Handbook for Public Librarians* (Washington, D.C.: Public Library of the District of Columbia, 1975); Hagemeyer, *Celebrate Deaf Legacy @ Your Library: National Deaf History Month Kit*, www.folda .net/lib/Library_Deaf-Legacy.pdf; Friends of Libraries for Deaf Action (FOLDA), *The Red Notebook*, www.folda.net/home/index.html.

53. Gallaudet University, Laurent Clerc National Deaf Education Center, *Info to Go*, http://clerccenter.gallaudet.edu; Gallaudet University Library, *Research Help*, http://clerccenter.gallaudet.edu; Gallaudet University Library, *Frequently Asked Questions—Deaf-Related*, http://library.gallaudet.edu; Gallaudet University Library, *Deaf Research Guide: How to Get Started*, http://clerccenter.gallaudet.edu; Rochester Institute of Technology, Wallace Memorial Library, *Deaf Studies Internet Resources*, http://library.rit.edu.

54. Gallaudet University Library, *Communicating in the Library with People Who Are Deaf or Hard of Hearing*, http://library.gallaudet.edu; *Emerging Scholars*, 16, 29–30; E-Michigan Deaf and Hard of Hearing People, *Communication Tips with People Who Are Deaf or Hard of Hearing*, www.michdhh.org.

55. Deines-Jones, *Improving Library Services to People with Disabilities*; Melanie J. Norton and Gail Lukovalik, eds., "Libraries Serving an Underserved Population: Deaf and Hearing-Impaired Patrons," (Special issue) *Library Trends* 41 (Summer 1992): 1–176; Norton, "Effective Bibliographic Instruction for Deaf and Hearing-Impaired College Students," *Library Trends* 41 (Summer 1992): 118–50.

56. ALA, ASCLA, *Guidelines for Library and Information Services for the American Deaf Community* (Chicago: ALA, 1995); John Michael Day, *Guidelines for Library Services to Deaf People*, IFLA Professional Reports No. 62, http://archive.ifla.org.

57. Postsecondary Education Programs Network (PEPNeT), *About PEPNeT*, www.pepnet.org/about.asp; PEPNeT Dissemination Center, www.pepnet.org; Rochester Institute of Technology (RIT), National Technical Institute for the Deaf (NTID), *What Is NTID?* www.ntid.rit.edu; RIT, Wallace Memorial Library, *Deaf Studies Internet Resources*, http://library.rit.edu; California State University, Northridge (CSUN), National Center of Deafness (NCOD), *Mission, Vision, and Organizations*, www.csun.edu; PEPNeT, *Helpful Link*, www.pepnet.org.

58. San Francisco Public Library, Deaf Services Center, http://sfpl.org; District of Columbia Public Library, *Library Services for the Deaf and Hard-of-Hearing*, http://dclibrary.org; Pinellas, Florida, Public Library Cooperative, *Literacy Services in Pinellas County*, www.pplc.us; Hennepin County, Minnesota, Library, *Deaf and Hard of Hearing—Resources*, www.hclib.org; FOLDA, www.folda.net.

59. National Institute on Deafness and Other Communication Disorders, www.nidcd.nih.gov; Alexander Graham Bell Association for the Deaf, www.agbell.org; American Deafness and Rehabilitation Association, www.adara.org; Deafsign, www.deafsign.com; Michigan State University, *American Sign Language Browser*, http://aslbrowser.commtechlab.msu.edu/browser.htm; Hearing Loss Association of America, *Self Help for Hard of Hearing People*, http://shhh.org; NLS Reference Circulars, *Deaf-Blindness: National Resources and Organizations 2004*, www.loc.gov/nls/reference/circulars/deafblind.html; National Consortium on Deaf-Blindness, www.nationaldb.org; American Association of the Deaf-Blind, www.aadb.org.

60. Turnbull, Turnbull, and Wehmeyer, *Exceptional Lives*, 370.

61. Gerald Jahoda, *How Do I Do This When I Can't See What I'm Doing? Information Processing for the Visually Disabled* (Washington, D.C.: LC, NLS, 1993); Kevin Carey, "Library Services to People with Special Needs: A Discussion of Blind and Visually Impaired People as an Exemplar," in *Improving Library Services to People with Disabilities*, 21–43; Carey, "The Opportunities and Challenges of the Digital Age: A Blind User's Perspective," *Library Trends* 55, no. 4 (2007): 767–84.

62. American Foundation for the Blind, *Etiquette*, www.afb.org; Deines-Jones, *Improving Library Services to People with Disabilities*; Rubin, *Planning for Library Services to People with Disabilities*, 76–77; AFB, *Bridging the Gap: Best Practices for Instructing Adults Who Are Visually Impaired and Have Low Literacy Skills*, www.afb.org/btglogin.asp.

63. R. Kavanaugh and B.C. Skold, *Libraries for the Blind in the Information Age: Guidelines for Development*, IFLA Professional Reports No. 86, www.ifla.org; ALA, ASCLA, *Revised Standards and Guidelines of Service for the Library of Congress Network of Libraries for the Blind and the Physically Handicapped* (Chicago: ALA, 2005).

64. National Library Service for the Blind and Physically Handicapped, www.loc.gov/nls; Bookshare, http://bookshare.org; Perkins Braille and Talking Books Library and the Minnesota Braille and Talking Book Library, *Info Eyes Information Service* (virtual reference service), www.infoeyes.org.

65. Deines-Jones, *Improving Library Services to People with Disabilities*; Rubin, *Planning for Library Services to People with Disabilities*, 78; NLS, *Physical Handicaps: A Selective Bibliography*, www.loc.gov/nls; NLS, *Physical Disabilities: Information and Advocacy Organizations*, www.loc.gov/nls.

66. Turnbull, Turnbull, and Wehmeyer, *Exceptional Lives*, 106–9.

67. Deines-Jones, *Improving Library Services to People with Disabilities*; Sandy Guild, "LD Accommodations in the School Library," *Knowledge Quest* 37, no. 1 (2008): 24–29; Virginia Ross and Lynn Akin, "Children with Learning Disabilities and

Public Libraries: An E-Survey of Services, Programs, Resources, and Training," *Public Libraries Quarterly* 21, no. 4 (2002): 9–18; Kaplan, *Pathways for Exceptional Children*, 191–211; Turnbull, Turnbull, and Wehmeyer, *Exceptional Lives*, 104–28; Landmark College, www.landmark.edu; Landmark College, Institute for Research and Training, www.landmark.edu/institute/; Beacon College, www.beaconcollege.edu.

68. National Center for Learning Disabilities, http://ncld.org; Learning Disabilities Association of America, www.ldaamerica.org; Learning Disabilities Worldwide, www.ldam.org; Learning Disabilities Association, www.ldanatl.org; Perspectives Network, www.tbi.org; *All Kinds of Minds*, www.allkindsofmind.org; *LD Resources*, www.ldresources.com; NLS Reference Circulars, *Learning Disabilities: National Organizations and Resources*, www.loc.gov; LD Online, *National Organizations*, www.ldonline.org.

69. Turnbull, Turnbull, and Wehmeyer, *Exceptional Lives*, 182–91.

70. Attention! Children and Adults with Attention Deficit Disorders, www.chadd.org; NLS Reference Circulars, *Learning Disabilities: National Organizations and Resources*, www.loc.gov.

71. Turnbull, Turnbull, and Wehmeyer, *Exceptional Lives*, 260–63.

72. Debra Lau Whelan, "The Equal Opportunity Disorder," *School Library Journal* 55, no. 8 (2009): 32; *Emerging Scholars*, 24; Turnbull, Turnbull, and Wehmeyer, *Exceptional Lives*, 272–76; Scotch Plains, New Jersey, Public Library and Fanwood Memorial Library, *Libraries and Autism: We're Connected*, www.thejointlibrary.org/autism/; Autism Society of America (ASA), www.autism-society.org; Autism Speaks, www.autismspeaks.org; Online Asperger Syndrome Information and Support (OASIS), www.aspergersyndrome.org.

73. Turnbull, Turnbull, and Wehmeyer, *Exceptional Lives*, 208–11.

74. Kaplan, *Pathways for Exceptional Children*, 142–51, 159–61; Turnbull, Turnbull, and Wehmeyer, *Exceptional Lives*, 215–24; Dennis Norlin, "Helping Adults with Mental Retardation Satisfy Their Information Needs," in *Information Services for People with Developmental Disabilities*, ed. Linda Lucas Walling and Marilyn M. Irwin (Westport, Conn.: Greenwood, 1995), 181–95.

75. Norlin, "We're Not Stupid, You Know: Library Services for Adults with Mental Retardation," *Research Strategies* 10, no. 2 (1992): 56–68; Linda Lucas Walling and Marilyn M. Irwin, eds., *Information Services for People with Developmental Disabilities* (Westport, Conn.: Greenwood, 1995); ALA, ASCLA, *Library Services for People with Mental Retardation* (Chicago: ALA, 1999).

76. Public Library of Cincinnati and Hamilton County, *Outreach Services*, www.cincinnatilibrary.org.

77. Johnson County, Kansas, Community College, *College Learning Experience Activities and Resources (CLEAR)*, www.jccc.edu; Ohio State University, Nisonger Center, *The Next Chapter Book Club*, www.nextchapterbookclub.org.

78. The ARC of the United States, www.thearc.org; National Association of Councils on Developmental Disabilities, http://nacdd.org; National Down Syndrome Society, www.ndss.org.

79. Turnbull, Turnbull, and Wehmeyer, *Exceptional Lives*, 158–62.

80. Jennifer Murray, "Library Psychiatry: Is There a Place for the Mentally Ill in Your Law Library?" *AALL Spectrum* 14, no. 2 (2009): 10–13; *Emerging Scholars*, 27; Turnbull, Turnbull, and Wehmeyer, *Exceptional Lives*, 171–73.

81. ALA, ASCLA, *Guidelines for Library Services for People with Mental Illnesses* (Chicago: ALA, 2007); National Institute of Mental Health, www.nimh.nih.gov; Mental Health America, www.nmha.org.

82. Turnbull, Turnbull, and Wehmeyer, *Exceptional Lives*, 314–17.

83. NLS, *Learning Disabilities: National Organizations and Resources*, www.loc.gov/nls/reference/circulars/learning.html.

6

Planning, Administration, Coordination, Evaluation

For instructional programs, public librarians can use what is known as the PACE system: plan, administer, coordinate, and evaluate. This chapter describes four models of instruction that public libraries can follow, four planning modes, and Information Literacy Instruction (ILI) resources to begin with. Information on planning using goals, objectives, and outcomes is also provided, along with information on Bloom's taxonomy. The chapter also covers evaluation, marketing, staffing, and what a good instructional program looks like.

MODELS OF INSTRUCTION

Public libraries can pursue at least four different instructional models in planning for instruction: the teaching library, the learning library, the traditional public library (reflecting information, education, and guidance), and libraries as gateways to new information technologies through direct and indirect instruction.

The Teaching Library

Public libraries could become mainly teaching libraries, like their academic and school counterparts, with an emphasis on the types of instructional activities found in other educational settings. Programs would usually be based on standards and follow instructional plans similar to those used by academic and school leaders in ILI. The more extensive plans would require funding, specialized equipment and electronic instructional classrooms, commitment, and dedicated staff in order to plan, execute, evaluate, and oversee all of this activity. Following this model could also have a huge impact on cultural programming. Small libraries can pursue this option, but bulk helps here. This support can come in the form of larger public library systems or of consortia or networks with other libraries and institutions. For more information on the teaching library model of planning, see *Creating and Promoting Lifelong Learning in Public Libraries: Tools and Tips for Practitioners.*

The Learning Library

There are several ways that public libraries can promote themselves as learning libraries:

- Instruction for one.
- Other help for independent learners.
- Ties to informal education and to lifelong learning.

Public, academic, and school librarians have always done some instruction at the reference desk in order to help library users with research demanding several steps. A 1994 article investigating this in detail is "Students and the Information Search Process: Zones of Intervention for Librarians" by Carol Kuhlthau, which describes how librarians can instruct students both in the classroom and at the reference desk as they progress through their research strategies. More recent articles on instruction at the reference desk include "Fostering Self-Regulated Learning at the Reference Desk" by Edward J. Eckel and "Assessment of Student Learning from Reference Service" by Gillian S. Gremmels and Karen Shostrom Hehman. Both explore ways that reference librarians can reinforce what students learn in their formal Information Literacy (IL) classes by encouraging them to design and refine their research strategies.[1]

Eckel asks whether more instruction should be incorporated into the reference encounter, and if so, how. Gremmels and Lehman compare student reports on what they learned in reference encounters with what they have been learning in more formal IL classes. Both articles are concerned with the best ways of tutoring and scaffolding students who are learning to be independent researchers.

With the rise and development of virtual reference, librarians have created online forms to help them and their patrons in the reference interview. These forms can incorporate questions to encourage patrons to take several steps as they carefully think through their research strategies. These strategies will be discussed more in *Creating and Promoting Lifelong Learning in Public Libraries: Tools and Tips for Practitioners.*

Public librarians have long used readers' advisory services and bibliotherapy to help patrons find popular and other materials interesting and useful to them. These services are also part of "instruction for one." However, the readers' advisory movement has become a full-fledged one, including book discussion groups and many other activities with more implications for instruction. Independent learners can also be helped through indirect means, such as pathfinders and bibliographies, handbook information, well-constructed websites, building design, and signage. Public libraries can also be tied into many forms of lifelong learning, including the promotion of leisure reading and study circles and work with "Universities of the Third Age," which have been created in a number of countries to encourage elders to further explore their own learning. (For more information on combining reader's advisory services with ILI, see chapter 7 of this volume, as well as *Creating and Promoting Lifelong Learning in Public Libraries: Tools and Tips for Practitioners*.)

The learning library is a phenomenon that has been emerging in various forms for some time. The promotion of independent learning by public librarians is a fulfillment of Louis Shores's idea of the "library college" and the idea of public libraries as "people's universities."

The Traditional Public Library

Another possibility would be libraries that want to add instruction to their extensive cultural programming and other activities. There are at least three ways of accomplishing this. Many public libraries offer a combination of cultural programs, literacy and ESL programs, and hardcore information literacy and promote it all as programming to the public. A second approach is to incorporate instruction into more traditional programs where appropriate. Some instruction can be done with literacy and ESL classes. With current events and book discussion groups, librarians can either instruct on where and how to find similar materials, create pathfinders and other handouts, or have exhibits or displays. A third approach would be to use some cultural programming techniques, such as storytelling or puppetry, to promote ILI. (For more on combining ILI with traditional public library programming , see chapters 7 and 8 of this volume.)

Gateways to New Information Technologies

Libraries have been called on to introduce their patrons to new information technologies. Some are introducing elders and other adults to computers and to the Internet. Another approach is to introduce all citizens in a geographic area to the use of broadband technology. In addition, public libraries can create instructional classrooms and information commons to help their public learn about and use a wide range of media information and technology. This is already happening in many academic libraries because of the changing needs of Millennial Generation students, those born

1982–2000, who are now coming of age as adults. Some public libraries have created computer laboratories, learning centers, homework help programs, and "net squares" to help their patrons with similar issues. Public librarians are beginning to consider whether and how their reference services should be redesigned. Some are finding it necessary to keep traditional services for their older patrons and to design new services for their younger users. School media specialists are going through similar changes in dealing with their students, faculty, and administrators.[2] It will be interesting to see whether public libraries also acquire or become electronic information commons and how they may eventually combine their traditional services with new ones.

MODES OF PLANNING

Public libraries can plan for instruction in several ways:

- Formal planning, specifically for instruction, using existing ILI goals and standards and following exemplary programs.
- Organic approaches—using elements of ILI to improve and to extend more traditional public library programming and activities.
- Combining formal and organic approaches by using public library planning and marketing guides to plan library collections and activities in general, including instruction and evaluating these through the use of Outcome-Based Evaluation (OBE) or logic models.
- Experimental approaches.

Formal Planning

Public librarians can find standards, guidelines, criteria for excellent programs, and examples of exemplary programs in a number of places. The most important for our purposes are the ALA standards, in *Information Literacy Competency Standards for Higher Education* by the Association of College and Research Libraries (ACRL), and *Standards for the 21st-Century Learner* and *Information Literacy Standards for Student Learning*, both by the American Association of School Librarians (AASL).[3] Another useful standard is the *Australia and New Zealand Information Literacy Framework* by ANZIIL[4]

Applying these standards or patterning one's planning after an instructional program of a large, well-funded educational institution without using planning checklists and other supportive material is like jumping off the diving board into the deep end of the pool. This is not an ideal approach for nonswimmers, beginners, or the timid. However, these documents can give public librarians many ideas and criteria that can be helpful in their own planning.

Some guidelines provide easier approaches for planning an instructional program. Students at the University of Rhode Island (URI) are assigned to design an instructional program for a library of their choice by doing the following:

Write a proposal to create a complete instructional program for an academic, public, school, or special library, including:

1. A brief description of your library, institution, and community. Draw on secondary sources for this information. What is the purpose of your institution? What are the characteristics of your community? How do these things affect the instruction goals of your library and your students?
2. Rationale, goals, and objectives.
   a. Why do you want to establish this program?
   b. Are there existing goals, objectives, and standards from professional associations, the state, accrediting agencies, and other sources that can be useful here?
   c. What are your own goals and objectives? How will you be able to tell that your patrons are "information literate?"
3. Types of instruction planned.
   a. What will be the subject of your instruction? Assessing information needs? Finding information? Evaluating information? Anything else?
   b. How will you present your instruction?
   c. Formal presentations through one-shot lectures? Course-integrated instruction? Full courses?
   d. Occasional workshops as needs arise? Programming? Other informal activities?
   e. Indirect instruction via guidebooks, bibliographies, pathfinders, or Web pages?
   f. What audiences will you be reaching? What is your general public like? Are there subgroups within your population (like preschoolers, continuing education students, or a particular ethnic, immigrant, or international community) that you may want to target in a particular way?
4. Evaluation and assessment.
   a. How will you evaluate each activity and event?
   b. How will you evaluate the entire instructional program?
   c. How can you use assessment tools to see whether, how, and how much your patrons may be benefiting from this program?

This proposal can be used for a single program or a whole range of instructional programs. It works equally well with large public library systems, small library branches, and small, isolated libraries. It can be adapted to fit the particular situation of your library and can also be amended to be more relevant for your purposes. It is also doable—URI students who mostly work full time in libraries write this proposal as part of their term projects along with several other assignments. This proposal is designed to get librarians new to ILI to think through their approaches to instruction.

A more complex planning document is *Creating a Comprehensive Information Literacy Plan* by Johanna M. Burkhardt, Mary C. MacDonald, and Andree Rathmacher.[5] This is geared more to academic and school libraries and emphasizes the work of committees, but it has many useful ideas, such as different ways to do needs assessments, what to emphasize in the plan for which audiences, how to describe trends and needs in your institution, assessment strategies, marketing through public relations, and the creation of progress reports. This guide has an excellent section on terminologies, definitions, and core competencies in this field, with an extensive list of resources. It also includes a comprehensive toolkit that includes an overview of IL, a needs assessment bibliography, information on peer institutions, more sources of IL definitions, a list of relevant organizations, standards and guidelines, a marketing bibliography, some websites concerning IL for specific disciplines and regional accreditation, and examples of instructional plans in one school media center and a variety of academic libraries. Also helpful are criteria for exemplary programs. Criteria for best practices can be found in ACRL's "Characteristics of Programs of Information Literacy That Illustrate Best Practices: A Guideline."[6] (For more on formal planning, see *Lifelong Learning in Public Libraries: Tools and Tips for Practitioners*.)

Organic Approaches

Elements of ILI can be used to improve what public librarians have always done using these approaches: research strategies or conceptual frameworks for public libraries; extensions of traditional public library programming, such as literacy, ESL, citizenship classes, and book discussion groups; approaches from cultural programs, such as storytelling or puppet shows; more indirect instruction; tie-ins with guidance and learning activities; information and referral (I&R), community outreach, and networking; and marketing and public relations.

There are many advantages to taking an organic approach. This is comparable to wading into the swimming pool from the shallow end, enabling librarians new to ILI to get their feet wet. This approach can be done fairly easily in small, isolated libraries with relatively few resources. It is more experimental. Activities that may or may not work can be easily kept, expanded, improved, or dropped, as needed.

The organic approach can be compared to early bibliographic instruction done in academic libraries in the 1970s that then consisted mostly of tours, orientations, and one-shot lectures or single presentations. Many of these librarians started with the classes of professors who were already interested in instruction. They also targeted introductory survey classes, research classes, and capstone courses in traditional disciplines. The new multidisciplinary disciplines in area, gender, and ethnic studies and other fields, such as conflict management, peace studies, and management information systems, were also good places to start ILI, since this activity would tie together thought and materials from the more traditional disciplines contributing to these new fields. Public librarians have similar audiences, including genealogists, elders needing computer and other instruction, business people, people needing business information on investments, people who are job seeking or interested in career or retirement planning, high school seniors preparing for college and for life, and parents and teachers who can all be instructed directly, indirectly, in a group, or more individually. Organic approaches can also be legitimately used in libraries that prefer to emphasize a lot of traditional cultural programming.

There are two caveats to the organic approach, however, affecting staffing and program design. A dedicated librarian or two can initiate instruction using a few resources, but unless the entire staff is committed to instructional programs, activities can disappear as these librarians transfer or retire. It is also important that ILI be viewed as a systematic program, not just as a group of unrelated or disjointed activities. However, it is possible to incorporate a lot of instruction into activities that public libraries already do without changing their basic character or interfering with cultural programs.

Combining Formal and Organic Approaches

Public libraries can use planning and marketing resources, like *Strategic Planning for Results* from the Public Library Association or *Marketing the Library* from the Ohio Library Foundation, to plan their collections and activities in general and design instruction that would support these activities. They can evaluate these activities using methods from the field of ILI and Outcome-Based Evaluation (OBE) or logic models—methods used by public libraries and not-for-profit agencies, respectively. These approaches will be described in more detail later in this chapter. (For more ideas on how to combine formal and organic approaches, see chapters 7 and 8 of this volume.)

Experimental Approaches

Some libraries, such as the Cerritos Library in California, have experimented with ways to promote the independent learning of their patrons. Some, such as the Public Library of Charlotte and Mecklenburg County (PLCMC) in North Carolina, have created tools like Library 2.0 that have many implications for both direct and indirect instruction. Other libraries are helping to create electronic networks to connect their public to the Internet. There are many experimental ways that public libraries can promote the information literacy of their patrons, including initiatives neither created yet nor described here.

Before attempting to create standards similar to their school or academic counterparts, public librarians should address a number of issues. They need the time, for example, to consider all that they are doing and to experiment. However, they do not have to recreate the wheel. They can draw on the extensive work of their academic and school counterparts, redesign it for their own purposes, and make these tools their own.

STARTUP RESOURCES FOR ILI

Research Strategies and Other Conceptual Frameworks

The core of Information Literacy Instruction has been the emphasis on the search, evaluation, and use of information (mostly nonfiction and literary). A number of researchers have discovered and described what people do as they look for information.

Kuhlthau mentions several steps in the "information process approach," including *defining* the need for information, *locating* and *selecting* information, *organizing* ideas, and *presenting* and *assessing* the results.[7] Alice Yucht created a research strategy called FLIPit! Her four steps are *Focus* or specifying an information need; *Links* or strategizing; *Input* or the sorting, sifting, and storing of information; and *Payoff* or solving problems and showing results. "If/then" can be used at any step to determine what students already know and where to go from there.[8]

The most influential research strategy among school media specialists has been the Big 6 created by Mike Eisenberg and Bob Berkowitz. The Big 6 focuses on task definition, information seeking strategies, location and access, use of information, synthesis or organizing and presenting the information, and evaluation.[9] To help teachers and school media specialists implement this approach, the strategy includes courses and a wide variety of resources. Eisenberg and Berkowitz have also created the Super 3 for younger students, focusing on determining information needs, finding information, and then using and evaluating information. The Big 6 and Super 3 can be applied well in all library settings.

Several researchers, including Peter Jarvis, John Holford, Colin Griffin, Robert Millis Gagne, and Malcolm Knowles, have investigated the characteristics of self-directed, independent learners.[10] Gagne's steps to learning are very similar to research processes described by Kuhlthau, Yucht, Eisenberg, and Berkowitz. They include engagement or getting interested in the topic, planning for research, exploration, reflection, generalization and implementation, and evaluation. All of these research strategies are important as we consider ILI standards created by several professional associations.

ILI Standards, Goals, and Objectives

In the United States, the most influential ILI standards have been created by two major divisions of the American Library Association (ALA): the Association of College and Research Libraries (ACRL) and the American Association of School Librarians (AASL). Other standards to be described here include the *Australian and New Zealand Information Literacy Framework* from the Australian and New Zealand Institute for Information Literacy (ANZIIL) and *The 25 Theses* from the Information Architecture Institute.

Information Literacy Competency Standards for Higher Education from ACRL focuses on the information-seeking strategies described by the researchers above, with an emphasis on defining, accessing, evaluating, and using information.[11] The *Australian and New Zealand Information Literacy Framework* has similar standards, with a focus on determining information needs and then finding, evaluating, managing, applying, and using information.[12] These standards mention the creation of new knowledge and understanding with new information.

AASL has created two sets of standards with applications to public libraries. Their earlier standards, *Information Literacy Standards for Student Learning*, mention the assessing, evaluation, and use of information, as do the standards mentioned above. They also mention two other concerns not emphasized as much elsewhere but relevant to public libraries: independent learning, including an appreciation for literature and for culture, and especially social responsibility.[13] A strength but a possible weakness of these standards is that they are relatively open-ended. However, public librarians can work with these to incorporate all of their goals for service.

AASL replaced the earlier standards with *Standards for the 21st-Century Learner*, with a focus on using critical thinking to gain knowledge, creating and applying new knowledge, ethically sharing information, and pursuing personal and aesthetic growth.[14] These standards present a much more detailed list of skills, demonstration of skills, responsibilities, and self-assessment strategies. There is still a focus on democratic participation and on "personal and aesthetic growth," but with specific objectives more oriented to formal education. Both AASL standards can be helpful to public librarians who are concerned with information provision and education as well as with cultural guidance.

The 25 Theses is a philosophical statement for professionals involved in the new field of Information Architecture (IA).[15] IA emerged at the same time as ILI and for many of the same reasons. According to *The 25 Theses*, information architecture "designs structures of information rather than bricks, wood, plastic, and stone" (Thesis 8). This field emerged to enable people to build superior websites on the Internet, but it extends beyond that. "One goal of information architecture is to shape information into an environment that allows users to create, manage and share its very substance" (Thesis 12). Another goal is "to enable users to communicate, collaborate, and experience each other" (Thesis 13).

The 25 Theses stress people's need for information. According to Thesis 1 and 2, people not only need information but also "need the right information at the right time." According to Thesis 16, "all people have a right to know where they are and where they are going and how to get what they need." Thesis 4 maintains that "the Internet has changed how we live with information."

The rest of the theses describe major characteristics of IA. According to Thesis 15, people come first and technology second. Even though IA began as a reaction to the emergence of the Internet, Thesis 19 states that this field may not always be tied to this particular technology. IA "accomplishes tasks with whatever tools are necessary" (Thesis 20). These tools are "fashioned by many people. . . . They all bring different perspectives and they all add flavor to the stew. They are all necessary" (Thesis 21). "These tools come in many forms and methods" (Thesis 22). Thesis 24 defines Information Architecture as "first an act, than a practice, then a discipline."

The implications of this document for public library instruction are important, not only in libraries' own website design, but in their other indirect and direct instruction. The broader philosophy expressed in The 25 Theses meshes very well with the philosophies and realities of public library services in general and public library instruction in particular. It also fits in with many of the general philosophies and goals of ILI, especially the use and sharing of information.

More Philosophical Works on ILI

Also useful when starting to think about ILI are two of the more philosophical and theoretical works treating the subject: The Seven Faces of Information Literacy by Christine Bruce and the article "Information Literacy as a Liberal Art" by Jeremy Shapiro and Shelley K. Hughes. In some ways, Bruce's work is a more theoretical and business-oriented version of the Big 6 and similar frameworks. The "7 Faces" are metaphors describing the experiences of people as they take steps to define, find, and use information. These faces include the IT Experience, the Information Source Experience, the Information Process Experience, the Information Control Experience, the Knowledge Construction Experience, the Knowledge Extension Experience, and the Wisdom Experience.[16]

In the Information Technology (IT) experience, people use IT in order to be aware of information. Bruce views the IT experience as being a social one, not an individualistic one. The Information Source experience would be roughly equivalent to using principles of Bibliographic Instruction (BI) and IL to look for information from printed and electronic sources, people, and organizations. The Information Processing experience entails using information to solve problems and to make decisions, and the Information Control experience includes recognizing and managing information and making connections between this information, projects, and people.

The Knowledge Construction experience is learning by using critical thinking in order to gain knowledge and a personal perspective on the information. Knowledge Extension is a combination of personal knowledge, experience, and creative insight or intuition. New knowledge and creative solutions come from these steps. Bruce sees people of the Wisdom experience combining their knowledge with their values and ethics and using their information to benefit others.

Shapiro and Hughes, in "Information Literacy as a Liberal Art," argue that ILI should go far beyond many of the goals discussed, so far to become a true part of the liberal arts.[17] The seven skills that they recommend are:

- Tool literacy—understanding and using information technology relevant to education and to professional life.
- Resource literacy—the use of printed, electronic, and human information sources. This is roughly equivalent to many librarians' definitions of BI and IL.
- Social-structural literacy—understanding how information is created, generated, disseminated, evaluated, and used in a society.
- Research literacy—the ability to understand and use information technology related to scholarly work in a discipline.
- Publishing literacy—the ability to publish ideas electronically.
- Emerging technology literacy—the ability to understand, evaluate, and use new technologies as they emerge.
- Critical literacy—the ability to critically evaluate information technologies using historical, philosophical, sociopolitical, and cultural perspectives.

Shapiro and Hughes have since expanded this argument to state that information literate people must be able to "communicate with others in a world mediated by technology" and to "manage the complexity that a constant connection to technology generates."[18] Their approach would teach people not only how to determine their information needs and how to find, evaluate, disseminate, and use information but also how to put all of these activities into a broader social context. Both *The Seven Faces of Information Literacy* and "Information Literacy as a Liberal Art" raise excellent questions about the ultimate goals and purposes of ILI in any setting. Since public libraries serve people "from the cradle to the grave" and are concerned about democracy and society in general, these questions are particularly germane in this setting.

PLANNING FOR GOALS, OBJECTIVES, AND OUTCOMES

Goals

Goals, objectives, and outcomes are unavoidable if one teaches.[19] What we want to teach is the goal. The objectives are methods we use to teach, as well as the intermediate steps taken by library users as they learn. Outcomes are thinking or behavior that has changed as a result of the teaching. If more than one person is teaching a group of people, it is important to write down the goals, objectives, and outcomes.

Goals are what perfection looks like, and they represent the ultimate reasons for doing anything, especially teaching. Goals are usually broad, abstract, and general statements. They tend to outline what should be as a result of people obeying or pursuing them. In public libraries, goals can often be found in their mission statements.

Objectives and Outcomes

Objectives are much more specific and behavioral than goals. Program objectives represent particular steps teachers take in instructing students, and instructional objectives show that students are making progress. Objectives can be observed, measured, and evaluated. They can also be referred to as performance indicators or enabling objectives. They show how goals are to be achieved.

Outcomes are more specific objectives measuring changes in thinking and especially behavior as a result of the teaching. For instance, a goal may be to teach children how to use a library collection to find information. Objectives would include activities and teaching techniques to help the class meet this goal, as well as the students' responses during their learning. Outcomes may include children successfully using the library's catalog to locate three or four books on the shelf or using periodical databases to find several articles. Outcomes are also called terminal objectives and show the result of learning at the end of instruction. They show when goals have been achieved.

Both objectives and outcomes are written in behavioral form and describe what students should be able to think or to do after the instruction. However, outcomes are usually more specific than objectives, and there can be several outcomes for each objective.

Goals, Objectives, and Bloom's Taxonomy

Public librarians can draw on several completely different sets of goals and objectives in planning their instruction. These include existing ILI goals from ALA and other professional library associations; informational, educational, and cultural goals from public libraries; goals created by librarians themselves; and the more general educational goals and objectives from Bloom's Taxonomy. All of these can affect specific instruction that public librarians plan.

The original version of Bloom's *Taxonomy of Educational Objectives* was published in two volumes, in 1956 and 1964.[20] Volume 1 lists goals and objectives related to steps in the cognitive domain that build on each other—knowledge, comprehension, application, analysis, synthesis, and evaluation. These steps are strikingly similar to most of the core goals for ILI. Volume 2 describes the more emotional goals of receiving and paying attention to information, responding, valuing, and organizing this information and incorporating it into one's own values.

Some educators and librarians have used Bloom's Taxonomy in order to plan instructional programs. This was especially true before the creation of the current ACRL and AASL standards. Bloom and his associates assumed that all students can learn with the right set of objectives. In addition, when these objectives are applied well, learning can also be evaluated. There are disadvantages to Bloom's Taxonomy. People can be treated as objects, and not everybody responds well to this approach. Also, it is difficult to use these goals with a direct application to ILI.[21] However, these goals may still be worth investigating. (For more information on how to write goals and objectives and incorporate rubrics, see *Creating and Promoting Lifelong Learning in Public Libraries: Tools and Tips for Practitioners*.)

EVALUATION

Kinds of Evaluation

Evaluation can be macro or micro, formal or informal, normative (or ongoing) or summative, quantitative or qualitative, norm referenced or criteria referenced, or based on thinking/learning or feelings/opinions. Some evaluations focus on the outcomes of programming activities. Evaluation tools can range widely, from the informal observation of body language and other behavior in the classroom to exercises, surveys, questionnaires, interviews, pre-tests, post-tests, and the separate assessments of teacher performance and student products, such as research journals, paper trails, or bibliographies that are the results of instruction.[22]

Micro evaluation would be the evaluation of specific instructional activities, such as a presentation, a presentation series, or a pathfinder. Macro evaluation would be designed to evaluate all instructional activities in a library. It would be a combination of micro evaluations and an overview to ascertain whether all activities fulfill the library's goals for instruction and whether they support or complement each other.

Informal evaluation would include the observation of students' behavior and body language in the classroom and teachers' responses to that. Students can be asked questions or asked for responses during the presentations. Their response is an indication of their interest and understanding. For instance, as librarians do a simulated search, they can ask the class for suggestions for search strategies. Grassian and Kaplowitz describe a number of Classroom Assessment Techniques (CATs), including exercises in class, worksheets, and hands-on practice.[23] CATs enable students to reflect on what they are thinking and learning as the class proceeds. One type of CAT is the "One-Minute Paper," a note reflecting what students are learning and any questions they may still have. One-minute papers can be either oral or written.

Normative or ongoing evaluation is assessment that occurs during the class session or series. It is designed to let the teacher know how well things are going and enables the teacher to make necessary changes. Two forms of normative evaluation are especially helpful to instructors: peer evaluation and "lesson study" or quality circles for educators, an idea from Japan. Summative evaluation occurs at the end of the session or series. It is designed to enable the librarian to look at the instructional activity as a whole to see what went well or poorly.

However, there are methods to evaluate instruction before it is given to its target audiences. This is especially true for many modes of indirect instruction such as explanatory Web pages or tutorials. Instruction can be evaluated ahead of time by using "focus groups" of library staff, library trustees, students, school or university instructors, and volunteers from the public to "test drive" the instruction.

Evaluation can be quantitative or qualitative. With quantitative evaluations, such as the use of five-point rubrics or averaging the grades of students, members are assigned to quantify the quality of students' work. Opinion surveys on a five-point scale also attempt to quantify results, as do objective tests to measure students' knowledge. Quantitative evaluations are based on methodologies in the sciences and measure "how much" and "how many."

More qualitative evaluation would include open-ended questions, Outcome-Based Evaluation (OBE), interviews, and paper trails or journals of student library research. This approach is based more on disciplines such as anthropology and measure "how" and "how well."

Evaluation may be norm referenced or criteria referenced. Norm-referenced evaluation is very similar to grading on a curve, with students being compared to each other. With criteria-referenced assessment, students are evaluated on how well they are fulfilling the goals and objectives of the instruction. (For more information on how to use tools for evaluation, see *Creating and Promoting Lifelong Learning in Public Libraries: Tools and Tips for Practitioners*.)

Public library instruction would be designed to answer these three questions:

- What did students learn from the instruction?
- How do they feel about the instruction?
- What difference does this make?

What People Learn and How They Feel

Most ILI evaluation is designed to measure either what people are learning or have learned or their opinions about the instruction. These approaches measure two different things and should probably be done separately. The two do not always correlate with each other, but both are important. Evaluation that measures what people learn lets you know how effective your instruction has been. However, measuring people's attitudes will let you know whether they would want more instruction like this and whether they would recommend this to a friend.

An excellent source for designing evaluation to measure student learning is *Information Literacy Assessment: Standard-Based Tools and Assignments* by Teresa V. Neely.[24] This source includes detailed information on how to apply the ACRL standards to instruction, how to evaluate during and after instruction, and how to design evaluation instruments. It ends with an extensive bibliography of assessment tools.

A useful source in designing evaluations for measuring attitudes and opinions of users is *Evaluating Library Instruction: Sample Questions, Forms, and Strategies for Practical Use* by Diana Shonrock and the Research Committee of ALA's Library Instruction Round Table (LIRT).[25] Shonrock includes questionnaires asking users about their opinions on many aspects of ILI, including single and multiple presentations, tours, instruction at the reference desk, and term paper assistance or consultation. There is an emphasis on evaluating presentations, with questions on course materials and activities, procedures, and content, points stressed during lectures, and exercises, assignments, examinations, and grading. Questions for students assess their opinions of the librarian's or teaching assistant's instruction as well as their grade expectations, workload, and effects of the instruction. This source also briefly describes designing pre- and post-tests to see what students learn from the sessions, and there are questions for professors or teachers to assess resources important to them, instructors' interactions with librarians, and the appropriateness of library instruction for their classes. Teachers are also asked whether they would continue to use this service, whether they would recommend it to other faculty, whether the

instruction has served its purpose, and whether their students are using libraries more. Both students and faculty are asked what was the most useful
information, and what should be added or omitted.

These two books can be very helpful for librarians designing evaluations
measuring student learning and attitudes, respectively.

The Difference This Makes: Outcome-Based
Evaluation (OBE) and Logic Models

So far, we have focused on the characteristics of goals, objectives, and
outcomes and examined the similarities, differences, and relationships
among all three. Two similar methods of evaluation that consider all of
these things and more are Outcome-Based Evaluation (OBE) and logic
models.

OBE emerged first in community agencies, such as the United Way, and
more recently in public libraries. According to Joan C. Durrance and Karen
E. Fisher, OBE emerged because public and other libraries have been ignored as institutions by other organizations, the government, and foundations.[26] OBE enables public librarians to better tell their stories and describe
their services to the public.

Libraries and other nonprofit organizations are facing increasing demands for accountability, with both pressure and encouragement from
federal, state, and local governments. The passage of the Government
Performance and Results Act (GPRA) by the federal government has had
a major impact, both on how government agencies are evaluated and on
how the federal government evaluates the services of nonprofit organizations, particularly those seeking government funding.[27] The GPRA would
be a major impetus for the development of both OBE and logic models. In
addition, the Institute of Museum and Library Services (IMLS) has funded
several projects related to OBE, and there has been funded research by other
sources.[28]

Two formulas or outcomes models used in OBE are the United Way
Outcomes Model and a similar model that emerged from the Durrance and
Fisher study *How Libraries and Librarians Help* (HLLH).[29] The United Way
model focuses on inputs or resources of organizations, their activities, their
outputs (or statistics), and their outcomes. The HLLH models investigate
library services, users, traditional outputs, and outcomes. Library services
would include specific activities, professional contributions from the staff,
and other inputs and resources used to do the program. User characteristics
investigated would include information needs, attitudes, perceptions, and
behavior. Traditional outputs are statistics on how many programs occurred
and how many people participated in the program, and the outcomes are
changes in people's lives in their "skill, knowledge, attitude, behavior, con-

dition, or life status." The focus of this research is on user responses and other outcomes of programs.

Public library mission statements can be compared to goals. They are very general, indicating what perfection should look like, but they can also lay the groundwork for much more specific outcome indicators. Output measures can be compared to objectives in some respects but are much more quantitative, measuring how many and how much. Many of these measures have been correlated to library circulation, while not enough attention has been paid to other library programs and activities. However, output measures can still provide some useful information on how many people participate in programs and activities or how many activities are scheduled and what kinds. Outcome indicators in the context of OBE are similar to outcomes elsewhere. Many of these outcomes are more qualitative than those found in other evaluation research and tend to come directly from the people served in the form of comments, stories, and testimonials. Questions in OBE are kept relatively open to encourage honest responses from library users. These responses can be positive or negative, expected or unexpected. After this research is done, practitioners analyze the responses to the questions, looking for patterns. This is almost opposite to the design of scaled instruments to measure audience reactions. Output measures and outcome indicators supplement each other. Output measures tell us how many or how much, while outcome indicators put human faces on the statistics. They show libraries and other institutions make a difference in people's lives and specifically how they accomplish this.[30]

Outcomes have been divided into categories by libraries and other institutions. The Annie E. Casey Foundation describes outcomes that promote informal social networks and economic opportunity, build neighborhood assets, and promote child and family well-being. Outcomes can affect individuals, families, neighborhoods, and communities at large.[31] They can also connect broad information literacy goals with public libraries' promotion of community, social capital, and democracy.

The Durrance and Fisher HLLH study was funded by the IMLS and conducted by researchers from the University of Michigan and the University of Washington.[32] The services examined included those for immigrants, after-school community technology programs for teenagers, community networks, I&R services, ethnic programs, and consumer health information services. ILI can be integrated into all of these programs.

They also described in detail how OBE helps libraries, librarians, and the broader community, and they included comments from other researchers.[33] OBE can help librarians focus on and clarify their goals and objectives. Librarians can look at their program results to find effective practices and exemplary programs and can use critical thinking on what is working—or not. Results of using outcomes include enhanced record keeping; better programs; evidence to enable librarians to expand, replicate, improve, or eliminate programs; more funding; much better publicity for libraries; more effective advocacy; and more community partnerships and collaborations.

Durrance and Fisher articulated nine ways that the results of OBE can be used: to enable librarians to better communicate with other agencies; to articulate the public library's role in civic society; to improve strategic planning; to "narrate the library story"; to better compete for scarce funds; to use marketing in promoting library service; to identify negative outcomes to improve service; to brand services; and to show public librarians as "primary engines of our democratic society."[34] They also give extensive guidance on how to do OBE in preparing for the study, collecting data, analyzing the data, and using the results of the study.[35] To help researchers get started, Durrance and Fisher urge them to determine the scope of their evaluation, including services to be evaluated, specific activities, user groups, and stakeholders affected by the activity. Researchers are encouraged to start thinking about positive and negative outcomes.

Durrance and Fisher discuss using and maximizing the results of the study through marketing, long-term assessment, improving services or programs, and allocating or reallocating resources. Marketing in this context would include identifying audiences, matching audiences with outcomes, determining dissemination strategies, and developing a graphical representation of the outcomes. Long-term assessment can be used to determine whether the program or activity has met its goals. Positive, negative, expected, or unexpected outcomes can be used to improve, enhance, replicate, or eliminate programs, which would affect allocation of resources.

OBE is designed to evaluate the broad diverse goals of public library services. Instructional activities and services can be evaluated by combining this approach with other methods of evaluation described above, including tests to see what people are learning and user opinions. OBE as described by Durrance and Fisher is an excellent approach to evaluation for public librarians.

Logic models, which are used by other nonprofit organizations, carry this process a step further and can be comparable to designing a 3–5 level rubric.[36] Like OBE, logic models look at program resources, activities, outputs, and customers reached. They also investigate short, intermediate, and longer-term outcomes and consider relevant external influences. The purposes of logic models are very similar to those of OBE—they communicate goals and needs of programs, communicate the place of the program in the organization or field, help professionals to design or improve their programs, and "point to a balanced set of key performance measurement points and evaluation issues." They also meet the requirements of GPRA. Logic models are also called "chains of reasoning," "theory of action," and "performance frameworks," and these are all related to program theory, which "guides an evaluation by identifying key program elements and articulating how these elements are expected to relate to each other."[37] The emphasis here is on showing how resources lead to activities, leading to outputs, leading to short-term, intermediate, and long-term outcomes, leading to the next cycle of the same. Logic models attempt to tie all of these things together.

Jack A. McLaughlin and Gretchen Jordan give an excellent introduction and overview of logic models.[38] There are also several Internet sites with information on logic models and detailed instruction on how to build them. The University of Wisconsin Extension has an introductory Web page explaining logic models as well as a separate workshop on how to build one. The W.K. Kellogg Foundation has a *Logic Model Development Guide.*[39] Eric Graig has created an online tutorial on this subject, and the United Way has published a book on outcome measurement that can be helpful. (For more information on incorporating OBE and logic models, see *Creating and Promoting Lifelong Learning in Public Libraries: Tools and Tips for Practitioners.*)

MARKETING AND NEEDS ASSESSMENT

Marketing

Most marketing texts refer to the "four Ps of marketing"—Product, Place, Price, and Promotion. This text would add People to the mix and put them first. Public libraries have historically marketed their services by using all five Ps. Library surveys and other planning documents are early steps in market research. Public libraries have long practiced demographic and geographic market segmentation, with youth services, other services for specialized groups, outreach, and library branches. Public librarians can use their planning documents and other materials to determine all of the following:

- *People*—their characteristics and their informational, instruction, and cultural needs.
- *Product*—the kinds of direct and indirect instruction to meet these needs.
- *Place*—where and how to do this instruction. In person at the library or in the community? Online? Indirectly through printed materials, signage, or building design?
- *Promotion*—the best ways to promote these services to the public.

Marketing is an alternative approach to the modes of planning found in academic and school libraries. Public librarians can do needs assessments and use public library planning guides in order to determine both the characteristics of their population and their information needs. As professionals plan their collections, services, and programs, they can also plan many modes of instruction designed to take care of these information needs. This approach would not be a great departure from activities that they have always done. In addition, public librarians can also use OBE to evaluate their instruction and supplement this with other forms of evaluation. These are excellent strategies for traditional public libraries combining formal planning with a more organic approach to instruction.

ILI Literature on Needs Assessment

A number of ILI publications provide useful information on how librarians can determine the informational and especially the instructional needs of their clientele. They include Grassian and Kaplowitz's *Information Literacy Instruction* and two chapters in *The LIRT Library Handbook*, one by Mary Loe and Betsy Elkins, and one by Kathleen G. Woods, Helen T. Burns, and Marilyn Barr. Karen E. Downing, Barbara McNair, and Darlene P. Nichols translate many of these approaches to an academic setting. They state that community analyses should present a picture of what the community looks like and a list of the community's needs. Loe and Elkins state that before beginning this research, librarians should determine questions to be answered, the extent and quality of existing information on the community, the quantity and type of data needed, available resources, and staffing needed to collect and analyze data.[40]

All of these sources describe needed information on library users and nonusers, characteristics of the service area, and the institutional climate and circumstances in the library, itself. Information needed on library users and nonusers includes:

- Demographics—sex, ethnicity, age, family life cycle, education, socioeconomic characteristics, occupations, language proficiencies.
- Users, libraries, and information—how users use libraries, barriers to library use for nonusers, and other opinions about libraries. Current information would incorporate whether people have computers and how they use them at home, work, and elsewhere. Do people in the community use basic computer resources like Microsoft Office, Internet search tools and other resources on Internet 1.0, or blogs, wikis, and other social networking tools that are part of Internet 2.0?
- Where people live and work and the transportation that they use.
- Informational, cultural, and instructional needs.
- Preferred modes of learning.

More specific information that is needed about children and teens includes:

- Levels and types of schools in the area.
- School curricula or what is taught and when.
- Subjects covered by high stakes testing.
- Characteristics of home schoolers, their families, and their supporting organizations.
- After-school and summer activities in the area, including reading lists from schools.
- Needs and status of preschoolers.
- Transitional needs of graduating high school seniors.

Needed information on the characteristics of the town, city, or county served would include:

- Whether the area is rural, suburban, urban, or inner city and whether this is changing.
- The economic, social, political, and cultural climate of the area.
- General news and trends affecting the area.
- Issues affecting the community as a whole as well as more specific groups.
- Formal and informal educational developments on all educational levels, from preschool to adult and graduate.
- Community organizations, their leaders, and their activities.
- Local politicians, administration, and government.

Different types of institutions and agencies should be considered in any community analysis.[41] Representatives from these groups should be on any major library planning committee or at least included in surveys and interviews. The organizations and institutions include:

- Chambers of commerce and other business and economic organizations.
- Community service organizations or clubs like the Rotary Club, United Way, or YMCA.
- Cultural groups.
- Educational organizations.
- Ethnic organizations.
- Family service organizations.
- Financial representatives.
- Government and political representatives.
- Health organizations.

- Legal organizations.
- Library representatives from other kinds of libraries.
- Media representatives.
- Organizations serving the disabled.
- Professional groups.
- Religious groups.
- Senior centers or service organizations.
- Youth services organizations.

These organizations can also be the source of very useful secondary data and statistics, and their media can later be used to promote library programs relevant to their clientele.

Earlier ILI literature also mentions institutional climate in the library and ILI developments in other libraries.[42] Library characteristics to be investigated include existing mission, goals, objectives, and philosophy; whether and how IL is mentioned and defined; how the library relates to its geographic service areas; potential partners and supporters; how libraries already meet community needs; the impact of proposed programs on existing services and activities; and existing library resources, facilities, space, staffing, and budget.

The earlier library ILI literature also describes and discusses useful techniques in collecting this information, including informal research, secondary research, and formal primary research. It is quite possible to do a needs assessment based on the information in earlier books on library ILI. This approach is especially recommended when librarians want to focus specifically on how ILI can be integrated with other activities. (For more on this, see *Lifelong Learning in Public Libraries: Tools and Tips for Practitioners.*) However public librarians can also incorporate questions and conclusions about ILI as they use manuals and guides like *Strategic Planning for Results* in their general planning.

PUBLIC LIBRARY STANDARDS AND PLANNING GUIDES

Outcome Based Evaluation considers library inputs, user characteristics and needs, and library outputs and outcomes, with a focus on the outcomes. Outcomes are based on users' opinions of the program and on changes in users' thinking or behavior as a result of the program. Logic models take OBE a little further by studying short-term, intermediate, and long-term outcomes, by considering external factors affecting libraries and their programs, by relating all of these things together, and by weaving them into a cycle.

Over time, public library standards and planning documents have focused on specific elements of OBE and logic models. Early public library standards, such as *Minimum Standards for Public Libraries* (1966) and *Your Public Library: Standards for Service* (1969), which explained these standards to the public, emphasized and focused on the quantity and quality of public library *inputs*, including the structure and governance of library services, the establishment and evaluation of these services, collection development, personnel, and physical facilities. These early standards established an essential framework and foundation on which to later build and develop more sophisticated library services, but these inputs alone were not enough. Several standards committees that were created by ALA's Public Library Association (PLA) in the 1970s investigated user needs and concluded that the PLA should develop a process to enable any public library or public library system to set its own standards and to plan and evaluate programs appropriate to the needs of their own service areas. More attention was being paid to *user needs and characteristics* and to *library outputs*.[43]

The earlier standards were meant to promote both consistency and a certain amount of uniformity where "one size fits all." It is still necessary to have standards in schools and universities that are concerned that all graduates of their programs have a consistent if not identical base of knowledge and that they are all achieving at a given level.

Public libraries not only serve a vast variety of people of all ages, but their communities or service areas differ greatly from each other. Neighboring public library systems in one state serving similar-sized populations may have totally different programs and activities, because their communities are so different. Branches of big-city libraries within walking distance of each other may also have totally different programs. As a result, public librarians have been working with planning documents instead of standards since 1980. They use these materials to determine the characteristics of their communities, users, nonusers, and libraries; to determine information needs; and to plan programs, collections, and activities and then evaluate them. Public librarians choose sets of strategies best suited for their particular population and circumstances. One size does *not* fit all in this context.

Planning guides cover much of the same kinds of issues, including organizing and orienting a committee to undertake a study; gathering data on the community; determining community needs; investigating library programs and ways that they can better fulfill these needs; establishing priorities for programs; writing mission statements, goals, and objectives; and writing the library plan and evaluating that plan. Planning guides have become simpler, more streamlined, and easier to use over time, and the latest versions incorporate information literacy.

Public library planning guides include *A Planning Guide for Public Libraries* (1980), *Planning and Role-Setting for Public Libraries* (1998), *Planning for*

Results (1998), *The New Planning for Results* (2001), and *Strategic Planning for Results* (2008).[44] The last title is the best place to start, especially for people new to this process. It is the most explicit of all of these documents.

Strategic Planning for Results is organized into four parts: the Planning Process, Public Library Service Responses, Tool Kits, and Work Forms. The first chapter, "Planning to Plan," like the manual *Creating a Comprehensive Information Literacy Plan* by Burkhardt, MacDonald, and Rathmacher, focuses on organizing and managing the planning committee.[45] It is essential that this committee represent a very broad and representative cross-section of library staff and community members and leaders. They will create and determine the community vision or the ultimate goals of the library, and this vision will drive all other aspects of the planning.

The second chapter, "Identifying Service Priorities," describes how to create a community vision, how to collect data on the community, and how to identify community needs by defining current conditions in the community, listing community needs, reviewing services already offered by the library, and selecting needs that the library can address through the use of service responses. The rest of this chapter discusses how the committee should choose and prioritize the service responses to be emphasized. Eighteen service responses are introduced in this chapter and explained more in part 2:

- Be an Informed Citizen: Local, National, and World Affairs
- Build Successful Enterprises: Business and Nonprofit
- Celebrate Diversity: Cultural Awareness
- Connect to the Online World: Public Internet Access
- Create Young Readers: Early Literacy
- Discover Your Roots: Genealogy and Local History
- Express Creativity: Create and Share Content
- Get Facts Fast: Ready Reference
- Know Your Community: Community Resources and Services
- Learn to Read and Write: Adult, Teen, and Family Literacy
- Make Career Choices: Job and Career Development
- Make Informed Decisions: Health, Wealth, and Other Life Choices
- Satisfy Curiosity: Lifelong Learning
- Stimulate Imagination: Reading Viewing, and Listening for Pleasure
- Succeed in School: Homework Help
- Understand How to Find, Evaluate, and Use Information: Information Fluency
- Visit a Comfortable Place: Physical and Virtual Spaces
- Welcome to the United States: Services for New Immigrants

One of the service responses, Information Fluency, is a combination of information literacy, computer literacy, and critical thinking and emphasizes ILI as applied to computers. The service response on Public Internet Access is a subset of Information Fluency. ILI can be combined in various ways with all of the other service responses in the form of face-to-face sessions and series; the use of pathfinders, tutorials, and other resources online; outreach; collaboration with other agencies; and exhibits and displays. ILI sessions and series can be held to promote Business and Nonprofit Support, Cultural Diversity and Awareness, Genealogy and Local History, Community Resources and Services, Job and Career Decisions, and Making Informed Decisions. Aspects of ILI can be integrated into the literacy service responses Early Literacy, Adult, Teen, and Family Literacy, and Services to New Immigrants as well as Local, National, and World Affairs, Homework Help, Lifelong Learning, and research questions at the reference desk. Much of Lifelong Learning and Create and Share Content would be incorporated into cultural programs, and Reading, Viewing, and Listening for Pleasure into readers' advisory services, book discussion groups, and similar programs. Cultural programs and book discussion groups can be supplemented with ILI sessions on how to find more information or resources related to the activity as well as with pathfinders and handouts. Tours and other orientation information in print and online can be used to promote the library's physical and virtual spaces.

Chapter 3 of *Strategic Planning for Results* describes how to assess the library's readiness for change, how to create a positive environment for change, and how to train supervisors and managers. It ends by describing how to define the library's values, mission, and tagline. Chapter 4 discusses how to write goals and objectives and how to determine the library's competencies and initiatives. Chapter 5 is on how to write and communicate the plan and chapter 6 describes another volume, *Implementing for Results*, with more information on how to implement these plans.

Another excellent resource is the online guide *Marketing the Library*, created by the Ohio Library Foundation.[46] This guide has many of the same steps as *Strategic Planning for Results*, but these are organized differently. It is an especially outstanding source for librarians new to library marketing. It can be used by people working in libraries of all sizes and is designed to be used by individuals or small groups. *Marketing the Library* is organized into six chapters—Overview, Planning, Products, Promotion, the Internet, and Activities—each with a brief introduction, some exercises, and other suggested reading.

The chapter on planning discusses library mission statements, marketing audits that analyze the state of libraries, and market research on users and their communities. The product chapter incorporates three of the four Ps found in the marketing literature—Product, Place, and Price. It describes the many programs and activities of libraries, discusses the importance of "thinking like a user," and considers how these services can be evaluated by performance, quality, durability, reliability, image, and trends. This chapter is roughly comparable to the section on service responses in *Strategic Planning for Results.*

The chapter on promotion describes how libraries can communicate information about their activities by matching their audiences to media and methods. It elaborates on the use of advertising and public relations and discusses at some length the use of image, branding, slogans, mottos, and positioning to promote library collections and activities. *Strategic Planning for Results* starts with exercises to promote the library vision and soon discusses the setting of priorities; the promotion chapter of *Marketing the Library* ends with these points.

The Internet chapter discusses the use of blogs, wikis, gaming, RSS feeds, photo sharing, and social bookmarking to attract young people from the Millennial Generation. The last chapter shows successful library marketing in Ohio. Public librarians can use either ILI needs assessment information or public library planning documents to plan and implement their instruction.

STAFFING FOR INSTRUCTION

For the most part, instruction is planned, executed, and evaluated by librarians, particularly those in public services. In the smallest, most isolated libraries with relatively few resources, individual librarians can still instruct by creating handbook or orientation information about their libraries, planning personal or written tours, designing pathfinders, instructing individual classes or groups as requested, combining instruction with other activities, and putting instructional materials on their websites. Tours may be led by library staff, students, or volunteers, but librarians plan these, including the routing and points to be shown or described. Tours can be designed even for small one-room libraries, which often contain a surprising variety of useful materials for the public.

For more extensive planning, especially when it involves more than one library, a committee is necessary, and this group should be a cross-section of library staff and especially people from the community. In school media centers, instruction and other activities are often coordinated system-wide by a librarian responsible for this, even though the instruction is done by media specialists in their own schools. In academic libraries, there may be a coordinator of instruction for the entire library, or more likely, a reference librarian performing this function for her or his section in addition to other duties. The coordinator receives requests for new instruction, assigns librarians to teach these classes, holds training sessions (especially for new librarians), keeps all librarians current with new trends and developments, coordinates instruction done by more than one librarian for large courses with many sections, keeps track of needed equipment, and evaluates instruction. In academic libraries, staff, students, and volunteers can lead tours. Sometimes technical service librarians can be involved in instruction as well, but most instruction is carried out by public service librarians.

Most public library instruction would be carried out by public service librarians, including general reference librarians, librarians in youth services, and specialized librarians, especially in areas like business or genealogy and local history. Public libraries that plan and do extensive instruction should hire an administrator dedicated to coordinating this service. Just as many public libraries have coordinators or supervisors of youth services or of their branches. Librarians are also needed to coordinate instruction activities.

Instruction coordinators can work in larger public library systems, for library consortia in an area, or in some cases for the state library. They can help with overall planning, training, equipment and supplies, and evaluation of instructors and their instruction. Qualifications for managing or coordinating ILI would include both knowledge and experience in education or ILI and a full appreciation of the multiple roles of public libraries. Experience in doing cultural programs can also be helpful. ACRL has published *Standards for Proficiencies for Instruction Librarians and Coordinators*, an extensive set of standards, especially concerning qualifications, duties, and responsibilities of instructional librarians, coordinators, and supervisors.[47] Public librarians should consider as many of these standards as appropriate in planning and administering their own instruction.

WHAT A GOOD INSTRUCTION PROGRAM LOOKS LIKE

Good instructional programs include goals and objectives, a variety of methods for a very varied audience, an integrated plan, and several modes of evaluation. Some instruction should include the IL goals reflected in the ACRL standards or the Big 6. At the very least, there should be some instruction on how to determine information needs, how to find information, and how to evaluate and use information. But as cultural institutions with cultural and social goals, public library instruction can combine these hardcore IL goals with cultural and community building goals. Having a mission and goals sets the direction for objectives and for specific programs and activities. Goals, objectives, and outcomes should also be related to the general mission of the public library.

Public librarians can instruct in a wide variety of ways. The same creativity needed and used for cultural programming can also be applied to instruction. Public library instruction can be direct, with interactive presentations either in person or online, or indirect, with printed materials, signage, the Web, displays, and exhibits. Instruction sessions can be either dedicated to ILI or in some cases combined with other activities, and instruction can be either with a group or with individuals. Instruction can also be on all kinds of materials—scholarly, popular, printed, electronic, and other media. Cultural programming is important in its own right. One does not have to combine instruction with *everything*. However, to consider this activity to be ILI, there should be *some* instruction in the program series, even if it is along the lines of "How to Find More . . . " or "How to Find Out More About . . . " Instruction should be an integrated plan, not just a series of disjointed activities. It can be organized as a separate series of programs or activities or integrated into the library's general programming plan. Instructional activities should be systematically organized, regardless of format.

Evaluation of instruction and other activities is also very important. This can range from informal observation to questionnaires and surveys measuring what users learn and how they feel to formal OBE and logic models. Individual activities should be evaluated during and afterward, and some instruction, like indirect instruction, should be test driven ahead of time by volunteers or focus groups. It is also important to look at instructional programs as a whole.

Last and most important, do not forget that public librarians already instruct in many ways. More elements of instruction can be incorporated into individual assistance: indirect instruction, such as signage, building design, pathfinders, and websites; tours and orientations; literacy programs; book discussion groups; and some cultural programs. Characteristics of good instruction in this context include goals, teaching to these goals, evaluation, and integration into a program. ILI can grow out of both formal planning and the traditional activities of public libraries. (Public libraries as agents of nonformal education will be discussed in chapter 7.)

NOTES

1. Carol Collier Kuhlthau, "Students and the Information Search Process: Zones of Intervention for Librarians," *Advances in Librarianship* 18 (1994): 57–72; Edward J. Eckel, "Fostering Self-Regulated Learning at the Reference Desk," *Reference and User Services Quarterly* 47, no. 1 (2007): 16–20; Gillian S. Gremmels and Karen Shostrom Lehman, "Assessment of Student Learning from Reference Service," *College and Research Libraries* 68, no. 6 (2007): 488–501.

2. Carolyn Jones, "Baby Boomers and Generation Y in the Public Library: An Australian Perspective," in *Our New Public, a Changing Clientele: Bewildering Issues or New Challenges for Managing Libraries*, ed. James R. Kennedy, Lisa Vardaman, and Gerard B. McCabe (Westport, Conn.: Libraries Unlimited, 2008), 31–45; Lesley Boon, "I Want It All and I Want It Now! The Changing Face of School Libraries," in *Our New Public, a Changing Clientele*, 173–79.

3. Association of College and Research Libraries (ACRL), *Information Literacy Competency Standards for Higher Education* (Chicago: ALA), www.ala.org; American Association of School Librarians (AASL), *Standards for the 21st-Century Learner,* www.ala.org; AASL and Association for Educational Communications and Technology (AECT), *Information Literacy Standards for Student Learning: Standards and Indicators* (Chicago: ALA, 1998). Also in AASL and AECT, *Information Power: Building Partnerships for Learning* (Chicago: ALA, 1998), 8–44.

4. Australia and New Zealand Institute for Information Literacy (ANZIIL), *Australia and New Zealand Information Literacy Framework* (Adelaide, Australia: ANZIIL, 2004).

5. Joanna M. Burkhardt, Mary C. MacDonald, and Andre J. Rathmacher, *Creating a Comprehensive Information Literacy Plan* (New York: Neal-Schuman, 2005).

6. ACRL, "Characteristics of Programs of Information Literacy That Illustrate Best Practices: A Guideline," www.ala.org.

7. Carol Kuhlthau, "Implementing a Process Approach to Information Skills: A Study Identifying Indicators of Success in Library Media Programs," *School Library Media Quarterly* 22, no. 1 (1993): 11–18.

8. Alice Yucht, *Alice in InfoLand: FLIPit,* www.aliceinfo.org.

9. The Big 6, "What Is the Big 6?" www.big6.com.

10. Peter Jarvis, John Holford, and Colin Griffin, *The Theory and Practice of Learning* (London: Kogan Page, 1998); Robert Mills Gagne, *The Conditions of Learning* (New York: Holt, Rinehart and Winston, 1985); Malcolm Knowles, *The Adult Learner: A Neglected Species* (Houston: Gulf, 1991); Sarah McNicol and Pete Daltton, "Broadening Perspectives on the Learning Process in Public Libraries," *New Review of Libraries and Lifelong Learning* (2003): 27–43.

11. ACRL, *Information Literacy Competency Standards for Higher Education,* www.ala.org.

12. ANZIIL, *Australia and New Zealand Information Literacy Framework.*

13. AASL and AECT, *Information Literacy Standards for Student Learning: Standards and Indicators* (Chicago: ALA, 1998). Also in AASL and AECT, *Information Power,* 8–44.

14. AASL, *Standards for the 21st-Century Learner.*

15. Information Architecture Institute, *The 25 Theses,* http://iainstitute.org.

16. Christine Bruce, *The 7 Faces of Information Literacy* (Adelaide, Australia: Auslib, 1997), http://web.bit.mah.se/konferens/ck2/cabinet/bruce/netsc/Bruce_Malmox/sld017.htm.

17. Jeremy J. Shapiro and Shelley K. Hughes, "Information Literacy as a Liberal Art," http://net.educause.edu/apps/er/review/reviewArticles/31231.html.

18. Anne-Marie Deitering. "Reflection and Thinking and All of That Stuff: Learning, Engagement, and the Net Generation," in Kennedy, Vardaman, and McCabe, *Our New Public, a Changing Clientele,* 26.

19. Esther S. Grassian and Joan R. Kaplowitz, *Information Literacy Instruction: Theory and Practice,* 2nd ed. (New York: Neal-Schuman, 2009), 116–17; Sandy Ready et al., "Library Instruction in Academic Libraries, Including Graduate Four-Year and Two-Year Institutions," in *The LIRT Library Instruction Handbook,* ed. May Brottman and Mary Loe (Englewood, Colo.: Libraries Unlimited, 1990), 25–28; Teresa Y. Neely and Katy Sullivan, "Integrating the ACRL Standards," in *Information Literacy Assessment: Standards-Based Tools and Assignments,* ed. Teresa Neely (Chicago: ALA, 2006), 6–18.

20. Benjamin S. Bloom et al., eds., *Taxonomy of Educational Objectives: The Classification of Educational Goals. Handbook 1: Cognitive Domain* (New York: David McKay, 1956); David R. Krathwohl, Benjamin S. Bloom, and Bertram B. Mason, *Taxonomy of Educational Objectives: The Classification of Educational Goals. Handbook II: Affective Domain* (New York: David McKay, 1964).

21. Grassian and Kaplowitz, *Information Literacy Instruction*, 116–21.

22. Grassian and Kaplowitz, *Information Literacy Instruction*, 208–12.

23. Grassian and Kaplowitz, *Information Literacy Instruction*, 211.

24. Teresa Y. Neely, *Information Literacy Assessment: Standards-Based Tools and Assignments* (Chicago: ALA, 2006).

25. Diana Shonrock, *Evaluating Library Instruction: Simple Questions, Forms, and Strategies for Practical Use* (Chicago: ALA. LIRT, 1996).

26. Joan C. Durrance and Karen E. Fisher, with Marian Birch Hinton, *How Libraries and Librarians Help: A Guide to Identifying User-Centered Outcomes* (Chicago: ALA, 2005), 3–5.

27. John A. McLaughlin and Gretchen B. Jordan, "Logic Models: A Tool for Telling Your Program's Performance Story," *Evaluation and Program Planning* 22 (1999): 65; Tamara S. Davis, "The Federal GPRA Mandate: Is Social Work Ready?" *Social Policy Journal* 1, no. 3 (2002): 51–74; James R. Kautz III, F. Ellen Netting, Ruth Huber, Kevin Borders, and Tamara S. Davis, "The Government Performance and Results Act of 1993: Implications for Social Work Practice," *Social Work* 42, no. 4 (1997): 364–73; Jonathan D. Breul, "GPRA: A Foundation for Performance Budgeting," *Public Performance and Management Review* 30, no. 3 (2007): 312–31.

28. Durrance and Fisher, *How Libraries and Librarians Help*, 5.

29. Durrance and Fisher, *How Libraries and Librarians Help*, 24–30.

30. Durrance and Fisher, *How Libraries and Librarians Help*, 5–10.

31. Durrance and Fisher, *How Libraries and Librarians Help*, 14–15.

32. Durrance and Fisher, *How Libraries and Librarians Help*, 16.

33. Durrance and Fisher, *How Libraries and Librarians Help*, 20–21.

34. Durrance and Fisher, *How Libraries and Librarians Help*, 21–22.

35. Durrance and Fisher, *How Libraries and Librarians Help*, 33–83.

36. McLaughlin and Jordan, "Logic Models," 65–66.

37. Leslie J. Cooksey, Paige Gill, and P. Adam Kelly, "The Program Logic Model as an Integrative Framework for a Multimethod Evaluation," *Evaluation and Program Planning* 24 (2001): 119.

38. McLaughlin and Jordan, "Logic Models," 66–72.

39. University of Wisconsin Extension, Program Development and Evaluation, *Logic Models*, www.uwex.edu; University of Wisconsin Extension, *Enhancing Program Performance with Logic Models*, www.uwex.edu; W.K. Kellogg Foundation, *Logic Model Development Guide*, www.osswa.org.

40. Grassian and Kaplowitz, *Information Literacy Instruction*, 112–16; Mary Loe and Betsy Elkins, "Developing Programs in Library Use Instruction for Library Learning: An Overview," in Brottman and Loe, *The LIRT Library Instruction Handbook*, 7–8; Kathleen G. Woods, Helen T. Burns, and Marilyn Barr, "Planning an Instruction Program in a Public Library," in *The LIRT Library Instruction Handbook*, 49–50; Karen E. Downing, Barbara MacAdam, and Darlene P. Nichols, *Reaching*

a Multicultural Student Community: A Handbook for Academic Librarians (Westport, Conn.: Greenwood, 1993): 13–26.

41. Sandra Nelson for the Public Library Association, *Strategic Planning for Results* (Chicago: ALA, 2008), 23.

42. Grassian and Kaplowitz, *Information Literacy Instruction,* 113–16; Loe and El-kins, "Developing Programs in Library Use Instruction for Lifelong Learning," 7–8; Woods, Burns, and Barr, "Planning an Instruction Program in a Public Library," 49–50; Downing, MacAdam, and Nichols, *Reaching a Multicultural Student Community,* 13–26.

43. Public Library Association (PLA), Standards Committee, *Minimum Standards for Public Libraries* (Chicago: ALA, 1967); Alice Norton, *Your Public Library: Standards for Service* (Chicago: ALA, 1969); PLA, Goals, Guidelines, and Standards Commit-tee, *The Public Library Mission Statement and Its Imperative for Service* (Chicago: ALA, 1979), iv–vii.

44. Vernon Palmour, Marcia C. Bellassai, and Nancy V. DeVath, *A Planning Pro-cess for Public Libraries* (Chicago: ALA, 1980); Charles R. McClure, Amy Owen, Doug-las C. Zweizig, Mary Jo Lynch, and Nancy A. Van House, *Planning and Role-Setting for Public Libraries: A Manual of Operations and Procedures* (Chicago: ALA, 1987); Ethel Himmel and William James Wilson, *Planning for Results: A Public Library Transfor-mation Process* (Chicago: ALA, 2001); Sandra Nelson, *The New Planning for Results: A Streamlined Approach* (Chicago: ALA, 2001); Nelson, *Strategic Planning for Results* (Chicago: ALA, 2008).

45. Burkhardt, MacDonald, and Rathmacher, *Creating a Comprehensive Informa-tion Literacy Plan.*

46. Ohio Library Foundation, *Marketing the Library,* www.olc.org.

47. ACRL, *Standards for Proficiencies for Instruction Librarians and Coordinators,* www.ala.org.

7

Public Libraries as Nonformal Cultural Institutions: Programming and Instruction

Public libraries differ from their academic counterparts in their audiences, purposes, and philosophical bases. While schools and universities are more focused on people in particular age groups and have very well-defined audiences, public libraries serve people "from the cradle to the grave" and sometimes work with families as units. The purpose of schools and universities is to promote formal education, and their libraries also emphasize this. The purpose of public libraries is to provide information, guidance, and education, and much of their education is informal or nonformal rather than formal. In their instruction, librarians in different kinds of libraries would also draw from different philosophies and learning theories. Traditional academic ILI draws heavily from behaviorism and constructivism, ending with constructivism. Public library instruction begins with constructivism and draws more from educational humanism or humanistic approaches to education, even as it uses behaviorist principles to organize instruction. Academic ILI reflects characteristics of formal, mandatory education. Adhering to the model of "the teaching library," public librarians would follow the lead of their academic counterparts as much as possible. Or they can use more organic approaches, reflecting their roles as informal or nonformal, voluntary educational and cultural institutions.

This chapter discusses the characteristics of informal/nonformal and formal education. It emphasizes characteristics of institutions offering nonformal education, with a look at religious organizations, museums, and public libraries. It also discusses how traditional public library programming relates to Information Literacy Instruction (ILI).

TYPES OF EDUCATION

Formal Education

Learning can be through formal education or through informal or non-formal education.[1] Formal learning is "institutionalized, chronological, graded, and hierarchical." It includes K–12 education, community colleges, four-year colleges, and universities, and it results in diplomas, certificates, and degrees. Most students participating in formal education are children, teens, or young adults, but many older adults also pursue higher education.

Formal education that occurs in most schools can be characterized by planned, written curricula and formal evaluation and assessment. Curricula for most public schools come from either the state department of education or local school districts, and textbooks reflect these planned curricula, which are also affected by what is covered on "high stakes" testing. Curriculum guides include information that define fields of study and reasons for covering them, the scope and sequence of the instruction, recommended instructional activities, and information on how students will be evaluated. There are several kinds of curricula: the taught or formal curriculum, the informal curriculum, the extra curriculum, and the null curriculum.[2]

The taught or formal curriculum is the official one that teachers teach. The informal curriculum is information that teachers pass on to students that is not part of a lesson plan, curriculum guide, or standards. Extra curricula are cultural or recreational activities that are not part of formal curricula but are sponsored by schools, usually after normal school hours. The null curriculum is what is not taught—but should possibly be, in some cases.

Teachers use a variety of methodologies to provide information to their students, and most use lesson plans to accomplish this. They describe either a single lesson on a topic to be covered in a particular day or a unit or series of related lessons on a topic. Lesson plans are generally written down, and many are available online and from other sources. One good thing about creating lesson plans is that if a teacher is absent but leaves a lesson plan, the substitute teacher can use this to teach the class. It is also a record of what is (or should be) covered in a class that can be used as a tool for later evaluation. Lesson plans include the subject to be taught, the grade level, goals and objectives of the lesson or unit, a lecture outline, and a list of activities, relevant sources, and methods to be used to assess whether and how well students learned the lesson.

Students and their work are informally assessed during instruction through questioning and observation to ascertain if they understand the lesson. More formal evaluation includes grading of assignments, tests designed by teachers, standardized testing, and the use of rubrics. Standardized testing and other methods are also used to see how well teachers and school are performing.

Some formal education is mandatory, with captive audiences. For many jobs, one must graduate from high school or prove that one has those credentials. To enter many professions, one must graduate from a college or university. The use of testing, evaluation, and formal assessment is very important in this context, with an increasing formalization in formal education since 1980. This formalization can be seen in the use of high-stakes testing, teaching to the standards and the tests, an emphasis on reading and mathematics, and a deemphasis on other subjects.

Traditional ILI in academic settings reflects these characteristics, with formal standards, goals, and objectives and the heavy use of assessment to evaluate instruction. Public libraries using the model of the teaching library would incorporate as much of this as possible, which would make their instruction more consistent with their academic counterparts and would encourage more cooperation between librarians from different kinds of libraries. However, the teaching library model does not reflect the more varied roles and purposes of public libraries.

Informal or Nonformal Education

There are two kinds of informal or nonformal education—self-teaching or being taught by others. People pursuing informal education determine what they want to learn (which could be anything) and either teach themselves in various ways or go to an expert who can teach them a skill. Informal education is the ultimate expression of both independent learning and educational humanism, and it is totally voluntary on the student's part. Informal lifelong learning incorporates all kinds of interests and subjects, from the popular and practical to the scholarly, and from self-study and practice to the pursuit of formal certificates, diplomas, and degrees. Students pursuing informal or nonformal learning determine their own curriculum, which they follow as long as they are interested. Their main measure of evaluation is how satisfied they are with what they are doing.

Some informal learning is incidental or even accidental. This is information learned in the process of doing something else, like reading fiction, watching television, or answering other questions. Sometimes this new knowledge is not recognized by the learner until later.

Students pursuing their own education can use human experts, books, online sources, and many other approaches to teach themselves. Public libraries serve as agents of informal education in their collections, reference services, printed and online bibliographies and guides, traditional programming, and outreach. Individuals can use any or all of these library services for their own purposes.

Other agents of nonformal education are religious bodies, groups such as scouting organizations, and museums and other organizations that use interpretation activities. Nonformal educational institutions borrow heavily from formal education in different respects. Churches use church lectionaries, museums use interpretation standards and guidelines, and scouting uses badge systems to recognize the achievements of young people. This influences much of their curricula, programming, and methods of presenting information.

Participation in nonformal educational organizations is voluntary, and many of these organizations use various forms of marketing to attract an audience. Assessment and evaluation are more informal than in formal educational institutions, with the main concerns being the following: What are people learning? How do they feel about their instruction? Would they do this again or recommend this activity to a friend? How is the attendance? What difference does participating in this activity make to audience members? Outcome Based Evaluation (OBE) and logic models have been created by nonprofit organizations to answer this last question.

Informal or nonformal educational institutions are varied and experiential in their approach to education. They often work with people throughout the life span and sometimes work with families as units. The rest of this chapter will investigate religious organizations and museums as agents of nonformal education. Then it will discuss how nonformal education relates to public library programming and instruction and will argue for a more organic approach to public library instruction.

CHURCHES AND OTHER RELIGIOUS BODIES AS AGENTS OF NONFORMAL EDUCATION

Churches serve as agents of nonformal education through their worship services, Sunday Schools or church schools, other Christian education, and their other organizations. Many denominations use the Bible as their curriculum and lectionaries as lesson plans. Lectionaries are lists of Bible readings for every Sunday over a span of several years. They are designed to take congregants and students through most of the Bible in this time frame. Priests and ministers choose these Bible readings for their sermon topics. Church musicians can look up the readings for the day and then check the index to scriptural references in the back of their hymnals to choose music that will connect to the themes of the sermon. An excellent example of a church lectionary is the United Methodist lectionary.[3] Not only does it list the Bible readings for each Sunday, but it has detailed ideas for incorporating the theme of the day into worship and other activities. In this regard, it is very similar to detailed lesson plans and curriculum guides designed by formal educators. A particularly thorough scriptural index to hymns can be found in *Worship and Rejoice,* an evangelical hymnal.

Church school curriculum is also tied to lectionaries. The same scriptural passages are the basis of the lessons that students learn in church school. Many Protestant denominations use Sunday School quarterlies (published four times a year) as textbooks, which are available for different age groups and grade levels, and may have the same or similar lessons for all groups. The quarterlies enable church schools to combine classes of different age groups where necessary and yet also enable students to learn at their own age and reading level. Each lesson consists of the Bible reading for the day, commentary written for specific age groups, and follow-up questions, exercises, and activities. In all of these respects, church schools are strongly influenced by the practices of secular formal education.

As agents of nonformal education, churches also educate through Christian education and through their schools, clubs, and organizations. The African Methodist Episcopal Church, for example, considers all educational activities of the church to be part of Christian education, including church schools, youth ministry, music ministry, and scouting.[4] Other church organizations, such as the Lay Organization and the Women's Missionary Society, incorporate educational activities within their local meetings and especially their regional and international conferences. Club members learn not only by study but by doing, or fulfilling the goals of their organizations. Christian educators are influenced by formal education in that they are interested in the learning styles of students and using computers to teach. They also reflect nonformal education by looking at the changing characteristics of their members and how this phenomenon affects what they do.

Religious bodies of all faiths have several other characteristics of nonformal educational institutions. They serve people from the cradle to the grave with ceremonies marking birth, coming of age, marriage, and death. They often serve families as units and appeal to all age groups. Participation in religious activities is usually voluntary, but members may have to go through confirmation or other procedures, rites, initiations, and ceremonies to qualify as full members as adults. Religious bodies tend to do much more formal credentialing of their leaders through seminaries or other training institutions and various procedures.

Christian churches market their services through missionary and other outreach, designing activities for different age groups, and specialized ministries. Marketing to children attracts young people as they are today, young people as future consumers, and their parents. Another way to promote growth is through the use of classes and small groups. In the class system created by the Wesley brothers, the founders of Methodism more than two hundred years ago, classes would meet on a regular basis and be led by a lay class leader. Alcoholics Anonymous and other self-help groups are based on the class system. Evangelical churches have used small groups to promote church growth, and the Evangelical scholar George Barna has conducted a number of market and trend studies of interest to many denominations.[5] His books discuss general trends in churches and in society that can affect how churches reach out to their communities. In all of these respects, religious institutions act as agents of nonformal education.

MUSEUMS AND PUBLIC LIBRARIES AS AGENTS OF NONFORMAL EDUCATION

Public Libraries and Museums Compared

Both museums and public libraries are agents of informal or nonformal education. Museums have emphasized raising the cultural standards of their surrounding communities. Public libraries provide nonformal or informal ways for people of all ages to extend their education beyond what is learned in public schools. Public libraries also emphasize raising the cultural standards of their communities through the selection of classics and "best books" for their collections, the use of reading lists, and the development of readers' advisory services, book discussion groups, and cultural programming.

Both museums and public libraries have been reaching out to a more diverse public in recent decades. Both institutions work with people of all ages, as well as with family or intergenerational groups. Unless a learner is sent by a boss, teacher, or parent, attendance at a public library or museum is voluntary, and people informally learn what they wish to within those settings. Public libraries promote informal learning through their collections, reference services, pathfinders and other printed and online guides, programming, and outreach. Museums do the same through their collections, displays, and educational activities known as interpretation. Both libraries and museums are clients of the Institute of Museum and Library Services (IMLS), a major funding arm of the federal government.

Like public librarians, interpreters also use marketing to plan and evaluate their instruction. Museums do surveys of their users and sometimes network with other organizations. They can encourage stakeholders to participate in their planning, evaluation, and feedback, and they can use focus groups to find out about audience needs and preferences. Then they use this information to plan their activities. As they do their programming and teaching, interpreters do ongoing evaluations of visitors' reactions and then use Outcome Based Evaluation (OBE) and logic models to evaluate their activities.

Interpretation

Interpretation is defined by Freeman Tilden as "an educational activity which aims to reveal meanings and relationships through the use of original objects, by first-hand experience and by illustrating media rather than simply to communicate factual information." Interpretation teaches people about real objects that they can see (and sometimes handle) or at least facsimiles of them. According to Alison L. Grinder and E. Sue McCoy, interpreters assist visitors with hands-on experiences, create environments, tell stories, act or do reenactments, conduct experiments, and demonstrate objects or animals. They educate by using factual information on labels, and through workshops, guided tours, outreach programs, and exhibits that are interactive, both physically and intellectually.[6]

Interpretation takes place in all kinds of museums, zoos, aquariums, and parks, as well as camps and playgrounds. Like many traditional public library activities, interpretation is a type of nonformal education. Interpreters, like public librarians, use a combination of formal and nonformal classroom techniques as well as marketing. Like more formal educators, interpreters use goals, objectives, and instructional design to plan their teaching. They are influenced by several of the educational theories described in chapter 3, especially constructivism, which promotes students building their knowledge base by integrating new information with what they already know. Constuctivists like Jean Piaget, John Dewey, and Jerome Bruner have emphasized learning by discovery and by doing, and this approach is especially used in science and children's museums.[7]

Methods of interpretation vary by setting. Art museums are the most traditional in their approach with their use of lectures, classes in art appreciation and art history, and direct experience with contemporary art. Historical sites and industrial museums show evidence of social history through demonstrations, participation, and animation. Interpreters demonstrate by showing and describing real objects or their facsimiles, encouraging visitors' participation, and providing an environment through animation, as in Colonial Williamsburg, Old Sturbridge Village, or Disneyland. Interpreters in historic settings also do reenactments, role playing, and story-telling. Interpreters in science and children's museums instruct through demonstrating objects or animals, conducting experiments, and in some cases helping to plan, design, and interpret interactive displays that visitors are encouraged to touch. Displays may be designed to help visitors teach themselves through their own explorations.

There are also ethnic museums, museums of ideas, and museums of conscience that use a variety of techniques to instruct their visitors. Examples include the Holocaust Museum in Washington, D.C., the Birmingham Civil Rights Institute, the National Civil Rights Museum in Memphis, the Museum of the African Diaspora in San Francisco, the Museum of Tolerance in Los Angeles, the Lower Eastside Tenement Museum and the Museo del Barrio, both in New York City, the National Underground Railroad Freedom Center in Cincinnati, and Constitution Hall in South Africa.[8]

Interpreters use lectures, guided tours, workshops, school projects, and audiovisual presentations to instruct. Interpretive techniques described by Grinder and McCoy include lecture-discussions, inquiry-discussions, guided discovery, and guided involvement.[9] Lecture discussions stress lecturing with little opportunity for interaction between visitors and guides. Grinder and McCoy recommend this approach for adults over age thirty as well as for visitors from abroad. Inquiry-discussion is more of a dialog between guides and visitors and is recommended for young people between the ages of eight and thirty, as well as families and members of minority groups. Guided discovery is a structured activity that allows visitors to make their own directions and connections. It is recommended especially for young people between the ages of three and eighteen and their families. Guided involvement is similar to guided discovery but briefer, more structured, and designed especially for children between the ages of three and seven. In this way, museums, like public libraries, try to accommodate people throughout the life cycle as well as several generations. Interpreters also use games, improvisation, hands-on materials, project-directed activities, story-telling, audiovisual aids, films, and interactive exhibits to enhance their tours.

Important classic texts on interpretation include *Interpreting Our Heritage* by Freeman Tilden and *The Good Guide: A Sourcebook for Interpreters, Docents, and Tour Guides* by Alison L. Grinder and E. Sue McCoy. More recent work has been by John H. Falk and Lynn Dierking, Barry Lord, and Gary Machlis and Donald R. Field.[10] An important organization is the National Association for Interpretation, which has published standards on the training of interpreters, interpretive methods, interpretive organizations, and planning for interpretation.[11] All of this information is available on their website.

ILI and Interpretation

There are similarities between ILI and interpretation, as well as some definite differences. Both use a variety of teaching techniques to reach their audiences. Both are concerned about constructivism, or starting with students were they are and helping them to build a base of knowledge, and they both start from a base of information.

However, ILI has been oriented to nonfiction and to some extent literary fiction. It is very intellectually oriented, with an emphasis on evaluating information for accuracy. The chief aim of ILI is to find and use information and to verify whether it is true or accurate. Interpretation blends truth with fiction, especially for reenactments and story-telling. While it is based on information, it tries to find a larger truth behind the facts. The chief aim of interpretation is not information but provocation![12]

In some respects, interpretation is closer to the traditional cultural and book discussion programs of public libraries than to ILI, especially as it has evolved from school and academic libraries. While ILI is almost strictly intellectual, traditional public library activities and interpretation incorporate both the intellect and emotions. One tells us what happened while the other tells us how that felt. (Similar points about nonfiction and fiction will be discussed at the end of this chapter.)

Impact of Public Libraries and Museums on Each Other

Both public libraries and museums interact quite a bit with school systems, and both have been affected by the No Child Left Behind legislation and the increasing formalization of education.[13] Museums have reacted to this formalization in two very different ways. One approach has been to plan visits and activities for classes that are directly linked to school curricula, standards, and testing. The Washington State Library recently took a similar approach in working with school systems. A very different approach is the establishment of new museum schools by museums, often in collaboration with charter schools and other organizations. Some public libraries do similar things, both by promoting their cultural and other activities to school systems and by their work with groups of home-schoolers. (These activities will be further discussed in chapter 8.)

Public librarians can learn several things from museum interpreters, including more effective touring techniques and exhibit design. They may be able to find out more about computer and other indirect instruction and signage. Interpreters have also done research on how families react and interact as they attend camps or visit museums together, and that can be very relevant to public librarians.[14] However, interpreters and other museum professionals are also inspired by public library services to families and see them as a model to be followed as well.[15]

TRADITIONAL PUBLIC LIBRARY PROGRAMMING AND ILI

Trends in Public Library Programming

Public libraries have promoted nonformal education by developing several kinds of programs, including literacy programs, cultural programs, and various forms of readers' advisory services for individuals and groups.[16] Book discussion groups and cultural programs have been consistently held in public libraries. Readers' advisory services started during World War I as an outreach to soldiers and was especially popular from 1920 to 1950. These services went into a gradual decline after that but experienced a renaissance starting around 1995. Readers' advisory services and programming are flourishing now.

General literacy programs were promoted among immigrants at the turn of the twentieth century. They have been the major focus of public library instructional activities since 1960. In addition, public libraries had many ties with the adult education movement during the first half of the twentieth century. All of these activities have been an outgrowth of public librarians fulfilling needs of their communities.

Where Guidance Meets Instruction

ILI and readers' advisory services are largely on parallel tracks but not mutually exclusive. The purpose of ILI is to promote learning. It exists to feed the mind, help people to solve problems, and teach them how to think and reason. It emphasizes learning and growth, focuses mainly on nonfiction and sometimes literary fiction, and is generally tied to conceptual frameworks or models of information seeking. ILI reflects the formal educational mission of academic libraries and is influenced mainly by the learning theories of behaviorism, cognitive science, and constructivism. (These theories are explained more in chapter 3.)

The purpose of reader's advisory services, book talks, book discussion groups, and bibliotherapy is to help people find enjoyment and fulfillment. These guidance activities feed the soul, promote healing, and teach people how to feel. They emphasize self-actualization, fulfillment, satisfaction, and entertainment and focus on popular literature as well as literary fiction and nonfiction. These initiatives are tied to informal and more individualized instruction and reflect the traditional guidance, cultural, and educational missions of public libraries. They are influenced by constructivism and humanistic aspects of psychology and education. In these respects, these activities also relate to interpretation.

ILI and readers' advisory services and programs exist in parallel universes in many ways. Formal information literacy classes can be compared to book talks and to book discussion groups. Term paper clinics, individualized instruction, and instruction at the reference desk can be compared to readers' advisory services and to bibliotherapy.

These universes can come together in several ways. Both ILI and readers' advisory services can be found on the Web. Just as people can be taught to raise questions and then find, evaluate, and use related nonfiction and literature, they can also learn to apply this procedure to more popular materials, graphic novels, Internet sites, social networking, and other media such as television or movies. This information literacy is in addition to approaches that already exist in the field of readers' advisory services. Videos, gaming, story-telling, or puppet shows can also be used to teach about Information Literacy (IL). Learning can be fun, and fun enlightening. They are different, but not mutually exclusive. Other activities that combine aspects of ILI with guidance include a session on how to use readers' advisory websites to find and evaluate genre fiction; how to find, evaluate, and use good books for one's children; and the use of critical thinking in a Great Books program.

Public libraries are cultural as well as informational and informal or nonformal educational institutions. Cultural programs are important in their own right as they stand now, without the addition of other elements. However, a reason not to ignore or disregard these activities is because of the renaissance, explosion, and new golden age for readers' advisory services since 1995. This development has led to new print and electronic tools to enable librarians and other readers to find materials, and to the creation of book discussion groups in and outside of libraries, as well as the activities of Nancy Pearl, the author of *Book Lust*, and the existence of several periodicals that have reported on this trend. Pearl has also organized the One Book program, where individuals in a whole campus, town, or state choose one book for all to read, with support discussions and other programming about it.[17] This has evolved into the Big Read, a similar program supported by the National Endowment of the Humanities. Several periodicals, such as *Book: A Magazine for the Reading Life*, *Black Issues Book Review*, and *Bookmarks*, report on trends in the book world for general readers, and some have regularly reported on the activities of reading groups as well.

Various book groups have been paying attention to nonfiction as well as fiction—which brings us back to ILI. In addition to techniques already being used in the readers' advisory field, the basic ILI questions can be slightly revised and used in this situation as well. Are there similar books? Where can I find them? Which are the best ones and how do I know this? What can I learn from this activity and how can I use what I learn?

There is evidence that some people learn as much from fiction as from nonfiction. Jessica E. Moyer did a survey of leisure adult readers from two midwestern public libraries and a local university.[18] All of her respondents believed that they learned from reading fiction and that this was more fun than other types of learning. They learned about people and relationships, other countries and cultures, history, faith and religion, personal problems and therapy, news and current events, and different perspectives. Readers in this survey also acquired an expanded vocabulary. They were lifelong readers who watched relatively little television. According to Moyer, reading fiction enriched the lives of her respondents, stimulated their imaginations, made them want to learn more, and led them to other books, both fiction and nonfiction.

While nonfiction teaches the facts about a situation, a good work of fiction teaches how it feels to be in that situation. It puts the reader there! Reading both fiction and nonfiction about the U.S. Civil War, the Holocaust during World War II, or life in African countries, especially during and immediately after the end of colonization, can really enhance learning, and using basic principles of ILI to analyze both can be very helpful. One can argue that there are three kinds of bibliotherapy: clinical, to help people through crises; developmental, to help children through normal childhood issues, like a new sibling or the death of a grandparent; and educational, in which carefully chosen fiction and nonfiction are used to teach about and to discuss a subject or an era. Educational bibliotherapy is another possibility for ILI.

Public library instruction does not always have to grow out of the formal, traditional ILI in academic settings. It can emerge from the more traditional activities of public libraries as well. (More ideas on how this can be implemented will be found in chapter 8.)

NOTES

1. Bruce Findsen, *Learning Later* (Malabar, Fla.: Krieger, 2005): 10–11; John C. Shirk, "The Library Learning Inventory: A Process for Understanding the Adult Learner," in *Educating the Public Library User*, ed. John Lubans Jr. (Chicago: ALA, 1983), 57–61.

2. David Cruickshank, Deborah Bainer, and Kim Metcalf, *The Art of Teaching* (New York: McGraw-Hill, 1995), 133–34; Sarah Davis Powell, *An Introduction to Education: Choosing Your Career Path* (Upper Saddle River, N.J.: Pearson, 2009): 113–23.

3. United Methodist Church, General Board of Discipleship (GBOD), "Lectionary Planning Helps for Sundays," www.gbod.org; *Worship and Rejoice*, "Scriptural Index," 805–16.

4. African Methodist Episcopal Church, *Journal of Christian Education* (Spring 2004); Marcia L. Conner, "What's Your Learning Style?" *Journal of Christian Education* (Winter 2009): 4–5; Richard H. Gentzler Jr., "Four Generations of Adult Learners," *Journal of Christian Education* (Winter 2009): 2–3; Tim Gossett, "10 Christian Education Trends for 2010 and Beyond," *Journal of Christian Education* (Spring 2010): 22–23.

5. George Barna, *Revolution* (Carol Stream, Ill: Tyndale House, 2006); Barna, *Grow Your Church from the Outside In: Understanding the Unchurched and How to Reach Them* (Ventura, Calif.: Regal, 2002); Barna, *Futurecast: What Today's Trends Mean for Tomorrow's World* (Carol Stream, Ill.: Barnabooks, 2011).

6. Freeman Tilden, *Interpreting Our Heritage* (Chapel Hill: University of North Carolina Press, 1977), 3; Alison L. Grinder and E. Sue McCoy, *The Good Guide: A*

Sourcebook for Interpreters, Docents, and Tour Guides (Scottsdale, Ariz.: Ironwood, 1985), 5.

7. Grinder and McCoy, *The Good Guide*, 22–39.

8. Barry Lord, "What Is Museum Learning?" in *The Manual of Museum Learning*, ed. Barry Lord (Lanham, Md.: AltaMira, 2007), 13–19; Tilden, *Interpreting Our Heritage*, 68–77; Spencer R. Crew, "Involving the Community," in *The Manual of Museum Learning*, 107–33.

9. Grinder and McCoy, *The Good Guide*, 56–71, 90–116, 78–81.

10. Freeman Tilden, *Interpreting Our Heritage*; Grinder and McCoy, *The Good Guide*; John H. Falk, Lynn D. Dierking, and Susan Foutz, eds., *In Principle, In Practice: Museums as Learning Institutions* (Lanham, Md.: AltaMira, 2007); Falk and Dierking, *Learning in Museums* (Lanham, Md.: AltaMira, 2000); Lord, *The Manual of Museum Learning*; Gary E. Machlis and Donald R. Field, eds., *On Interpretation: Sociology for Interpreters of Natural and Cultural History* (Corvallis: Oregon State University, 1992.

11. National Association for Interpretation, www.interpnet.com.

12. Tilden, *Interpreting Our Heritage*, 32–46.

13. Brad King, "New Relationships with the Formal Education Sector," in *The Manual of Museum Learning*, 77–105.

14. Gary E. Machlis, "The Social Organization of Family Camping: Implications for Interpretation," in *On Interpretation*; Kirsten M. Ellenbogen, Jessica J Luke, and Lynn D. Dierking, "Family Learning in Museums: Perspectives on a Decade of Research," in *In Principle, In Practice*, 17–30; Claudia Haas, "Families and Children Challenging Museums," in *The Manual of Museum Learning*, 49–75.

15. Elaine Heumann Gunian, "The Potential of Museum Learning: The Essential Museum," in *The Manual of Museum Learning*, 21–41, especially 24–26.

16. Kathleen de la Pena McCook and Peggy Barber, "Public Policy as a Factor Influencing Adult Lifelong Learning, Adult Literacy, and Public Libraries," *Reference and User Services Quarterly* 42, no. 1 (2002): 60–75; McCook and Barber, *Chronology of Milestones for Libraries and Adult Lifelong Learning and Literacy*, prepared for the ALA Committee on Literacy, 2002 (ERIC 458888).

17. Nancy Pearl, *Book Lust* (Seattle: Sasquatch, 2003).

18. Jessica E. Moyer, "Learning from Leisure Reading: A Study of Adult Public Library Patrons," *Reference and User Services Quarterly* 46, no. 4 (2007): 66–79.

8

Instructing Throughout the Life Cycle

Public libraries differ from their academic counterparts in purpose, philosophy, and populations served. Instruction given in academic settings is based on one set of mandatory skills, with all or most students headed in the same general direction. Public library instruction can consist of different activities in the same time period for very diverse groups of people, different age groups and circumstances, as well as families and other groups in a completely voluntary setting. A public library actively doing ILI may focus on literacy and cultural programming for preschoolers, on choosing picture books or educational materials for their caregivers, visiting schools and doing workshops for local public school teachers, doing a combined cultural and information literacy session for home-schoolers, having sessions for adults on finding business or genealogical information, and having sessions for seniors on using search tools, the library Online Public Access Catalog (OPAC), and periodical databases to find travel information. A lot of this instruction may be combined with cultural and other programming, and some would be in the form of pathfinders and information on the website. Public library ILI often does not look like that found in other settings. This chapter will describe approaches to ILI from the cradle to the grave (or from hatch to dispatch), looking at preschoolers and their caregivers, families, schoolchildren and teens, young people in transition, adult learners, and elders. Special attention will be paid to what is happening today as Millennial Generation young adults come of age.

PRESCHOOLERS AND THEIR CAREGIVERS

Before planning instruction for young people, there are a number of questions to ask. Existing community surveys and other sources may provide data. General questions include the following: Are there general statistics on children and young people in the area? If so, who is compiling them? For instance, there are books of statistics on children in the *Kids Count* series, compiled by the Annie E. Casey Foundation and other groups with national and state statistics.[1] Also, public schools often keep excellent statistics on their students. Are there any interagency groups in the area that are concerned with children and families? What about agencies or organizations such as WIC or the Boys and Girls clubs? What kind of demographic and other information can be drawn from this data?

It is important to know the characteristics of babies and preschoolers in the area. For instance, if many of the babies have teen parents, outreach to both may be appropriate. Are there day care centers and preschools? Well-baby clinics? What are their needs and requirements? In the case of older children and teens, information about area schools as well as any home schooling becomes very important. You may already have this information to plan your collections and cultural programs, but now you are looking to see what instructional needs for information literacy there may be.

Story Hours and Story Times

Once upon a time, not too long ago or too far away, children's librarians held regular story hours for children age three to five. These children were just beyond the toddler stage but not quite ready to start school. Librarians would read from picture books and tell the children fairy and folk tales. They would supplement these with songs, finger plays, and nursery rhymes. Once in a while, they would use concept books, including alphabet and counting books and books about shapes and colors. Librarians would choose their own stories, songs, and rhymes and create their own programming. By providing story times, they were promoting both cultural and general literacy.

Story hours have really changed in the last thirty years. In addition to story hours for preschoolers, there are now "lap sits" and "bounce" sessions for very young babies. Just as teachers can now consult collections of lesson plans to plan their teaching, children's librarians can consult several source books with ideas for storytelling programs to find book titles, music, and finger plays on specific themes.[2] However, the biggest change has probably been the impact of preschool and family literacy programs.

General Literacy Programs for Preschoolers

In 2000, the Public Library Association (PLA) and the Association of Library Services to Children (ALSC) noted research by the National Institute of Child Health and Human Development (NICHD) on how early childhood development promotes general literacy.[3] In the fall of 2001, PLA and ALSC formed a partnership in order to develop a research-based curriculum for parents and other caregivers to help them promote early general literacy to their children.

The organizations published a toolkit and started the website Every Child Ready to Read@Your Library (ECRR). They urged librarians to work with parents and other caregivers to promote early literacy. Two researchers in emergent literacy identified six prereading skills: narrative skills, print motivation, vocabulary, phonological awareness, letter knowledge, and print awareness (a "Big 6" for general reading literacy). These skills have been promoted by librarians in a number of ways: outreach to parents at WIC meetings and elsewhere in the community; talking to parents at story hours; newsletters to youth librarians and childcare providers; blogs, national and local websites, workshops, and other networking with agencies; packets and kits to new parents and teen parents; home visits by literacy experts to families at risk; and kits sent to teachers. These skills have also been promoted at story hours.

These library activities spilled over into other outreach to parents and families. Schools and school media centers have hosted family literacy and family reading nights.[4] Evenings can include a presentation and resources for parents, a separate story hour with activities for the children, and then joint activities with parents and children, and other incentives for both at the end of the evening.

In some public libraries, there are joint story hours for parents and their children where parents are taught to do story sessions with their children and encouraged to do this activity at home. In some cases, parents are taught literacy along with their children. Some libraries have multicultural and multilingual story hours, sometimes in partnership with community agencies. Story-telling source books and other kits are shared with parents, who are encouraged to have family and bedtime stories at home, and *The Family-Centered Library Handbook* has a lot of valuable information on all aspects of reaching out to young children and their families.[5]

ILI for Preschoolers and Their Caregivers

Can and should preschoolers be instructed in Information Literacy (IL)? One can say that it is much more important to stress general and cultural literacy at this age. It is difficult to be information literate without this. The picture book *San, Bangs, and Moonshine* discusses the difference between facts and "moonshine," or fiction, that can lead to a discussion on the difference between fiction and nonfiction, but this is as far as one should go with this age group. Information Literacy becomes more relevant as children reach elementary school, are able to read, and begin to write papers. The Super 3 exist to instruct children in the primary grades, and more teaching can follow as students go through school.

However, more can be done to integrate nonfiction into story hours. For example, use concept books, have story hours on certain themes, and use both fiction and nonfiction (but point out the difference). Conduct book talks on nonfiction subjects, and co-sponsor programs or story sessions with a community agency on a nonfiction subject, such as animal safety or first aid. The best thing that librarians can do for this age group is introduce the children to both imaginative stories and nonfiction that can answer their questions about the world.

On the other hand, the children's parents, teachers, and caregivers make good audiences for ILI related to the care of their children and to other subjects of interest. There can be sessions, handouts, and tutorials on how to help children prepare for preschool or school; how to find, evaluate, choose, and use picture books; more general information on child rearing; and how to find information on developmental bibliotherapeutic issues, such as new siblings or the illness or death of a grandparent. This instruction can be combined with other types of programming and activities.

There can be similar outreach and activities for other adults and teens who work with young children as camp counselors, playground aids, babysitters, and in other capacities. This group can be reached with occasional workshops, bibliographies, kits, and buckets of books. Information Literacy can be promoted by discussing information needs, where to find information, and how to evaluate and use it.

CHILDREN, TEENS, AND FAMILY OUTREACH

Questions to Begin With

Most children and teenagers in the United States between the ages of five and eighteen are either in schools or are being home-schooled. Schooling is a major part of their lives. Any ILI for this age group depends largely on what is happening in school. Questions to ask about K–12 education in your area include the following: What public, charter, private, and parochial schools are there in your area? What grade levels do they serve? If there are no high schools in the area, where do local teens go to high school?

What is covered in the curriculum, and when does this happen, both during the school year and by grade level? Is the curriculum changing or about to change in any way? Do students take achievement tests and high-stakes examinations? What subjects are covered?

Is ILI offered in all of the schools in the area? If so, what is covered (or not)? What do students learn that they apply in your library? Can you tell who has received ILI? How can you tell? On what grade level is ILI offered: elementary, middle school, high school?

Does the library have anything not in school media centers in your area? The public library may have a different classification system or materials and resources that schools do not. If any of this is the case, there should be supplementary public library instruction even if this is online, and this activity should be advertised.

What networking or outreach opportunities may there be with area schools? This can include ILI and other outreach to teachers and media specialists or cooperation between public, school, and sometimes college librarians in planning joint instruction.

ILI with Schools and School Systems

All of these factors would affect any formal ILI for this age group and, if implemented, how much, for what grades, and on what subjects. If the local school system has a good instructional program, public librarians can supplement and support them, but they should not be duplicating this. However, they can work with local school media specialists to plan computer tutorials, transitional instruction for high school seniors, or to promote ILI in other ways.

It would make more sense to concentrate on schools with no libraries or poor programs, as well as on home-schoolers. Private and parochial schools tend to have their own ways of dealing with libraries and ILI, and it may be necessary to work with each school as a special case.

Charter schools tend to have curricula that focus on particular subjects, themes, or points of emphasis, which would also affect instruction for them. Look for capstone courses or research assignments involving many students, especially in pivotal grades like grades 3, 4, 8, or 12.

In addition to traditional book talks, there are several ILI techniques that can be used during school visits. Public librarians can take a laptop computer and show students their library's website, online tours, the OPAC, and some databases. Some librarians, like those from the Multnomah County Public Library or the Providence Public Library, have also done outreach with teachers that includes book discussions, kits, buckets of books, and sometimes ILI related to their teaching. Do not forget to promote your cultural and reading programs, homework help, tutoring, and other activities. Instruction upon request, orientations, and other activities can also be done with classes that visit the library. Public library children's and teen's

Web pages are good locations for tutorials, pathfinders, and other information. Some public libraries have also created packets for teachers on public
library services and procedures. Much instructional information can also be
on the public library's general website.

Home-Schoolers

There are several ways to interact with home-schoolers. One approach
is to treat them as independent researchers. Another is to work through
national home-schooling groups. A very practical approach is to work with
local home-schooling groups to combine ILI with other kinds of programming.

Families choose to pursue home-schooling for a variety of reasons. Conservative Christians have home-schooled on religious grounds, in protest
over perceived secular humanism in public schools. Raymond and Dorothy Moore are founders of this branch of home-schooling. They started
the Hewitt-Moore Child Development Center and wrote *Schools Can Wait*.
Those who are more liberal or libertarian have chosen to home-school on
pedagogical grounds, protesting the rigidity of public schools. They take
a more humanistic approach to education, believing that students should
learn what they want to. Their founding father, John Holt was the author
of *Teach Your Own* and other books.[6]

Some parents home-school their children because they do not like the
social atmosphere in their public schools. Some high school students want
to accelerate their studies so that they can attend college earlier, and other
children have other unusual learning styles or special needs not well accommodated by local schools.

Home-schooling families vary in the curricula they follow. Some start
with curricula like the Christian Hewitt-Moore one or the more secular
Calvert School curriculum, which has long been used by Americans abroad.
Some experiment with other approaches, depending on their children's
interests and learning styles. Others keep up with the official public school
curriculum in their geographic areas and with testing requirements as well
as state regulations and requirements. Some families consider the public
library's collection to be their curriculum. In many cases, learners and their
parents determine what and how they study, and the whole world can literally be their classroom.[7]

Public libraries have been helping home-schoolers in different ways:
through website information, through networking, and through programming and outreach, including ILI. Libraries have been building resource
collections for home-schoolers and other interested library patrons (such
as other parents and teachers), which includes kits and curricular materials.
Some libraries offer circulating kits and bins of books. They may put infor-

mation on standards, benchmarks, testing, bibliographies, resource lists, and pathfinders on their websites, as well as bulletin boards, newsletters, blogs, and current information.

In networking, some public libraries work with local home-schooling organizations. They may keep a database of relevant organizations, use home-schooled teens as volunteers, and advertise activities through the library's website. There may be a Home-Schooler's Forum to discuss issues, and some libraries do ILI for home-schoolers and their parents. A few libraries have offered Home Education or Schooling Fairs or Open Houses for the general public. They have sponsored academic team competitions, including science and Internet fairs, spelling and geographic bees, and other events.

Some home-schoolers participate in evening and weekend family programs for the general public. In other cases, there are programs specifically for home-schoolers during the school day. Public libraries have found this group of students and parents to be very enthusiastic library users. Resources and programming developed for home-schoolers have benefitted the general public as well.

Home-schooling resources organized by public libraries include the Home School Resource Center at the Johnsburg Public Library, Illinois, and *The Quarterly List of Educational Books for Homeschooling Families and Children K–12* published by the Cleveland Public Library. Organizations include the Alternative Education Resource Organization, National Home Education Network, National Home Education Research Institute, and Home School Legal Defense Association.[8]

Cultural Programs: Reaching Out to Children, Teens, and Families

Cultural programs for children, teens, and families should be advertised at schools as much as possible. For older children and youth, this programming can include story hours, crafts, summer reading programs for children and reading lists for teens, gaming, homework centers, tutoring, and creative writing, history, or genealogy clubs.

Family programming can include festivals, story hours, book fairs, guest speakers or performers, family reading nights, and literary birthday parties. *El Dia de los Ninos: El Dia de los Libros / Day of Children: Day of Books* has been particularly popular in Latino communities around the country promoting family togetherness, bilingualism, and the love of books. This celebration has also spread to other communities. In addition, libraries in certain African American communities have sponsored events or programs, such as creative writing focusing on children and their grandparents. These programs can lead to opportunities for instruction, which can be offered on a limited basis, either as a form of gaming or as an activity in a program series on a particular subject.

ILI for Teens

Aside from supplementing and supporting existing ILI in local schools, working with other schools and institutions, and doing cultural program programming, there are a number of ways that public librarians can use ILI to support teens, whether or not they are bound for a four-year college. College-bound youths benefit from summer reading lists of good literature, whether they are compiled by local teachers or librarians. There may be book discussion groups on adult literary classics as well as YA literature, genre literature, graphic novels, and information on the Internet that can incorporate information on how to find, use, and evaluate this material and more.

ILI and other workshops on finding college, financial aid, and career information can be very helpful. Resources in public libraries are often similar to those at universities. Learning to use public library databases is a nice transition from high school to college. Students can also be taught basic steps in doing term papers. They can be introduced to the library website of colleges that they will be attending.

Teens not planning to attend a four-year college right away can be steered to career and vocational information. They can be told about community colleges, vocational schools, and apprenticeship programs, and they can be taken through the ILI process of raising questions and of finding, evaluating, and using information. Just learning how to analyze college and vocational school pages can be quite a lesson in itself. Teens can also be shown pros and cons of enlisting in the armed services, and it may be a good idea to form an entrepreneurial club to help teenagers write plans for their own businesses. Writing business plans is another research process amenable to ILI, along with participating in job-hunting workshops.

Another possible audience may be teens with special needs who have worked with teams of parents, teachers, and other professionals in designing their Individualized Education Plans (IEPs). Many of these teens are headed to college, and they may need assistance to make that transition. In spite of Disabled Student Services at most universities, students are much more on their own as they leave K–12 education for college. ILI to help with this may be useful.

COMING OF AGE: ROADS TO ADULTHOOD

From the High School Media Center to the University Library

School and college libraries do roughly the same thing but on different scales, and they even work together on committees and stay aware of developments in both kinds of libraries. Most high school graduates who had good ILI while in school can skillfully use their school media centers and their local public libraries. However, using a college library may be a whole other proposition. In small college towns, some students and faculty prefer to use the public library for scholarly research rather than their own college library, whether this is appropriate or not. There are several reasons for this preference.

Traditional college libraries are much bigger than school media centers and considerably larger than most public libraries. Instead of using the Dewey decimal classification to organize their materials, like most school and public libraries, most college libraries use the Library of Congress classification. College libraries have a wide range of materials not generally available in their school and public counterparts—government information and microfilms, for instance. They carry many more electronic databases, and most of those are more specialized by subject. For the most part, college library collections carry much more scholarly material than that found elsewhere. So, as many students move from high school to college, particularly four-year colleges and universities, they find that they are "not in Kansas, anymore," to quote Dorothy, the protagonist in *The Wizard of Oz*. Students are starting almost all over again, needing to be reoriented to their new libraries and needing more advanced ILI as they move through their courses. However, if they received good instruction in their school media centers, they come with a foundation that can be built on. If not, college librarians have to start from the beginning in their instruction.

In addition, scholarly literature by William Perry and researchers studying Women's Ways of Knowing has noted that many people do not move from concrete to abstract thinking until *after* they have graduated from high school. According to Perry, students move from dualism (one right answer to everything), to multiplicity (many answers, all equally good), to relativism (multiple answers, some better than others), to a commitment to relativism (using critical thinking to solve personal problems and to make decisions). This gradual move from concrete to more abstract thinking is another reason that college students often need to have ILI, both as first-year college students taking composition courses and later as students moving into specific majors and concentrations.

Constance Mellon and others have written about college students with library and information anxiety, and there has been more information on this phenomenon by Qun G. Jiao and Anthony John Onwuegbuzie, especially as this affects international students.[9] However, a new generation of students, the Millennials, are coming of age with different issues, needs, and demands.

Millennials and Other Digital Natives: An Earthquake in the Library

William Strauss and Neil Howe, as well as Jonathan Pontell, have written about the different needs of recent generations.[10] According to Strauss and Howe, there are four different kinds of generations: idealistic, reactive, heroic, and artistic. These generations experience different kinds of childhoods, come of age under different circumstances, deal with different sets of problems in middle age, and even experience old age in different ways and in different roles. Generations described by Strauss and Howe that are currently using and working in our libraries include the following:

- The GIs (Civic Heroes, born 1901–1924)—The younger, healthier members of this generation still come to libraries. In other cases, libraries may go to them in the form of outreach. GIs tend to be avid readers. Some in this generation were the technological experts of their era (e.g., Charles Lindbergh, Walt Disney), but this has been the last generation to largely escape the impact of the Internet.
- The Silent Generation (Artistic Mediators, born 1925–1942)—People from this generation are either retired or on the verge of it. Some library administrators and senior librarians are younger members of this group. Most active elders who currently travel and use libraries are in this generation. Many are now living into their eighties, which is becoming the new norm. They vary in their computer skills, with many needing basic instruction. Some were introduced to computers and the Internet before retiring, and this experience makes a positive difference.
- Boomers (Idealistic Prophets, born 1943–1960)—Members of the Baby Boom generation are just beginning to retire. Most administrators and senior librarians are now in this group. Most social scientists say that Boomers were born between 1946 and 1964, but one can state that Strauss and Howe are more accurate on this point. However, Jonathan Pontell considers people born 1954–1965 to be "Generation Jones," a transitional group between the Boomers and Generation X. They are more idealistic than Generation X, but more realistic than Boomers. U.S. President Barack Obama exemplifies these characteristics.
- Generation X (Reactive Warriors, born 1961–1981)—This group is also known as Gen X, the Thirteenth Generation, 13ers, or the Hip Hop Generation. Most librarians, graduate students, and recent college graduates are now from Gen X. Many of the technological trends that have come to full flower with Millennials started with them.
- Millennials (Civic Heroes, born 1982–2000)—This group is also known as Generation Y, Echo Boomers, Nintendogen, Boomlet, Nexters, or 14th Generation. Most current college undergraduates of traditional age, recent college graduates, and new librarians are from this generation, and younger members are still in high school and middle school. Older members are making a major impact as they enter the workforce. We cannot be sure whether this generation will turn out to

be a heroic one or a more artistic one. So far, Millennials are developing in many ways like their GI grandparents and great grandparents in their own youth. However, Millennials appear to be different from all earlier generations because we have moved from a modern industrial age to a postmodern information one.

One big question is how Millennials compare to the Hip Hop Generation or Generation X. Strauss and Howe see these generations as opposites, and they have certainly been treated very differently. Generation X was ignored and neglected and in some cases had to raise themselves. They have been dealing with the problems left by the idealistic Boomer generation. Generation X has not received enough attention, and Millennials may be getting too much. Millennials are optimistic team members, while Gen Xers tend to be relatively pessimistic loners and individualists. While Boomers are passionately large on ideas but short on application, Millennials are the opposite, just like their GI elders. It appears that they will be another great generation of doers and achievers.

However, Generation X and Millennials have several things in common. While Boomers represent the last modern generation of the industrial age, members of Generation X and Millennials are the first postmodern generations and the first real digital natives. They have always dealt with extensive technology in their homes. These two generations are also more ethnically diverse than their elders. Generation X represents the first generation of mixed race children whose parents could legally marry in all states, and prominent biracial people include Barack Obama, Soledad O'Brien, and Tiger Woods. Millennials also reflect this trend, as well as often being immigrants or the children of immigrants.

Now we can consider research on the new characteristics that Millennials bring to libraries and how academic libraries are reacting to these.[11] What Boomers call "high technology" has always been woven into the lives of Gen Xers and especially Millennials, who live online and literally carry technology with them. The Internet is the first place that many Millennials turn to for information, and they see this source as the most authoritative. Millennials are also used to social networking with interactive sources such as wikis, blogs, Facebook, and text messaging, and they use portable technology like cell phones, smart phones like the iPhone, and laptops. They respect authority that they experience with live people such as parents, teachers, and bosses but question it as they deal with information. ILI and critical thinking can be a hard sell to this group.

Unlike competitive Boomers or individualistic Gen Xers, Millennials are used to working together collaboratively in teams. This may also be a reflection of the kind of constructivist education that they have been receiving on the K–12 level. Millennials are visual students who also learn by experimenting and by doing. They usually prefer active learning to lectures. They multitask and get bored easily.

In the library, Millennials tend to trust Internet search tools to give them all the information that they need. They have to be told about OPACs and periodical databases, and they expect them to operate like search engines, with the most relevant results first. Millennials see themselves as consumers of information and want everything customized to them. They either tend to bypass libraries altogether or make new and different demands on them that have never been seen before—for customization, help with technology, and flexible space for both quiet study and for team projects and group study.

As researchers, Millennials want the latest information now and will sacrifice quality for speed and convenience. They look for bits of information without context, and their knowledge can be very fragmented. In many of these respects, Millennials are strikingly like their more field independent elders in the law, sciences, and especially business.

These characteristics have been confirmed in community college, school, and public library settings by Michael D. Rush, Lesley Boon, and Carolyn Jones.[12] Rush states that Millennial students do much of their learning through forms of gaming, which includes learning by doing and through trial and error. Not only do they make heavy use of technology and collaborate in groups, but they use technology to collaborate. Both Boon and Jones speak to the need of school and public libraries to provide more traditional services to older generations and newer services to the young.

According to Deborah Sheesley and Lauren Presley, librarians should be constructivist in starting with where Millennials are and what they already know.[13] Use students' research to demonstrate a search on Internet search tools first. Then demonstrate or have the students do a comparable search using periodical databases and OPACs. Introduce print sources last. A similar approach can be taken with encyclopedias—start with Wikipedia first, then show them other electronic encyclopedias, and cover print encyclopedias last, comparing procedures and results. Be sure to skillfully weave technology into your presentation. Present bite-sized information instead of long narratives, and have students work in cooperative groups as much as possible. Jamie Seeholzer, Frank J. Bove, and Delmus E. Williams urge librarians to teach skills that are often developed in video and computer games as well as analytical thinking that can lead to searching, discovering, and gaining knowledge.[14]

Susanne Markson suggests that libraries should accommodate new generations by evaluating the effectiveness of their services and resources, considering new roles and policies, keeping their own technology skills current, adopting new ways to provide access to resources and services, developing new ways to communicate and interact with library users, improving the library's website, collaborating with Millennial librarians and users to improve services, maintaining open communications with all staff, and encouraging more participatory methods of management. She warns librarians to beware of restricting the use of technology.[15]

Public library websites can be improved by adding appropriate social networking tools as well as ILI and other tutorials, chat software, and various forms of electronic reference. Seeholzer, Bove, and Williams recommend that digital networked services be merged with the Internet and that portals be used on websites to promote "one step shopping." They recommend 24/7 service that is both wireless and in person, as well as the "incorporation of collaborative and multitasking services."[16]

The use of space has become a major consideration in academic and other libraries. Glenda A. Thornton, Bruce Jeppeson, and George Lupone as well as Seeholzer, Bove, and Williams all recommend that libraries create flexible spaces for quiet study, group work, or socializing (in the form of lounges and cafes).[17] The ultimate expression of this trend in academic libraries has been the creation of information or knowledge commons, which are organized in different ways. In certain libraries, the information commons is a separate department from reference. In others, it is integrated with other library departments, especially those dealing with technology and sometimes media. Learning centers also include writing centers and other offices. A few libraries are completely reorganizing their public services to fully accommodate this model. The idea behind an information or a learning commons is that students can go to one place to get help with their electronic and other information searching, as well as with all technology necessary for them to do their work. Learning commons are comparable to computer labs that can now be found in public libraries. These are designed to be used by people with no other access to computers or the Internet. Through an enclosed lab, librarians can offer classes in basic computer literacy, basic adult literacy, ESL, GED preparation, and ILI. It may be possible to also design these labs as "electronic sandboxes" to enable people to explore, experiment with, and learn about a variety of applications.

Academic information commons incorporate many workstations with software that can be applied in many ways.[18] They usually have workspaces for individuals and groups, comfortable furniture, and staff that can help with both reference and technology questions. Some offer access to writing labs, media, and other services. Both social spaces like cafes and lounges and information or learning commons can promote a sense of community.

In planning instructional and other services for Millennials and other digital natives, public librarians should investigate how they can best meet the needs of young people in their communities. They should also adopt successful practices of college and school libraries that are the most applicable in a public library setting. As with other aspects of ILI, public libraries could go in any of several directions with these services. They may do best in merging the best of their current practices with new developments described here. Using focus groups of younger librarians, young adults, and teens will be another way to plan for the future.

ALL GROWN UP AND PLACES TO GO: ADULTS LEARNERS

If public library instruction is a shopping mall with many different instructional activities going on at the same time for widely different groups of people, as well as cultural and social activities, this is especially true of public library instruction for adults. Instead of one set of activities for one audience, there may be multiple modes of instruction for multiple audiences, many of them specialized in one way or another. Except for academics, business people, and other specialists, adults represent one group of people not served in this way by any other type of library. While public librarians can do a lot of creative instruction for children and teens, they should focus mainly on reaching adults, elders, and the caregivers of young children. This section will describe research on how ordinary adults learn in their daily lives, developmental tasks and learning characteristics of adults, how pedagogy compares to andragogy, instructional needs of adult learners in academic and public settings, and potential audiences for this instruction. Much of what is written here also applies to elders, but their more specific characteristics, needs, and issues will be described separately.

How Adults Learn Every Day When (Almost) Nobody Is Looking

Chapter 3 describes several sets of learning theories—behaviorist, cognitive, constructivist, and humanist, as well as the theories of modality, field dependence and independence, and multiple intelligences. Cognitive and constructivist psychologists and educators are especially interested in how people think, and much of their research has focused on how people learn in laboratory and classroom situations. However, a few researchers in other fields, such as Alan Tough, John C. Shirk, Patrick Penland, and Cyril Houle, have investigated ways in which ordinary people learn every day, regardless of where they are. This work is similar to John Holt's research on how children learn.

In 1970, Tough interviewed people from a wide variety of working-class and middle-class occupations to discover whether they do any informal, self-directed learning, and if so, in what ways.[19] He asked his respondents about learning activities they had done in the past year that included at least seven hours of highly deliberate learning within a six-month period.

Ninety percent of his sample had conducted at least one major learning effort during this time, and the average person did five distinct learning projects in the areas of knowledge, skills, or personal change. Of all of these activities, 20 percent were planned by professionals and 80 percent by "amateurs," including 73 percent by learners themselves, 3 percent by their friends, and 4 percent by a "demographic group of peers."

People tended to learn in order to prepare for, upgrade, or improve their *careers*, to improve their *home lives*, to promote *hobbies*, to deal with puzzling or upsetting *events*, or to answer *other questions*. Puzzling or upsetting events can include divorce, birth of exceptional children, other health issues, or other major life decisions. Other questions included current events, religious or philosophical beliefs, and other subjects of interest to the learner. Much adult learning is motivated by fairly immediate problems. One can state that to live *is* to learn, at least for healthy people. Informal learning is tied to the rest of life.

Tough also concluded that people chose self-learning or independent study because this kind of learning best suited their personalities and learning styles. Independent learning enabled these individuals to structure their own learning and to learn at their own pace. Difficulties with money or transportation and the physical availability of various learning resources also played a role. Tough also found that particular knowledge or skills sought by people could also be influenced by their stage in the life cycle and their level of humanitarian concern as well as their vocational, intellectual, moral, or ego development. He found that the amount and methods of learning were usually consistent in people over a lifetime, but the particular subject matter chosen may vary by age.

There have been studies done around the world since then on all kinds of people in a wide variety of occupations that confirmed the work of Tough. It would be interesting to see how the trends described here have been affected by the information age. One would guess that people not only spend significant amounts of time learning computer applications, but they also use these applications and the Internet to learn about all of the issues mentioned here and maybe more.

Shirk surveyed the staff of a branch of the Houston Public Library as well as eighty-one randomly selected members of the public to see what encouraged them to learn and how and what they learn.[20] People in his survey were often influenced to learn by others, and some pursued learning out of curiosity. The types of learning activities reported here were very similar to those in the Tough survey—job or career, home related, hobbies, religious development; current events, and more personal issues. Respondents in Shirk's survey got much of their information from friends, clergy, the library, teachers, counselors, club members, influential people in the community, and their own personal books. Even library staff did not always

depend on libraries for information. Shirk found that some of his respondents confused learning with schooling and underestimated their learning.
He believed that his results could be used to create "cottage learning centers
and other invisible circles of knowledge." Shirk envisioned learning taking
place in a wide variety of community settings and led by a variety of leaders
and professionals. In these ways, he anticipated the lifelong learning movement of the 1970s and beyond.

Shirk's research left him with six questions about adult learners:

1. Why are some people more involved in learning than others?
2. What incentives prevailed in one's environment or life space that
   caused one to seek various types of resources for their learning activities?
3. Who was to determine whether a learning project had quality—the
   respondent, his or her cohorts, or the researcher?
4. Were learners likely to use public libraries for certain learning categories more than others?
5. Were library users more likely to get involved in learning projects than
   nonusers?
6. Did library instruction have any influence on respondents' use of libraries as resources for their learning activities?"

Shirk's research certainly has many applications, especially in the use of
independent study by members of the public and libraries' support of this
activity. His questions can still be used to formulate further research into
what and how adults learn, especially as computers and the Internet are
integrated into this process, both as a subject of learning in themselves and
as a tool to use in studying other subjects.

Developmental Tasks and Learning Characteristics of Adults

Erik Erikson mentions three stages of adulthood, with a major task at
each stage: young adulthood, middle adulthood, and elderhood. According to him, young adults who are beginning careers and starting families
must either learn to be intimate or suffer isolation. Middle-aged adults who
are established in their careers and who have raised families must either
achieve generativity by mentoring others or experience stagnation. Elders
who are dealing with declining health, reviewing their lives, and trying to
pass wisdom to others must achieve either integrity or despair. Adults at
all of these stages are dealing with family, vocations, avocations, and often
some form of education.

Older, nontraditional college students return to school to pursue career
goals and other interests. Unlike younger students who live on college cam-

puses, college is *not* the center of their lives. Most older students are juggling at least several things at once: their families, jobs, community obligations, and schoolwork. Many are in the "sandwich" generation—they may be caring for children and elderly parents at the same time.

Adult learners know who they are, bring knowledge based on their own experiences to class, and are generally very motivated as students. They respond well to interactive, self-directed, and collaborative styles of learning and are more likely to ask questions and demand clarification. Adult learners are interested in skills that are directly applicable to their lives. Their time is limited, and they are much more likely to be distance learners, or at least to commute long distance, between home, school, work, and other commitments. They appear in academic libraries at unconventional times (evenings, weekends), if at all. Alternative methods of ILI like printed asynchronous instruction and tutorials and other materials online have always been a real necessity for this group. In addition, many distance students use their local public libraries as their academic libraries. This is especially true in geographically isolated areas. Esther Grassian and Joan Kaplowitz describe this group in more detail.[21]

Aside from Tough, other researchers with theories about what, how, and why adults learn include Houle and Malcolm Knowles. Tough emphasizes the specific nature of all adult learning. Houle states that people who pursue adult education do so for three reasons: they are either goal oriented, activity oriented, or learning oriented. Some pursue adult education to fulfill specific goals, such as a better position at work. Activity-oriented learners participate for social reasons, either to have something to do or to meet interesting people. Learning-oriented students participate mainly for the joy of learning something new. They also tend to be avid readers and watchers of educational television programs.[22]

Adult Learners in Public and Academic Libraries

Adult learners are the norm in public libraries. Many are invisible learners who work independently. These learners may be conducting projects for work, school, and home, satisfying their curiosity, or using the public library for fun and relaxation. Projects can include term papers, reports for work, business plans, and genealogical research. Many can benefit from indirect, asynchronous instruction—tutorials and other information on the Web, printed materials such as handbooks or pathfinders, signage and building design, instruction as part of electronic reference, or help in an information commons or computer learning center. In some cases, they can benefit from in-person IL workshops that are either general or tied to specific topics.

Traditional reference, cultural programming, reader's advisory services for individuals and groups, and other public library routines can all be important in supporting independent learners and lifelong learning. Other adults in public libraries include people in all kinds of literacy programs; those needing information and referral (I&R) services; parents and sometimes teachers needing information to help their children; people active in the community, including community leaders, gatekeepers, and their organizations; and people in Great Books and similar book discussion or current affairs groups.

Differences between adult college students and their younger counterparts are more pronounced in the academic library setting than in public libraries. Most college undergraduates between the ages of eighteen and twenty-two are still forming, and they are looking for their identities. They try on different roles and personas. Most of these students are learning for future applications. They may be studying educational psychology but probably will not apply this subject to real life for several more years. If they live on campus, their school is usually the center of their lives. Most undergraduates at this age are just beginning to acquire real-life experience.

On the other hand, older students are formed adults who know who they are and are more certain of their identity. Many are learning for immediate application. The teaching aide in the educational psychology class may apply what she learns at work the next day! In addition to juggling several other major responsibilities, adult students also bring more real-world experience with them and can challenge their teachers on these grounds.

Pedagogy and Andragogy

Knowles initially viewed and described pedagogy and andragogy as two almost mutually exclusive methods of education, the former for children and maybe college undergraduates and the later for adults. For younger students who are still forming an identity, there is pedagogy, where the teacher is the definite leader or "the sage on the stage." The teacher is the authority on the subject, and the students are treated more like blank slates to take in information from their professors. It is the students' responsibility to conform to their teachers. The curriculum is teacher and subject centered for the most part. Knowles states that pedagogy was first used in the Middle Ages to teach children to conform to religious doctrine.

For older students, usually adults who have formed an identity, there is andragogy, where the teacher is a more equal facilitator or "guide on the side." The teacher is seen as the slightly more qualified peer of the students, and relationships between teachers and students are more informal and equal. Students can challenge their teachers. It is the teachers' responsibility to conform to their students. The curriculum is more student centered as well as life, task, and problem centered, starting with specific needs of learners. Knowles traces andragogy back to Jesus and the ancient Greeks.[23]

Andragogy is increasingly being viewed as a humanistic approach to education that can be applied to people of all ages. It is not just for adults. In some situations, however, especially in introducing new materials, pedagogy may be appropriate for adults. Either or both can be useful, depending on the situation.

Potential Adult Audiences for ILI

Some adults may be willing and able to come to general ILI sessions, but the best approaches are either through online tutorials that can be accessed as people need them or as specialized sessions and activities for people already there to learn or to do something else. Good potential audiences would be groups interested in genealogy, local history, health, survival information, or business information. This latter can run the gamut from company research for investment or employment to financial planning or writing a business plan for a small, new business. People looking for job or career information may be another good potential audience. Adult students working on their GEDs or adult college students, especially isolated distance students who use their public library as their college library, may be other potential audiences, as well as people who need to access electronic government information.

People in literacy programs may be a good possibility depending on the kind of literacy program they are in, their proficiency with reading, and whether their literacy program is strictly job based or not. It is possible to use ILI even in this situation because it is sometimes necessary to use critical thinking and other aspects of information literacy to make good decisions at work. However, it is easier to work with literacy groups that can pursue any goals students are interested in.

Other audiences would include recreational readers with links to book discussion groups and similar activities, other independent learners, community leaders and gatekeepers, and their organizations. Informally, literacy can be promoted to these groups through hands-on sessions with pathfinders and other handouts, via tutorials on the Internet, and through other means.

ELDERHOOD

Elders tend to be retired or semiretired. They all must deal with aging and declining health, especially over a long period of time. Many are thinking about their lives and what they mean, and most want to pass on their wisdom and other legacies to others. To Erikson, elders must resolve the issue of integrity vs. despair. He sees a task, a virtue, and a corresponding social institution for every stage of life. Elders can be involved in any or all of these institutions. However, elders differ by personality, gender, and all of the demographic characteristics that affect everyone else (race, ethnicity, class, educational level, religious beliefs, and other factors). While all experience declining health over time, some stay in remarkably good condition well into their eighties and nineties.

Elders also differ by generation, aging differently and playing different roles. Strauss and Howe have found that those in the GI generation tend to be relatively wealthy as they age and are looked to for material resources, but not necessarily advice. They had usually formed affable communities among themselves, and many live in elder communities often far away from their families. Artistic generations often stay closer to families. Aging members of the Silent Generation tend to be around their children and may take grandchildren with them as they travel. This is also the generation that has participated heavily in educational organizations, like Elderhostel. Most idealistic generations have led their country through a major secular crisis as they aged (and participated in a religious or cultural awakening in their youth). Reactive generations, such as the Lost Generation born at the end of the nineteenth century, are often neglected all of their lives, and this neglect follows them into old age. They often sacrifice for everybody else and are seldom thanked or acknowledged for doing so. Middle-aged generals during secular crises, such as George Washington, Ulysses S. Grant, or Dwight Eisenhower, often come from reactive generations. The Hip Hop Generation may be another reactive group.

We are living in a time when there are three different generations in their old age: the very elderly GI Generation, the Silent Generation, and the Boomers who are just entering that stage of life and retiring. For the first time, many people in their sixties have at least one parent in their eighties who is still living, and sometimes two. The dominant generation at this time in the elder group is the Silent Generation.

Researchers who study learning in later life include Brian Findsen and Peter Laslett.[24] Laslett divides human life stages into four ages. The first age is childhood and adolescence, where the main focus of society is formal education and socialization. At this stage, students are dependent on others, and there is an emphasis on pedagogy. The second stage is young adulthood, where people are mainly concerned with work and family responsibilities for others. The third age is middle age and early old age, when people have raised their families and are retiring but are still healthy and active enough to pursue leisure, hobbies, volunteer work, and learning. The fourth age, advanced old age, is a period of declining health, dependency, and interdependency, when people can no longer readily go out but may still be learning. There has been a lot of attention paid to people in "the third age" in countries around the world with the establishment of Universities of the Third Age (U3A), which are managed by members of the third age themselves.

Institutions That Support the Learning of Elders

Universities of the Third Age began as a movement in France in 1973 and was tied to universities. This model of U3As originally emphasized the humanities and the arts but has diversified its curriculum. The "British model" of U3A, which can be found in the United Kingdom, Australia, and New Zealand, does not depend as much on universities but on autonomous institutions based on self-help, where groups or committees of elders determine their curricula and the methods used to implement them. There is little distinction between teachers and learners, and teachers may be experts on particular subjects who emerge from the learners. The British model of U3A usually has constitutions but as few rules as possible, and they keep their costs as low as possible. The U3As hold their learning events in a variety of places. Participation in U3As is completely voluntary, and learning is not assessed. This represents a form of nonformal educational humanism.

U3As have been criticized for their slow reactions to recent immigration in their respective countries and for being overwhelmingly white and middle class in orientation. Some have management issues, and some struggle with a lack of resources. There is a tension between whether they should be international or whether they should put more stress on the local. Dealing with new communications technology is another issue.[25]

Elderhostel, which initially developed in the United States and Canada, has become a real international movement. It began in 1975 as a fee-based initiative designed to support short-term residency college programs specifically for low- to middle-income adults over the age of sixty. Elderhostel has become a "travel and learn" program combining tourism and education and "making the world their classroom." It involves nearly 200,000 learners in ninety countries. Many early programs were relatively inexpensive ones that people could attend close to home. Elderhostel has become much more privatized, consumer driven, and geared to elders who are upper middle class or wealthy, with a "focus on meeting individual needs for intellectual and personal enhancement and expressive learning."[26]

The closest thing to U3As in the United States and Canada are Institutes for Learning in Retirement (ILRs). These started as a peer learning program at the New School for Social Research in 1962. Like the French U3As, ILRs are under the mantle of colleges and universities, especially their colleges of continuing education. They offer noncredit courses to an open membership, and like the British-model U3As, students plan and direct their own learning to suit their own needs and circumstances. Under the wings of the Elderhostel Institute Network (EIN), ILRs can now be found all over North

America. However, they often live an ambiguous existence at the margins of their host universities and must often be self-supporting and effectively managed in order to survive.[27]

Findsen concludes that organizations providing the best attention to seniors are independent, autonomous ones that are mainly focused on this age group. He also describes how seniors learn through their families, other forms of intergenerational learning, their places of worship, and the mass media.[28] According to him, educational gerontology differs from gerontological education. Educational gerontology, like the field of education in general, draws from psychology, history, philosophy, sociology, and economics. Scholars in this field investigate how older people learn, how senior adult education is designed, self-help instructional gerontology that helps learners to help themselves, and the development of learning groups, peer counseling, and other forms of self-help senior adult education. Gerontological education is more concerned with social gerontology and adult education, advocacy gerontology, professional gerontology, and gerontology education—in other words, training professionals of all ages to work with older people. An institution relevant to this issue is the Center for Creative Retirement in Asheville, North Carolina, which promotes "life-long learning, leadership, community service, and research by and about senior citizens" with "programs in the arts and humanities, the natural world, civic engagement, wellness, life transition and retirement relocation planning, intergenerational co-learning and research on trends in the reinvention of retirement."[29]

Information Needs

Elders, especially in the third age, have the same information needs as younger adults, but they also have unique needs as they grow older (and sometimes take care of even older relatives). According to Connie Van Fleet and Karen E. Antell, elders must "adjust to changing family relationships, forge intergenerational friendships, keep up with current events, plan for health changes, and overcome social isolation." Staying connected with peers is also very important.[30] Other needs include information on financial planning, retirement, part-time work, and volunteer opportunities and information on leisure, travel, and hobbies. Some elders are also independently learning about various subjects that they never had time to investigate before.

However, an important information need for seniors at this time is how to use computers and the Internet. Elders vary widely in their computer skills, from knowing nothing about computers to being expert on basic computer use, e-mail, the Internet, and even social networking in certain cases, as well as other applications. Some are drawn to the computer for the first time because they want to keep up with children, grandchildren, and other younger people. Others need to access government services on the Web. Most ILI for elders in public libraries has focused on computer and Internet use, and librarians are learning a lot about elders' learning styles and effective ways to teach them.

Bo Xie and Paul T. Jaeger maintain that public libraries are ideal institutions for doing this kind of instruction.[31] Public libraries have informational, cultural, and educational missions and serve people throughout the life cycle. They offer computers and Internet access and often accessible technology for people with disabilities. Public libraries are in many communities and are usually either close to public transportation or offer good parking. They also have a history of reaching out to seniors.

How Elders Learn: Insights from Librarians

As librarians instruct elders on computer and Internet use, they are finding that older people have their own styles of learning, including "selective memories," a focus on details, Automated Attention Response (AAR), and learning through practice, active learning, and peer teaching. With "selective memory," many older adults will intentionally remember only what they think they can use later. Information viewed as irrelevant is quickly forgotten. Older people focus more on details than on overviews in their learning, especially in comparison to younger people. In many cases, their AAR is either low or nonexistent. This means that older adults take longer to learn new tasks, and they must pay close attention to what they are doing. However, having a low to nonexistent AAR can also be an advantage. Mistakes are easier to deal with, for instance.

For elders, practice really does make perfect. In fact, older people benefit more from practice than do people in younger age groups. Like their Millennial grandchildren and great-grandchildren, older adults tend to respond well to active, hands-on learning and to working with peers. However, in being introduced to a subject new to them, they sometimes like to see presentations in familiar settings first.[32]

Tips for Instructing Elders on Computer and Internet Use

There are at least three levels of computer skills. The first level would be using the computer itself, including the mouse and programs like Windows Office Suite. The second level would be on how to use Internet search engines and directories to find information. Instruction on using library OPACs and periodical databases should also be integrated here, as appropriate. A third level of skill would be using social networking tools, such as wikis, blogs, Facebook, Twitter, YouTube, Second Life, and other applications viewed as especially relevant for the purposes of the group. How to access e-government forms and services is another very important topic for this age group. Many elders also want to know how to send pictures to others.

It may be a good idea to work with a focus group of elders and representatives of relevant organizations to design a survey to ascertain where people currently are in their computer skills and what they would like to learn next. Some surveys have asked older people to evaluate any past computer workshops that they have taken. Focus groups and surveys are also useful in planning future activities.

There are several decisions that should be part of any planning. Should seniors be instructed with other age groups or mainly with peers? From the library literature, it appears that computer instruction is more effective with peers, but other types of programming may be more amenable to adults of all ages, family groups, the community as a whole, or other configurations, such as grandparents and grandchildren.

Should workshops explain the internal workings of computers? There is disagreement on this issue in the literature. Van Fleet and Antell advise librarians to emphasize not what computers can do, but what learners will be able to do with the computers.[33] Workshop titles should be on practical subjects that can be investigated and presented with the help of computers and the Internet. They discourage librarians from going into too much detail about how the computer works. On the other hand, Puacz and Bradfield mention how they successfully did a presentation describing computer hardware and software as part of a series on computer use. Whether one introduces this subject would depend on the interests of the audience, how much they already know, and on how the workshop series is organized.

While most articles on this subject encourage librarians to do as much hands-on instruction with computers as possible, Puacz and Bradfield believe that this approach may be too intimidating for certain groups.[34] They describe how they did a four-part series on computer use. Sessions 1 and 3 were given in a familiar setting away from the library as presentations, while students worked in the computer lab in other sessions. This approach enables the librarian to be more informal and serve refreshments, which may attract and encourage some learners. Where and how to instruct would also depend on the interest and skills of the targeted group.

In planning any workshop or workshop series, there are several other considerations. What is the specific subject to be covered? What level of expertise will the workshop be based on? How will people with varying skills be incorporated into workshops? Will more experienced users be encouraged to help less experienced ones, and if so, what will they get out of the workshop? Will small groups work together? Will there be time for extra practice or more individualized attention for slower or less experienced users?

Then choose the settings and make sure that those are accessible to this audience. Determine what materials will be needed, and create some if necessary. Personalized workbooks that include basic points to be covered, with room for more notes and nonthreatening self-paced exercises, can be very useful. Do not forget to preview existing, related websites and tutorials at this time and get permission to use those. Advertise this activity to your proposed audience, and let them know what they will be able to do as a result of the workshop.[35]

In the workshops, be sure to emphasize practical, relevant subjects over computer applications. Examples may be how to plan for retirement, find travel information, or communicate with younger relatives. Emphasize self-pacing in the presentations, exercises, and activities. Give people plenty of time to practice, play, and explore. Learners may need to go "line by line" and "step by step" with exercises and with reading computer screens. Avoid jargon as much as possible. Brief glossaries that users can take with them may help.[36]

In certain cases, seniors can be compared with their Millennial grandchildren and great-grandchildren. Both groups respond well to learning from peers and working in groups. Both need hands-on experience to effectively use computers and the Internet. In both cases, you can be constructivist and start with where people are by using analogies, but your specific analogies may differ depending on the group. With today's elders, you can compare search engines and portals to newspapers, e-mail addresses to zip codes, and OPACs to card catalogs.[37] With today's young people, you would want to start with the latest Internet search tools and directories and compare those with OPACs, or with Wikipedia and compare that to more traditional electronic and print encyclopedias.

Remember to build confidence, encourage questions, focus on your learners rather than yourself, and share your own computer adventures and misadventures with your audience. Be sure to pay close attention to facial expressions and body language.[38]

Most of the early library computer workshops focused mainly on the basics of using a system like Microsoft Office, doing searches with Internet search tools, and using e-mail. However, with the development of social networking tools and many other computer applications, more follow-up is a real necessity.[39] Follow-up includes later workshops on more advanced or new topics by librarians, peer-led computer clubs, newsletters, and computer interest groups. It may be possible for several organizations, including the library, to network together to create and promote in-person and online workshops. Facebook and other networking tools may also be very important to keep people current, especially as the active younger elders of today have more difficulty getting out in their later years.

Beyond Computers: Other Programming and Instruction

ILI for elders can also grow out of other programming and activities and incorporate the use of computers, print, and other media. Groups of seniors interested in many topics such as retirement, financial planning, health information, genealogy, local history, or other topics of local concern can also have instructional sessions on how to raise related questions, how to find more information, how to evaluate it, and how to use it. Instruction could also be created in the form of tutorials or pathfinders. Some sessions and workshops can be taken "on the road" to retirement villages, senior centers, and other settings.

Some libraries have done extensive programming specifically for elders. For more than fifty years, the Boston Public Library has offered Never Too Late, a set of programs for senior citizens that includes book discussions, guest speakers, movies, and other activities. The library has also done out-reach to nursing homes and other organizations serving seniors, as well as to individuals confined to their homes. The Oshawa Public Library in Ontario province, Canada, works with a local senior center to sponsor a cultural series emphasizing the British Isles, a video discussion series, an afternoon matinee series to show documentaries, discussions of "books on a theme," band concerts, and a weekly discussion of the news. The Free Library of Philadelphia has created Central Senior Services at their main library, an information commons particularly for senior citizens. This center offers laptop computers, books and magazines in different formats, adaptive or assistive technology (AT), reference and I&R services, instruc-tion in computer use, and a wide variety of workshops and events on other subjects. These library systems serve elders who are still relatively healthy and active as well as those who either cannot go out or have dementia. Many of these programs can incorporate ILI. Most elders are facing declin-ing eyesight, and hearing and other difficulties. They can often use the same assistive technologies and services available to disabled people, such as large print and audio books, and be instructed on how to take advantage of these resources.

Using Guidelines to Develop Services

ALA's main guidelines on serving the elderly are the following:

1. Acquire current data about the older population and incorporate it into planning and budgeting.
2. Ensure that the special interests of older adults in your community are reflected in the library's collections, programs, and services.
3. Make the library's collections and physical facilities safe, comfortable, and inviting for all older adults.

4. Make the library a focal point for information services to older adults.
5. Target the older population in library programming.
6. Reach out to older adults in the community who are unable to travel to the library.
7. Train the library's staff to serve older people.

In addition to these general guidelines, ALA provides more specific objectives relevant for this purpose, especially under Guideline 5.0. In addition to recommending computer and Internet courses for this age group, the more specific objectives also recommend other programming specifically for seniors, programming taking the needs of different generations of elders into account, intergenerational programming, cooperative programming with community and senior centers, outreach to elders outside of the library, and other lifelong learning activities.[40] ILI can be incorporated into any or all of these programs, as needed and appropriate.

As with younger age groups, instructional programs can lead to other activities, which may lead to more (if different) instruction! There is a tremendous amount that can be done in this area for the entire lifespan of people. It is important to consider all possibilities and choose the best ones for your purposes.

This concludes the first volume of *Lifelong Learning in Public Libraries: Principles, Programs, and People.* This volume contains information on Information Literacy Instruction in public library and other settings and how this relates to other public library activities, tips on planning for instruction, and extensive information on developmental and learning theories and on instructing diverse people of all ages. The companion volume, *Creating and Promoting Lifelong Learning in Public Libraries: Tools and Tips for Practitioners,* will focus more on methods of promoting ILI and other forms of lifelong learning in public library settings, including choosing modes of instruction, lesson planning, execution, and evaluation in all formats, and instruction for one in the form of reader's advisory services, instruction at the reference desk, promoting learning for independent researchers, and other subjects.

NOTES

1. *Kids Count Data Book Online* (Baltimore, Md.: Annie E. Casey Foundation, 2006); *Kids Count Data Book* (Washington, D.C.: Center for the Study of Social Policy, 2006); *Rhode Island Kids Count Factbook* (Providence: Rhode Island Foundation, 1995); *Kids Count: A Pocket Guide on America's Youth* (Washington, D.C.: Produced for the Annie E. Casey Foundation by Population Reference Bureau, 2007).

2. Carolyn N. Cullum, *The Storytime Sourcebook II: A Compilation of 3500+ New Ideas and Resources for Storytellers* (New York: Neal-Schuman, 2007); Saroj Nadhami Ghoting, *Early Literacy Storytimes @ Your Library: Partnering with Caregivers for Success*

(Chicago: ALA, 2006); Jeri Kladder, *Story Hour: 55 Preschool Programs for Public Libraries* (Jefferson, N.C.: McFarland, 1995); Rob Reid, *Family Storytime:: Twenty-Four Creative Programs for All Ages* (Chicago: ALA, 1999).

3. Viki Ash and Elaine Meyers, "Every Child Ready to Read @ Your Library: How It All Began," *Children and Libraries* 7, no. 1 (2009): 3–7; Kim Snell, "Ready to Read Grant: How Columbus Metropolitan Library Got It and What They Learned," *Children and Libraries* 6, no. 2 (2008): 45–48.

4. Michelle McGahey, "Hosting a Family Literacy Night," *Teaching Librarian* 13, nos. 1–2 (2006): 52–59; Julie Rehmer, "Family Reading Night: A How-to Guide," *Library Media Connection* 25, no. 7 (2007): 16–17.

5. Renea Arnold and Nell Colburn, "Read to Me: Summer Reading Programs Are Now Catering to the Pre-School Set," *School Library Journal* 53, no. 7 (2007): 25; Colleen Langan, "Literacy Starts in the Cradle of Shoalhaven Libraries, New South Wales," *Aplis* 22, no. 1 (2000): 17–19; Susan Klingler, "Low Literacy: Breaking the Family Cycle," *Indiana Libraries* 27, no. 2 (2008): 36–39; Sue North, "Catching Them in the Cradle: Family Literacy Programs," *Aplis* 16, no. 2 (2003): 66–71; Sandra Feinberg, Barbara Jordan, Kathleen Deerr, Marcellina Byrne, and Lisa G. Krupp, *The Family-Centered Library Handbook* (New York: Neal-Schuman, 2007).

6. Raymond Moore and Dorothy Moore, *School Can Wait* (Provo, Utah: Brigham Young University, 1979); John Holt and Pat Farenga, *Teach Your Own: The John Holt Book of Homeschooling* (Cambridge, Mass.: Da Capo, 2003).

7. Ann Slattery, "In a Class of Their Own: As More Families Turn to Home-schooling, Public Libraries Can Be an Invaluable Resource," *School Library Journal* 51, no. 8 (2005): 44–46; Nann Blaine Hilyard, "Welcoming Homeschoolers to the Library" (special section), *Public Libraries* 47, no. 4 (2008): 17–27; Nancy Wikel, "A Community Connection: Public Libraries and Home Schoolers," *Emergency Librarian* 22, no. 3 (1995): 13–15; Susan B. Madden, "Learning at Home," *School Library Journal* 37, no. 7 (1991): 23–25; Jane A. Avner, "Home Schoolers: A Forgotten Clientele?" *School Library Journal* 35, no. 11 (1989): 29–33; Tamara Marquam, "Fable and Fact: Serving the Homeschool Population in Public Libraries," *Indiana Libraries* 27, no. 1 (2008): 12–18.

8. Johnsburg, Illinois, Public Library, Home School Resource Center, www.johnsburglibrary.org; Cleveland Public Library, *The Quarterly List of Educational Books for Homeschooling Families and Children K–12*, www.cpl.org; Alternative Education Resource Organization, www.educationrevolution.org; National Home Education Network, www.homeschool-curriculum-and-support.com; National Home Education Research Institute, www.nheri.org; Home School Legal Defense Association, PO Box 2091, Washington, DC 20013.

9. Constance Mellon, "Attitudes: The Forgotten Dimension in Library Instruction," *Library Journal* 113, no. 14 (1988): 137–39; Qun G. Jiao and Anthony John Onwuegbuzie, "Identifying Library Anxiety Through Students' Learning Modality Preferences," *Library Quarterly* 69, no. 2 (1999): 202–16; Jiao and Onwuegbuzie, "Is Library Anxiety Important?" *Library Review* 48, no. 6 (1999): 278–82; Jiao and Onwuegbuzie, "Library Anxiety and Characteristic Strengths and Weaknesses of Graduates' Study Habits," *Library Review* 50, no. 2 (2001): 73–80.

10. William Strauss and Neil Howe, *Generations: A History of America's Future, 1584–2069* (New York: Morrow, 1991); Strauss and Howe, *The Fourth Turning: An*

American Prophecy (New York: Broadway, 1997); Strauss and Howe, *13th Gen: Abort, Retry, Ignore, Fail?* (New York: Vintage, 1993); Strauss and Howe, *Millennials Rising: The Next Great Generation* (New York: Vintage, 2000); Jonathan Pontell, *Generation Jones*, www.jonathanpontell.com.

11. Deborah Sheesley, "The 'Net Generation: Characteristics of Traditional-Aged College Students and Implications for Academic Information Services," *College and Undergraduate Libraries* 9, no. 2 (2002): 25–42; Howe and Strauss, *Millennials Rising*; James R. Kennedy, Lisa Vardaman, and Gerard B. McCabe, eds., *Our New Public, a Changing Clientele: Bewildering Issues or New Challenges for Managing Libraries?* (Westport, Conn.: Libraries Unlimited, 2005); Carolyn Jones, "Baby Boomers and Generation Y in the Public Library: Keeping Them Both Happy—An Australian Perspective," in *Our New Public, a Changing Clientele*, 31–45; Lauren Presley, "Educating the Millennials User," in *Our New Public, a Changing Clientele*, 104–13; Glenda A. Thornton, Bruce Jeppeson, and George Lupone, "A Traditional Library Meets Twenty-First Century Users," in *Our New Public, a Changing Clientele*, 183–205; Jamie Seeholzer, Frank J. Bove, and Delmus E. Williams, "What's Old Is New Again: Library Services and the Millennials Student," in *Our New Public, a Changing Clientele*, 241–54.

12. Michael D. Rush, "Community College Libraries, Learning Resource Centers Meet the Generation Y Challenge," in *Our New Public, a Changing Clientele*, 161–72; Lesley Boon, "'I Want It All and I Want It Now!': The Changing Face of School Libraries," in *Our New Public, a Changing Clientele*, 173–79; Jones, "Baby Boomers and Generation Y in the Public Library," 38–42.

13. Sheesley, "The 'Net Generation," 25–42; Presley, "Educating the Millennials User," 108–11.

14. Seeholzer, Bove, and Williams, "What's Old Is New Again," 249–50.

15. Susanne Markgen, "Reaching Out to Generation Y: Adapting Library Roles and Policies to Meet the Information Needs of the Next Generation," in *Our New Public, a Changing Clientele*, 46–54.

16. Seeholzer, Bove, and Williams, "What's Old Is New Again," 247–49.

17. Thornton, Jeppeson, and Lupone, "A Traditional Library Needs Twenty-First Century Users," 186–88; Seeholzer, Bove, and Williams, "What's Old Is New Again," 250–52.

18. Seeholzer, Bove, and Williams, "What's Old Is New Again," 250–52.

19. Allen Tough, "Interests of Adult Learners," in *The Modern American College*, ed. Arthur W. Chickering (San Francisco: Jossey-Bass, 1981), 296–305; Lifelong Learning Act, 1976; Jarvis, Hollford, and Griffin, *The Theory and Practice of Learning*, 79–80.

20. John C. Shirk, "The Library Learning Inventory: A Process for Understanding the Adult Learner," in *Educating the Public Library User*, ed. John Lubans Jr. (Chicago: ALA, 1983), 57–61.

21. Esther Grassian and Joan Kaplowitz, *Information Literacy Instruction: Theory and Practice*, 2nd ed. (New York: Neal-Schuman, 2009), 257–58.

22. Jarvis, Holford, and Griffin, *The Theory and Practice of Learning*, 77–87.

23. Malcolm S. Knowles, Elwood F. Holton III, and Richard A. Swanson, *The Adult Learner: The Definitive Classic in Adult Education and Human Resource Development* (Houston: Gulf, 1998), 54–58, 61–70.

24. Brian Findsen, *Learning Later* (Malabar, Fla.: Krieger, 2005), 12–13; Peter Laslett, *A Fresh Map of Life: The Emergence of the Third Age* (Cambridge, Mass.: Harvard University Press, 1991).

25. Findsen, *Learning Later*, 90–92.

26. Findsen, *Learning Later*, 92–94.

27. Findsen, *Learning Later*, 94–95.

28. Findsen, *Learning Later*, 95–97, 100–8.

29. Findsen, *Learning Later*, 16–18; University of North Carolina, Asheville, North Carolina Center for Creative Retirement, www2.unca.edu.

30. Connie Van Fleet and Karen E. Antell, "Creating Cyber Seniors: Older Adult Learning and Its Implications for Computer Training," *Public Libraries* 41, no. 3 (2003): 149–51.

31. Bo Xie and Paul T. Jaeger, "Computer Training Programs for Older Adults at the Public Library," *Public Libraries* 47, no. 5 (2008): 52–53.

32. Van Fleet and Antell, "Creating Cyber Seniors," 150–151; Jeanne Holba Puacz and Chris Bradfield, "Surf's Up for Seniors: Introducing Older Patrons to the Web," *Computers in Libraries* 20, no. 8 (2000): 50–53, www.infotoday.com.

33. Van Fleet and Antell, "Creating Cyber Seniors," 151, 152; Puacz and Bradfield, "Surf's Up," 50–53.

34. Puacz and Bradfield, "Surf's Up," 50–53.

35. Puacz and Bradfield, "Surf's Up," 50–53; Xie and Jaeger, "Computer Training Programs for Older Adults at the Public Library," 54.

36. Van Fleet and Antell, "Creating Cyber Seniors," 151–54; Puacz and Bradfield, "Surf's Up," 50–53; Tammy Bobrowsky, "Seniors Increasingly Online: Tips for Helping Seniors Navigate the Information Highway," *LIRT News* (June 2005): 3; Lisa A. Burwell, "Too Old to Surf? No Way!: An Internet Course for Seniors," *American Libraries* 32, no. 10 (2001): 41–42.

37. Van Fleet and Antell, "Creating Cyber Seniors," 152; Burwell, "Too Old to Surf?" 42.

38. Burwell, "Too Old to Surf?" 42.

39. Puacz and Bradfield, "Surf's Up," 50–53; Xie and Jaeger, "Computer Training Programs for Older Adults at the Public Library," 53–57.

40. ALA, "Guidelines for Library and Information Services to Older Adults," *Reference and User Services Quarterly* 42, no. 2 (2008): 209–12.

Bibliography

Abdullahi, Ismail, ed. *Global Library and Information Science: A Textbook for Students and Educators*. Munich: K.G. Saur, 2009.

Abilities! www.abilitiesonline.org/Programs.aspx (15 March 2011).

Adams, Helen R. "Access for Students with Disabilities." *School Library Media Activities Monthly* 25, no. 10 (2009): 54.

African Methodist Episcopal Church. *Journal of Christian Education* 66, no. 1 (2004).

AJR (American Journalism Review) Newslink. www.ajr.org/Newspapers .asp?MediaType=1 (14 March 2011).

Albanese, Andrew Richard. "Campus Library 2.0." *Library Journal* 129, no. 7 (2004): 30–33.

Alexander, Otis D. "Library Services for the Unemployed and the Institute for Information Literacy." *Virginia Libraries* 52, no. 2 (2006): 34–35.

Alexander Graham Bell Association for the Deaf. www.agbell.org (15 March 2011).

All Kinds of Minds. www.allkindsofmind.org (15 March 2011).

Allen, Mary Beth. "International Students in Academic Libraries: A User Survey." *College and Research Libraries* 54, no. 4 (1993): 323–33.

Alternative Education Resource Organization. www.educationrevolution .org.

American Association of School Librarians (AASL). "AASL History: 1914–1951." www.ala.org/ala/mgrps/divs/aasl/aboutaasl/aaslhistory/aaslhistory 19141951.cfm (12 March 2011).

———, ed. *Empowering Learners: Guidelines for School Library Programs*. Chicago: ALA, 2009.

———, ed. *Information Standards for the 21st Century Learner*. Chicago: ALA, 2007. www.ala.org/ala/mgrps/divs/aasl/guidelinesandstandards/learning standards/AASL_Learning_Standards_2007.pdf (12 March 2011).

———, ed. *Information Standards for the 21st Century Learner in Action*. Chicago: ALA, 2009.

American Association of School Librarians (AASL) and Association for Educational Communications and Technology (AECT), eds. *Information Literacy Standards for Student Learning: Standards and Indicators*. Chicago: ALA, 1998.

———, *Information Power: Building Partnerships for Learning*. Chicago: ALA, 1998.

American Association of the Deaf-Blind. www.aadb.org/ (15 March 2011).

American Deafness and Rehabilitation Association. www.adara.org (15 March 2011).

American Foundation for the Blind (AFB). *Applied Technology*. www.afb.org/ Section.asp?SectionID=4&TopicID=31 (15 March 2011).

———. *Bridging the Gap: Best Practices for Instructing Adults Who Are Visually Impaired and Have Low Literacy Skills*. www.afb.org/btglogin.asp (15 March 2011).

———. *Etiquette*. www.afb.org/Section.asp?SectionID=36&TopicID=163 (15 March 2011).

American Library Association (ALA). "Guidelines for Library and Information Services to Older Adults." *Reference and User Services Quarterly* 42, no. 2 (2008): 209–12.

———. Association of Specialized and Cooperative Library Agencies (ASCLA). www.ala.org/ala/mgrps/divs/ascla/ascla.cfm (15 March 2011).

———. ASCLA. *Guidelines for Library and Information Services for the American Deaf Community*. Chicago: ALA, 1995.

———. ASCLA, *Guidelines for Library Services for People with Mental Illnesses*. Chicago: ALA, 2007; National Institute of Mental Health. www.nimh .nih.gov.

———. ASCLA. *Library Services for People with Disabilities Policy*. www.ala.org/ ala/mgrps/divs/ascla/asclaissues/libraryservices.cfm (15 March 2011).

———. ASCLA. *Library Services for People with Mental Retardation*. Chicago: ALA, 1999.

———. ASCLA. *Revised Standards and Guidelines of Service for the Library of Congress Network of Libraries for the Blind and Physically Handicapped*. Chicago: ALA, 2005.

———. Library Instruction Round Table (LIRT). "Top Twenty-Five of LIRT's Top Twenty Instruction Articles." http://fleetwood.baylor.edu/lirt/top25 .htm (12 March 2011).

———. Research Committee. *From Chalkboard to Keyboard: 25 Years of Library Instruction Research*. Chicago: ALA.

———. Presidential Commission on Information Literacy. *Final Report*. Chicago: ALA, 1989.

Anderson, David, Martin Storksdieck, and Michael Spock. "Understanding the Long-Term Impacts of Museum Experience." In *In Principle, In Practice: Museums as Learning Institutions*, ed. John H. Falk, Lynn D. Dierking, and Susan Foutz. Lanham, Md.: AltaMira, 2007, 197–215.

Angeley, Robin, and Jeff Purdue. "Information Literacy: An Overview." http://pandora.cii.wwu.edu/dialogue/issue6.html (12 March 2011).

Annie E. Casey Foundation. *Kids Count: A Pocket Guide on America's Youth*. Washington, D.C.: Produced for the Annie E. Casey Foundation by Population Reference Bureau, 2007.

———. *Kids Count Data Book*. Washington, D.C.: Center for the Study of Social Policy, 2006.

———. *Kids Count Data Book Online*. Baltimore, Md.: Annie E. Casey Foundation, 2006.

———. *Rhode Island Kids Count Factbook*. Providence: Rhode Island Foundation, 1995.

Anspaugh, Sheryl. "Public Libraries: Teaching the User?" In *Progress in Educating the Library User*. New York: Bowker, 1978.

ARC of the United States. www.thearc.org (15 March 2011).

———. *Internet Instruction for Librarians Serving People with Disabilities*. www.thearclink.org/forLibrarians/default.htm (15 March 2011).

Arnold, Renea, and Nell Colburn. "Read to Me!" *School Library Journal* 53, no. 7 (2007): 25.

Arp, Lori. "Information Literacy or Bibliographic Instruction: Semantics of Philosophy?" *RQ* 30, no. 1 (1990): 46–49.

Ash, Viki, and Elaine Meyers. "Every Child Ready to Read @ Your Library." *Children and Libraries* 7, no. 1 (2009): 3–7.

Asher, Curt, Emerson Case, and Ying Zhong. "Serving Generation 1.5: Academic Library Use and Students from Non-English-Speaking Households." *College and Research Libraries* 70, no. 3 (2009): 258–72.

Association for Educational Communications and Technology (AECT). "Association for Educational Communications and Technology in the Twentieth Century: A Brief History." www.aect.org/About/History (12 March 2011).

Association of College and Research Libraries (ACRL). *Standards for Proficiencies for Instruction Librarians and Coordinators*. www.ala.org/ala/mgrps/divs/acrl/standards/profstandards.cfm (12 March 2011).

———. *College and Research Libraries*. Chicago: American Library Association.

———. *Immersion '10 Program*. www.ala.org/ala/mgrps/divs/acrl/issues/infolit/professactivity/iil/immersion/immersion10.cfm (12 March 2011).

———. Bibliographic Instruction Section. *Evaluating Bibliographic Instruction: A Handbook*. Chicago: Author, 1983.

Association of College and Research Libraries and American Library Association. *Information Literacy Competency Standards for Higher Education*. Chicago: ACRL, 2000. www.ala.org/ala/mgrps/divs/acrl/standards/standards.pdf (12 March 2011).

Association on Higher Education and Disability (AHEAD). www.ahead.org (15 March 2011).

Attention! CHADD (Children and Adults with Attention Deficit Disorders). www.chadd.org (15 March 2011).

Augst, Thomas. "American Libraries and Agencies of Culture." *American Studies* 42, no. 3 (2001): 5–22.

Australia and New Zealand Institute for Information Literacy (ANZIIL). *Australia and New Zealand Information Literacy Framework*. Adelaide, Australia: Author, 2004.

"Australian Government Broadband Initiatives." www.thaicom.net/eng/press.aspx?id=174.

Ausubel, David Paul. *Educational Psychology: A Cognitive View*. New York: Holt, Rinehart and Winston, 1968.

———. *The Psychology of Meaningful Verbal Learning: An Introduction to School Learning*. New York: Grune and Stratton, 1963.

Autism Society of America (ASA). www.autism-society.org (15 March 2011).

Autism Speaks. www.autismspeaks.org (15 March 2011).

Avner, Jane A. "Home Schoolers: A Forgotten Clientele?" *School Library Journal* 35, no. 11 (1989): 29–33.

Bailey, Russell, and Barbara Tierney. "Information Commons Redux: Concept, Evolution, and Transcending the Tragedy of the Commons." *Journal of Academic Librarianship* 28, no. 5 (2002): 277–86.

Banks, James A. *An Introduction to Multicultural Education*. 4th ed. Boston: Pearson/Allyn and Bacon, 2008.

Barbe, Walter Burke, and Raymond H. Swassing. *Teaching Through Modality Strengths: Concepts and Practices*. Columbus, Ohio: Zaner-Bloser, 1988.

Barna, George. *Futurecast: What Today's Trends Mean for Tomorrow's World*. Carol Stream, Ill.: Barnabooks, 2011.

———. *Grow Your Church from the Outside In: Understanding the Unchurched and How to Reach Them*. Ventura, Calif.: Regal, 2002.

———. *Revolution*. Carol Stream, Ill.: Tyndale House, 2006.

Beacon College. www.beaconcollege.edu (15 March 2011).

Beagle, Donald. "Conceptualizing an Information Commons." *Journal of Academic Librarianship* 25, no. 2 (1999): 82–89.

Beaubien, Anne K., et al. *Learning the Library: Concepts and Methods for Effective Bibliographic Instruction*. New York: Bowker, 1982.

Behrens, Shirley J. "A Conceptual Analysis and Historical Overview of Information Literacy." *College and Research Libraries* 55, no. 4 (1994): 309–22.

Belenky, Mary Field, ed. *Women's Ways of Knowing: The Development of Self, Voice, and Mind.* 10th anniversary ed. New York: Basic, 1997.

Bell, Daniel. *The Coming of Post-Industrial Society: A Venture in Social Forecasting.* 1st Indian ed. New Delhi: Arnold-Heinemann, 1974.

Bennett, Christine I. *Comprehensive Multicultural Education: Theory and Practice.* 6th ed. Boston: Pearson/Allyn and Bacon, 2007.

Berkeley Public Library. *Resources for People with Disabilities.* www.berkeley publiclibrary.org/services_and_resources/disability_resources.php (15 March 2011).

Berry, John. "The Valley Library." *Library Journal* 124, no. 11 (1999): 38–41.

Bertini, Mario, Luigi Pizzamiglio, and Seymour Wapner, eds. *Field Dependence in Psychological Theory, Research, and Application: Two Symposia in Memory of Herman A. Witkin.* Hillsdale, N.J.: Lawrence Erlbaum, 1986.

———. "Some Implications of Field Dependence for Education." In *Field Dependence in Psychological Theory, Research, and Application,* 93–106.

Birdsong, Lark. "Information Literacy Training for All." *Searcher* 17, no. 9 (2009): 38–42.

Bjork, Daniel W. *B.F. Skinner: A Life.* Washington, D.C.: American Psychological Association, 1997.

Blaine-Hilyard, Nann. "Welcoming Homeschoolers to the Library." *Public Libraries* 47, no. 3 (2008): 17–27.

Bloom, Benjamin Samuel, ed. *Taxonomy of Educational Objectives: The Classification of Educational Goals.* New York: D. McKay, 1956.

Blowers, Helene, and Lori Reed. "The C's of Our Sea Change: Plans for Training Staff, from Core Competencies to Learning 2.0." *Computers in Libraries* 27, no. 2 (2007): 10–15.

Bly, Linda. "Library Skills: An Informal Survey." *Arkansas Libraries* 42 (June 1985): 21.

Bobrowsky, Tammy. "Seniors Increasingly Online: Tips for Helping Seniors Navigate the Information Highway." *LIRT News* (June 2005): 3.

Boeree, C. George. "Behaviorism." http://webspace.ship.edu/cgboer/beh.html (12 March 2011).

Bookshare. http://bookshare.org (15 March 2011).

Boon, Lesley. "I Want It All and I Want It Now! The Changing Face of School Libraries." In Kennedy, Vardaman, and McCabe, *Our New Public, a Changing Clientele,* 173–79.

Branscomb, Bennett Harvie. *Teaching with Books: A Study of College Libraries.* Hamden, Conn.: Shoe String, 1964.

Breivik, Patricia Senn, ed. *Libraries and the Search for Academic Excellence.* Metuchen, N.J.: Scarecrow, 1988.

Breivik, Patricia Senn, and E. Gordon Gee, eds. *Information Literacy: Revolution in the Library.* New York: Macmillan, 1989.

Breul, Jonathan D. "GPRA: A Foundation for Performance Budgeting." *Public Performance and Management Review* 30, no. 3 (2007): 312–31.

Brooklyn Public Library. *The Child's Place for Children with Special Needs.* www.brooklynpubliclibrary.org/childs_place.jsp (15 March 2011).

Brooks, Jacqueline Grennon, and Martin G. Brooks, eds. *In Search of Understanding: The Case for Constructivist Classrooms.* Alexandria, Va.: Association for Supervision and Curriculum Development, 1999.

Brooks, Jean. "User Education in Public Libraries." In *Seminar on User Education Activities: The State of the Art in Texas.* Bethesda, Md: ERIC, 1977. ED 138 249.

Brottman, May, and Mary Loe, eds. *The LIRT Library Instruction Handbook.* Englewood, Colo.: Libraries Unlimited, 1990.

Bruce, Christine. "Information Literacy Research: Dimensions of the Emerging Collective Consciousness." *Australian Academic and Research Libraries* 31, no. 2 (2000): 91–109.

———. *The Seven Faces of Information Literacy.* Adelaide: Auslib, 1997. http://web.bit.mah.se/konferens/ck2/cabinet/bruce/netsc/Bruce_Malmox/sld017.htm (12 March 2011).

Bruner, Jerome S. *Toward a Theory of Instruction.* Cambridge, Mass.: Belknap Press of Harvard University, 1982.

———. *In Search of Mind: Essays in Autobiography.* New York: Harper and Row, 1983.

Brunvand, Amy. "The Information Commons: Librarians vs. Libertarians." *American Libraries* 32, no. 4 (2001): 42–43.

Bundy, Mary Lee. "Metropolitan Public Library Use." *Wilson Library Bulletin* 41 (1967): 950–61.

Burgess, Kerrie. "Public Libraries and Egovernment." *APLIS* 19, no. 3 (2006): 118–25.

Burkhardt, Joanna M., Mary C. MacDonald, and Andree J. Rathmacher, eds. *Creating a Comprehensive Information Literacy Plan: A HOW-to-Do-It Manual and CD-ROM for Librarians.* New York: Neal-Schuman, 2005.

Burrell, Jennifer. "Now for the Hard Part: End User Education." *APLIS* 12, no. 3 (1999): 105–13.

Burwell, Lisa A. "Too Old to Surf? No Way! An Internet Course for Seniors." *American Libraries* 32, no. 10 (2001): 41–42.

California State University, Northridge (CSUN). National Center of Deafness (NCOD). *Mission, Vision, and Organizations.* www.csun.edu/ncod/programs/mission.html (15 March 2011).

———. NCOD. PEPNeT. *Helpful Links.* www.pepnet.org/pdc/Links.asp (15 March 2011).

Canadian Library Association. *Canadian Guidelines on Library and Information Services for People with Disabilities.* www.cla.ca/AM/Template.cfm?Section=Position_Statements&Template=/CM/ContentDisplay.cfm&ContentID=4065 (15 March 2011).

Carbone, Jerry. "Library Use Instruction in the Small and Medium Public Library: A Review of the Literature." *Reference Librarian*, no. 10 (1984): 149–57.

Carey, Kevin. "Library Services to People with Special Needs: A Discussion of Blind and Visually Impaired People as an Exemplar." In Deines-Jones, *Improving Library Services to People with Disabilities*, 21–43.

———. "The Opportunities and Challenges of the Digital Age: A Blind User's Perspective." *Library Trends* 55, no. 4 (2007): 767–84.

Carnegie Library of Pittsburgh. *Downtown and Business Events*. www.clpgh .org/locations/downtown/programs.cfm (12 March 2011).

Carroll, Frances Laverne, ed. *International Librarianship: Cooperation and Collaboration*. Lanham, Md.: Scarecrow, 2001.

Center for Accessible Technology. www.cforat.org (15 March 2011).

Center for Applied Special Technology (CAST). Universal Design for Learning (UDL). www.cast.org.

Chepesiuk, Ron. "Prognosis: Literacy." *American Libraries* 38, no. 11 (2007): 54–56.

Chickering, Arthur W., ed. *The Modern American College*. San Francisco: Jossey-Bass, 1981.

Chodock, Ted, and Elizabeth Dolinger. "Applying Universal Design to Information Literacy: Teaching Students Who Learn Differently at Landmark College." *Reference and User Services Quarterly* 49, no. 1 (2009): 24–32.

Christian Parents Special Kids/Alliance for Technology Access. *Technology Resources*. www.cp-sk.org/cpsktechnologyaccesscenters.htm (15 March 2011).

Cleveland Public Library. *Ohio Library for the Blind and Physically Disabled*. http://cpl.org/TheLibrary/OhioLibraryfortheBlindandPhysicallyDisabled .aspx (15 March 2011).

———. *The Quarterly List of Educational Books for Homeschooling Families and Children K–12*. www.cpl.org.

Closing the Gap. www.closingthegap.com/about_us.lasso (15 March 2011).

Collen, Lauren. "Teaching Information Literacy in the Public Library." *Knowledge Quest* 37, no. 1 (2008): 12–16.

Communications in Information Literacy. www.comminfolit.org.

Compton, Christopher. "Innovation in Library Instruction Applied to an Adult Education Course." In *Progress in Educating the Library User*, ed. John J. Lubans Jr. New York: Bowker, 1978, 135–37.

Concept to Classroom. *Constructivism as a Paradigm for Teaching and Learning*. www.thirteen.org/edonline/concept2class/constructivism/index .html (12 March 2011).

Conner, Marcia L. "What's Your Learning Style?" *Journal of Christian Education* (Winter 2009): 4–5.

Consortium for Libraries in Higher Education Networking to Improve Library Access for Disabled Users in South and Southwest England (CLAUD). www.bris.ac.uk/claud/welcome.html (15 March 2011).

Cooksey, Leslie J., Paige Gill, and P. Adam Kelly. "The Program Logic Model as an Integrative Framework for a Multimethod Evaluation." *Evaluation and Program Planning* 24 (2001): 119.

Cowgill, Alison, Joan Beam, and Lindsay Wess. "Implementing an Information Commons in a University Library." *Journal of Academic Librarianship* 27, no. 6 (2001): 432–39.

Crew, Spencer R. "Involving the Community: The Museum as Forum for Dialogue and Learning." In Lord, *The Manual of Museum Learning,* 107–33.

Crispen, Joanne L., ed. *The Americans with Disabilities Act: Its Impact on Libraries: The Library's Responses in "Doable" Steps.* Chicago: Association of Specialized and Cooperative Library Agencies, a division of ALA, 1993.

Cruickshank, Donald R., and Deborah Bainer Jenkins, eds. *The Act of Teaching.* New York: McGraw-Hill, 1995.

Cullum, Carolyn N. *The Storytime Sourcebook: A Compendium of Ideas and Resources for Storytellers.* New York: Neal-Schuman, 1990.

Davis, Tamara S. "The Federal GPRA Evaluation Mandate: Is Social Work Ready?" *CSA Social Services Abstracts* 1, no. 3 (2002): 51–74.

Day, John Michael. *Guidelines for Library Services to Deaf People.* IFLA Professional Reports No. 62.

Deafsign. www.deafsign.com (15 March 2011).

Dean College. Arch Learning Community. www.dean.edu/Academics/Arch .cfm (15 March 2011).

Deines-Jones, Courtney. *Improving Library Services to People with Disabilities.* Oxford: Chandos, 2007.

———. "Low Cost/No Cost Ways to Improve Service Right Now." In *Improving Services to People with Disabilities.* Oxford: Chandos, 2007, 123–47.

Deines-Jones, Courtney, and Connie Jean Van Fleet, eds. *Preparing Staff to Serve Patrons with Disabilities: A How-to-Do-It Manual.* New York: Neal-Schuman, 1995.

Deitering, Anne-Marie. "Reflection and Thinking and All of That Stuff: Learning, Engagement, and the Net Generation." In Kennedy, Vardaman, and McCabe, *Our New Public, a Changing Clientele,* 26.

Delpit, Lisa. *Other People's Children: Cultural Conflict in the Classroom.* New York: New Press; distributed by Norton, 2006.

Dembo, Myron H., ed. *Applying Educational Psychology in the Classroom.* 3rd ed. New York: Longman, 1988.

Diehl, Susan, and Terry L. Weech. "Library Use Instruction Research and the Public Library." *Public Libraries* 30, no. 1 (1991): 33–42.

DiMartino, Diane, and Linda Zoe. "International Students and the Library: New Tools, New Users, and New Instruction." In Jacobson and Williams, *Teaching the New Library to Today's Users,* 17–43.

Disability Info.gov. www.disability.gov.

District of Columbia Public Library. *Library Services for the Deaf and Hard-of-Hearing.* http://dclibrary.org.

Downing, Karen E. "Instruction in a Multicultural Setting: Teaching and Learning with Students of Color." In Jacobson and Williams, *Teaching the New Library to Today's Users,* 47–70.

Downing, Karen E., Barbara MacAdam, and Darlene Nichols, eds. *Reaching a Multicultural Student Community: A Handbook for Academic Librarians.* Westport, Conn.: Greenwood, 1993.

Durrance, Joan C., and Karen E. Fisher, eds. *How Libraries and Librarians Help: A Guide to Identifying User-Centered Outcomes.* Chicago: ALA, 2005.

EASI (Equal Access to Software and Information). http://people.rit.edu/easi (15 March 2011).

Eaton, Gale. "What the Public Children's Library Needs to Know About Locational Skills Instruction in Elementary Schools." *Journal of Youth Services in Libraries* 2 (Summer 1989): 357–66.

EBSCO. *Library, Information Science, and Technology Abstracts.* Ispwich, Mass.: EBSCO, 2005.

Eckel, Edward J. "Fostering Self-Regulated Learning at the Reference Desk." *Reference and User Services Quarterly* 47, no. 1 (2007): 16–20.

Edmonds, Leslie. "The Birth of a Research Project." *Top of the News* 43 (Spring 1987): 323–25.

Edmonds, Leslie, Paula Moore, and Kathleen Mehaffey Balcom. "An Investigation of the Effectiveness of an Online Catalog in Providing Bibliographic Access to Children in a Public Library Setting." Unpublished report submitted to ALA, 1988.

Educators' Spotlight Digest. Syracuse, N.Y.: S.O.S. for Information Literacy Syracuse University.

Edwards, Sherri. "Bibliographic Instruction Research: An Analysis of the Journal Literature from 1977 to 1991." *Research Strategies* 12 (Spring 1994): 68–78.

Eisenberg, Michael B., and Michael K. Brown. "Current Themes Regarding Library and Information Skills Instruction: Research Supporting and Research Lacking." *School Library Media Quarterly* 20 (Winter 1992): 103–9.

Ellenbogen, Kirsten M., Jessica J Luke, and Lynn D. Dierking. "Family Learning in Museums: Perspectives on a Decade of Research." In Falk, *In Principle, In Practice,* 17–30.

Elrick and Lavidge, Inc. *Public Library Usage in Illinois.* Illinois State Library Report No. 1. Springfield, Ill: Illinois State Library, 1977.

E-Michigan Deaf and Hard of Hearing People. *Communication Tips with People Who Are Deaf or Hard of Hearing.* www.michdhh.org/hearing/comm_tips.html (15 March 2011).

En Gauge. "21st Century Skills: Literacy in the Digital Age." www.grrec.ky.gov/SLC_grant/Engauge21st_Century_Skills.pdf (12 March 2011).

Encyclopedia of Library and Information Sciences. New York: Marcel Dekker, 1968–2003.

England, S.R. "The Consequences of Promoting an Educational Role for Today's Public Libraries." *Public Libraries* 46, no. 2 (2007): 55–63.

Erikson, Erik H. *Childhood and Society.* New York: Norton, 1993.

———. *Identity: Youth and Crisis.* New York: Norton, 1994.

Evans, Richard I. *B.F. Skinner: The Man and His Ideas.* New York: Dutton, 1968.

Ewert, Gisela. "The Beginnings of Instruction in Library Use: Selected German Examples from the 17th to 19th Centuries." *Research Strategies* 4 (Fall 1986): 177–84.

Faibisoff, S.G., and D.J. Willis. "Public Library Adult Learning Center Renewal." *Public Library Quarterly* 9, no. 2 (1989): 41–56.

Falk, John H., ed. *In Principle, In Practice: Museums as Learning Institutions.* Lanham, Md.: AltaMira, 2007.

Falk, John H., and Lynn D. Dierking. *Learning in Museums.* Lanham, Md.: AltaMira, 2000.

———, eds. *Lessons without Limit: How Free-Choice Learning Is Transforming Education.* Walnut Creek, Calif.: AltaMira, 2002.

Family Center on Technology and Disability. www.fctd.info (15 March 2011).

Farkas, Meredith. "A Roadmap to Learning 2.0." *American Libraries* 38, no. 2 (2007): 26.

Feinberg, Sandra, ed. *The Family-Centered Library Handbook.* New York: Neal-Schuman, 2007.

Feinberg, Sandra, Barbara Jordan, Kathleen Deerr, Marcellina Byrne, and Lisa G. Kropp. "Culturally Diverse Families." In Feinberg, *The Family-Centered Library Handbook*, 239–52.

Feldman, Sari, and Lev Gonick. "The Dream of OneCleveland." *Library Journal* 130, no. 14 (2005): 34–36.

Findsen, Brian. *Learning Later.* Malabar, Fla.: Krieger, 2005.

Foos, Donald D., ed. *How Libraries Must Comply with the Americans with Disabilities Act (ADA).* Phoenix, Ariz.: Oryx, 1992.

Freeman, Evelyn B., and Barbara A. Lehman, eds. *Global Perspectives in Children's Literature.* Boston, Mass.: Allyn and Bacon, 2001.

Freire, Paulo. *Pedagogy of the Oppressed.* 30th anniversary ed. New York: Continuum, 2000.

Friedman, Lawrence J. *Identity's Architect: A Biography of Erik H Erikson.* New York: Scribner, 1999.

Friend, Marilyn. *Special Education: Contemporary Perspectives for School Professionals.* 3rd ed. Boston: Pearson, 2011.

Friends of Libraries for Deaf Action (FOLDA). www.folda.net (15 March 2011).

Gagne, Robert M. *The Conditions of Learning and Theory of Instruction.* 4th ed. New York: Holt, Rinehart and Winston, 1985.

Gallaudet University. Laurent Clerc National Deaf Education Center. http:// clerccenter.gallaudet.edu/Clerc_Center/Information_and_Resources/ Info_to_Go.html (15 March 2011).

Gallaudet University Library. *Communicating in the Library with People Who Are Deaf or Hard of Hearing.* http://library.gallaudet.edu/Library/Deaf_ Research_Help/Communication_Tips_for_Librarians.html (15 March 2011).

———. *Deaf Research Guide: How to Get Started.* http://clerccenter.gallaudet .edu/Library/Deaf_Research_Help/Deaf_Research_Guide.html (15 March 2011).

———. *Frequently Asked Questions—Deaf-Related* http://library.gallaudet.edu/ Library/Deaf_Research_Help/Frequently_Asked_Questions_(FAQs).html (15 March 2011).

———. *Research Help.* http://clerccenter.gallaudet.edu/Library/Research_ Help.html (15 March 2011).

Gallup Organization. *The Role of Libraries in America.* Frankfurt: Kentucky Department of Libraries and Archives, 1976.

Gardner, Howard. *Frames of Mind: The Theory of Multiple Intelligences.* 20th anniversary ed. New York: Basic, 2004.

———. *Multiple Intelligences: The Theory in Practice.* New York: Basic, 1993.

Garrison, Dee. *Apostles of Culture: The Public Librarian and American Society, 1876–1920.* New York: Free Press, 1979.

Gentzler, Richard H., Jr. "Four Generations of Adult Learners." *Journal of Christian Education* (Winter 2009): 2–3.

Georgia Institute of Technology. Center for Assistive Technology and Environmental Access. *Assistive tech.net: National Public Website on Assistive Technology.* http://assistivetech.net.

Ghoting, Saroj Nadkarni, and Pamela Martin-Díaz, eds. *Early Literacy Storytimes @ Your Library: Partnering with Caregivers for Success.* Chicago: ALA, 2006.

Gilton, Donna Louise. "Culture Shock in the Library: Implications for Information Literacy Instruction." *Research Strategies* 20, no. 4 (2007): 424–25.

———. "Information Literacy as a Department Store: Applications for Public Teen Librarians." *Young Adult Library Services* 6, no. 2 (2008): 39–44.

———. "Instruction in Different Types of Libraries." *Teaching About Information.* www.uri.edu/artsci/lsc/Faculty/gilton/Instruction-CoverPage.htm.

———. *Multicultural and Ethnic Children's Literature in the United States.* Lanham, Md.: Scarecrow, 2007.

———. "A World of Difference: Preparing for Information Literacy Instruction for Diverse Groups." *MultiCultural Review* 3, no. 3 (1994): 54–62.

Goldberger, Nancy Rule, ed. *Knowledge, Difference, and Power: Essays Inspired by Women's Ways of Knowing.* New York: Basic, 1996.

Goodenough, David R. "History of the Field Dependence Construct." In Bertini, Pizzamiglio, and Wapner, *Field Dependence in Psychological Theory, Research, and Application,* 5–13.

Gossett, Tim. "10 Christian Education Trends for 2010 and Beyond." *Journal of Christian Education* (Spring 2010): 22–23.

Grassian, Esther S., and Joan R. Kaplowitz, eds. *Information Literacy Instruction: Theory and Practice.* 2nd ed. New York: Neal-Schuman, 2009.

———. "Teaching in a Diverse World: Knowledge, Respect, and Inclusion." In *Information Literacy Instruction: Theory and Practice.* 2nd ed. New York: Neal-Schuman, 2009, 247–66.

Green, Samuel Swett. "Personal Relations Between Librarians and Readers." *American Library Journal* 1 (October 1876): 74–81.

Gremmels, Gillian S., and Karen Shostrom Lehmann. "Assessment of Student Learning from Reference Service." *College and Research Libraries* 68, no. 6 (2007): 488–501.

Grinder, Alison L., and E. Sue McCoy, eds. *The Good Guide: A Sourcebook for Interpreters, Docents, and Tour Guides.* Scottsdale, Ariz.: Ironwood, 1985.

Groggin, Margaret, et al. *The Report on the Instruction in the Use of Libraries in Colorado Presented to the Colorado Council of Library Development by (Its) Committee on Insruction in the Use of Libraries.* Denver: The Committee, 1973.

Guild, Sandy. "LD Accommodations in the School Library." *Knowledge Quest* 37, no. 1 (2008): 24–29.

Gunian, Elaine Heumann. "The Potential of Museum Learning: The Essential Museum." In Lord, *The Manual of Museum Learning,* 21–41.

Gutek, Gerald L. "Froebel, Friedrich (1782–1852)." In *Encyclopedia of Education.* Vol. 3. 2nd ed. New York: Thomson/Gale, 2003, 903–6.

———. "Pestalozzi, Johann (1746–1827)." In *Encyclopedia of Education.* Vol. 5. 2nd ed. New York: Thomson/Gale, 2003, 1874–76.

H.W. Wilson Company. *Library Literature and Information Science.* New York: H.W. Wilson, 2000.

Haas, Claudia. "Families and Children Challenging Museums." In Lord, *The Manual of Museum Learning,* 49–75.

Hagemeyer, Alice Lougee, and Association of Specialized and Cooperative Library Agencies, eds. *The Legacy and Leadership of the Deaf Community: A Resource Guide for Librarians and Library Programs.* Chicago: Association of Specialized and Cooperative Library Agencies American Library Association, 1991.

Hall, Edward T. *Beyond Culture.* Garden City, N.Y.: Anchor, 1981.

———. *The Dance of Life: The Other Dimension of Time.* Garden City, N.Y.: Anchor/Doubleday, 1984.

——. *The Hidden Dimension.* New York: Anchor, 1990.

——. *The Silent Language.* New York: Anchor, 1990.

Hall, Patrick Andrew. "Developing Research Skills in African-American Students: A Case Note." *Journal of Academic Librarianship* 29, no. 3 (2003): 182–88.

——. "Peanuts: A Note on Intercultural Communication." *Journal of Academic Librarianship* 18, no. 4 (1992): 211.

——. "The Role of Affectivity in Instructing People of Color: Some Implications for Bibliographic Instruction." *Library Trends* 39, no. 3 (1991): 316–26.

Haras, Catherine, Edward M. Lopez, and Kristine Ferry. "Latino Students and the Library: A Case Study." *Journal of Academic Librarianship* 34, no. 5 (2008): 425–33.

Hargreaves, Andy, and Dennis Shirley. "Beyond Standardization: Powerful New Principles for Improvement." *Phi Delta Kappan* 90, no. 2 (2008): 135–43.

Harris, Cathryn. "Libraries with Lattes: The New Third Place." *Aplis* 20, no. 4 (2007): 145–52.

Harris, Roma H. "Bibliographic Instruction in Public Libraries: A Question of Philosophy." *RQ* 29 (Fall 1989): 92–98.

Harris, Roma H., and B. Gillian Michell. "The Social Context of Reference Work: Assessing the Effect of Gender and Communication Skill on Observers' Judgements of Competence." *Library and Information Science Research* 8 (January–March, 1986): 85–101.

Hart, Genevieve. "Public Librarians and Information Literacy Education: Views from Mpumalanga Province." *South African Journal of Library and Information Science* 72, no. 3 (2006): 172–84.

——. "Public Libraries in South Africa: Agents or Victims of Educational Change?" *South African Journal of Library and Information Science* 70, no. 2 (2004): 110–20.

Health Infonet of Alabama. http://healthinfonet.org (12 March 2011).

Hearing Loss Association of America. *Self-Help for Hard of Hearing People.* http://shhh.org.

Hennepin County Library. *Deaf and Hard of Hearing: Resources.* www.hclib .org/pub/search/fff/FullDisplay.cfm?ID=1162 (15 March 2011).

Hernon, Peter, ed. *Improving the Quality of Library Services for Students with Disabilities.* Westport, Conn.: Libraries Unlimited, 2006.

Hillenbrand, Candy. "Public Libraries as Developers of Social Capital." *Aplis* 18, no. 1 (2005): 4–12.

Himmel, Ethel E., and William James Wilson, eds. *Planning for Results: A Public Library Transformation Process.* Chicago: ALA, 1998.

Hogan, Robert. "Erik Erikson." In *Personality Theory: The Personological Tradition.* Englewood Cliffs, N.J.: Prentice-Hall, 1976, 164–86.

Holba Puacz, Jeanne. "Surf's Up for Seniors!" *Computers in Libraries* 20, no. 8 (2000): 50–53.

Holmes, Katherine "Use All Your Smarts: Multiple Intelligences for Diverse Library Users." http://lesley.edu/faculty/kholmes/presentations/MI.html (12 March 2011).

Holt, Cynthia, and Wanda Hole. "Training Rewards and Challenges of Serving Library Users with Disabilities." *Public Libraries* (January/February, 2003): 34–37.

Holt, John. *Freedom and Beyond*. Portsmouth, N.H.: Boynton/Cook, 1995.

———. *How Children Fail*. Reading, Mass.: Addison-Wesley, 1995.

———. *How Children Learn*. Reading, Mass.: Addison-Wesley, 1995.

———. *Instead of Education: Ways to Help People Do Things Better*. 2nd ed. Talent, Ore.: Sentient, 2003.

Holt, John, and Pat Farenga. *Teach Your Own: The John Holt Book of Homeschooling*. Cambridge, Mass.: Da Capo, 2003.

Home School Legal Defense Association. PO Box 2091, Washington, DC 20013.

Hooks, Bell. *Teaching to Transgress: Education as the Practice of Freedom*. New York: Routledge, 1994.

Hooten, Patricia A. "Online Catalogs: Will They Improve Children's Access?" *Journal of Youth Services in Libraries* 2 (1989): 270.

Howe, Neil, and William Strauss, eds. *13th Gen: Abort, Retry, Ignore, Fail?* New York: Vintage, 1993.

———. *Millennials Rising: The Next Great Generation*. New York: Vintage, 2000.

Huitt, W., and J. Hummel, "Piaget's Theory of Cognitive Development." *Educational Psychology Interactive*. Valdosta, Ga.: Valdosta State University. www.edpsycinteractive.org/topics/cogsys/piaget.html (12 March 2011).

Humes, Barbara. *Understanding Information Literacy*. Washington, D.C.: National Institute on Postsecondary Education, Libraries, and Lifelong Learning, 1999. www.libraryinstruction.com/infolit.html (12 March 2011)

Hunt, Nancy, and Kathleen J. Marshall, eds. *Exceptional Children and Youth: An Introduction to Special Education*. 4th updated ed. Boston: Houghton Mifflin, 2006.

Hunt, Peter, ed. *International Companion Encyclopedia of Children's Literature*. New York: Routledge, 2004.

IFLA/UNESCO Public Library Manifesto, 1994. www.ifla.org/VII/s8/unesco/eng.htm.

Independence Through Enhancement of Medicare and Medicaid (ITEM). *What Are Assistive Devices, Technologies, and Related Services?* www.itemcoalition.org/what_are_at.html (15 March 2011).

Information Architecture Institute. *The 25 Theses.* http://iainstitute.org/pg/25_theses.php (12 March 2011).

Information Competence for Black Studies. www.csulb.edu/~ttravis/BlackStudies/information.html (14 March 2011).

Information Competence for the Field of Chicano and Latino Studies. www.csulb.edu/~sluevano/chls/intro.html (14 March 2011).

International Federation of Library Assocations (IFLA). *Libraries Services to People with Special Needs Section.* www.ifla.org/en/lsn (15 March 2011).

Irvall, B., and G.S. Nielson. *IFLA Checklist: Access to Libraries for Persons with Disabilities.* IFLA Professional Reports No. 89. www.ifla.org/VII/s9/nd1/iflapr-89e.pdf (15 March 2011).

Ishizuka, Kathy. "Come Blog with Me." *School Library Journal* 52, no. 9 (2006): 22–23.

Jackson, Pamela A. "Incoming International Students and the Library: A Survey." *Reference Services Review* 33, no. 2 (2005): 197–209.

Jackson, Rebecca. "Cognitive Development." *Reference and User Services Quarterly* 46, no. 4 (2007): 28–32.

Jacobson, Trudi, and Helene C. Williams, eds. *Teaching the New Library to Today's Users: Reaching International, Minority, Senior Citizen, Gay/Lesbian, First Generation, At-Risk, Graduate and Returning Students, and Distance Learners.* New York: Neal-Schuman, 2000.

Jahoda, Gerald, ed. *How Do I Do This When I Can't See What I'm Doing? Information Processing for the Visually Disabled.* Washington: National Library Service for the Blind and Physically Handicapped, Library of Congress, 1993.

Jarvis, Peter, John Holford, and Colin Griffin, eds. *The Theory and Practice of Learning.* London: Kogan Page, 1998.

Jehlik, Theresa. "Information Literacy in the Public Library." *Nebraska Library Association Quarterly* 35, no. 4 (2004): 7–13.

Jiao, Qun G., and Anthony J. Onwuegbuzie. "Identifying Library Anxiety Through Students' Learning-Modality Preferences." *Library Quarterly* 69, no. 2 (1999): 202–16.

——. "Is Library Anxiety Important?" *Library Review* 48, no. 6 (1999): 278–82.

——. "Library Anxiety and Characteristic Strengths and Weaknesses of Graduate Students' Study Habits." *Library Review* 50, no. 1 (2001): 73–80.

Johnsburg Public Library. *Home School Resource Center.* www.johnsburglibrary.org/content/homeschool-resource-center (13 March 2011).

Johnson, B. Lamar, and American Library Association, eds. *Vitalizing a College Library.* Chicago: ALA, 1939.

Johnson County Community College. *College Learning Experience Activities and Resources (CLEAR).* www.jccc.edu/home/depts.php/5112 (15 March 2011).

Jones, Carolyn. "Baby Boomers and Generation Y in the Public Library: An Australian Perspective." In Kennedy, Vardaman, and McCabe, *Our New Public, a Changing Clientele*, 31–45.

Journal of Academic Librarianship. Ann Arbor, Mich.: Mountainside.

Journal of Information Literacy. http://jil.lboro.ac.uk.

Julien, Heidi, and Sandra Anderson. "The Public Library in Connecting Canadians" *Canadian Journal of Information and Library Sciences* 27, no. 4 (2003): 5–29.

Julien, Heidi, and Reegan D. Breu. "Instructional Practices in Canadian Public Libraries." *Library and Information Science Research* 27, no. 3 (2005): 281–301.

Kaplan, Paul. *Pathways for Exceptional Children: School, Home, and Culture*. Minneapolis/St. Paul: West, 1996.

Kathy Schrock's Guide for Educators. "Assessment and Rubric Information." http://school.discoveryeducation.com/schrockguide/assess.html (March 12, 2011).

Kaufman, Amy. "Marketing Museum Learning." In Lord, *The Manual of Museum Learning*, 253–72.

Kautz, James R., III, F. Ellen Netting, Ruth Huber, Kevin Borders, and Tamara S. Davis. "The Government Performance and Results Act of 1993: Implications for Social Work Practice." *Social Work* 42, no. 4 (1997): 364–73.

Kavanaugh, R., and B.C. Skold, *Libraries for the Blind in the Information Age: Guidelines for Development*. IFLA Professional Reports No. 86, 2005. www.ifla.org/VII/s31/pub/Profrep86.pdf (15 March 2011).

Kennedy, James R., Lisa Vardaman, and Gerard B. McCabe, eds. *Our New Public, a Changing Clientele: Bewildering Issues or New Challenges for Managing Libraries?* Westport, Conn.: Libraries Unlimited, 2008.

Kesselman, Martin Alan, ed. *Global Librarianship*. New York: Marcel Dekker, 2004.

King, Brad. "New Relationships with the Formal Education Sectors." In Lord, *The Manual of Museum Learning*, 2007, 77–105.

Kirkendall, Carolyn A., and Carla J. Stoffle. "Instruction." In *The Service Imperative for Libraries: Essays in Honor of Margaret E. Monroe*, ed. Gail A. Schlachter (Littleton, Colo.: Libraries Unlimited, 1982), 56.

Kladder, Jeri. *Story Hour: 55 Preschool Programs for Public Libraries*. Jefferson, N.C.: McFarland, 1995.

Klingler, Susan. "Low Literacy: Breaking the Family Cycle." *Indiana Libraries* 27, no. 2 (2008): 36–39.

Knowles, Malcolm S. *The Modern Practice of Adult Education: From Pedagogy to Andragogy*. Rev. ed. New York: Cambridge, the Adult Education Company, 1980.

———. *The Adult Learner: A Neglected Species*. 4th ed. Houston: Gulf, 1990.

Knowles, Malcolm S., and Richard A. Swanson, eds. *The Adult Learner: The Definitive Classic in Adult Education and Human Resource Development.* 6th ed. Boston: Elsevier, 2005.

Kobelski, Pamela, and Mary Reichel. "Conceptual Frameworks for Bibliographic Instruction." *Journal of Academic Librarianship* 7, no. 2 (1981): 73–77.

Kohl, Herbert R. *The Open Classroom: A Practical Guide to a New Way of Teaching.* New York: New York Review/Vintage, 1970.

———. *36 Children.* New York: New American Library, 1988.

———. *The Discipline of Hope: Learning from a Lifetime of Teaching.* New York: Simon and Schuster, 1998.

Koning, Alisa. "Information Literacy in New Zealand Public Libraries." *Aplis* 14, no. 3 (2001): 159–63.

Krzys, Richard, and Gaston Litton, eds. *World Librarianship: A Comparative Study.* New York: M. Dekker, 1983.

Kuhlthau, Carol C. "Implementing a Process Approach to Information Skills: A Study Identifying Indicators." *School Library Media Quarterly* 22, no. 1 (1993): 11–18.

———. *Information Skills for an Information Society: A Review of Research.* Syracuse, N.Y.: ERIC, 1987. ED 297.

———. "Students and the Information Search Process: Zones of Intervention for Librarians." *Advances in Librarianship* 18 (1994): 57–72.

Ladson-Billings, Gloria. *The Dreamkeeper: Successful Teachers of African American Students.* San Francisco: Jossey-Bass, 1994.

Landmark College. www.landmark.edu.

———. Institute for Research and Training. www.landmark.edu/institute/ (15 March 2011).

Lane, Patty. *A Beginner's Guide to Crossing Cultures: Making Friends in a Multicultural World.* Downer's Grove, Ill.: Intervarsity, 2002.

Langan, Colleen. "Literacy Starts in the Cradle of Shoalhaven Libraries New South Wales." *Aplis* 22, no. 1 (2009): 17–19.

Laslett, Peter. *A Fresh Map of Life: The Emergence of the Third Age.* Cambridge, Mass.: Harvard University Press, 1991.

Lavin, Michael R. *Business Information: How to Find It, How to Use It.* Phoenix, Ariz.: Oryx, 1992.

LD Online. www.ldonline.org (15 March 2011).

———. *National Organizations.* www.ldonline.org/finding_help/national_org/natorg_help.html (15 March 2011).

LD Resources. www.ldresources.com (15 March 2011).

Learning Disabilities Association. www.ldanatl.org (15 March 2011).

Learning Disabilities Association of America. www.ldaamerica.org (15 March 2011).

Learning Disabilities Worldwide. www.ldam.org (15 March 2011).

LeFever, Marlene. *Learning Styles: Reaching Everyone God Gave You to Teach.* Colorado Springs: David C. Cook, 1995, 99–107.

Liao, Yan, Mary Finn, and Jun Lu. "Information-Seeking Behavior of International Graduate Students vs. American Graduate Students: A User Study at Virginia Tech." *College and Research Libraries* 68, no. 1 (2007): 5–25.

Library Instruction Conference and Teresa B. Mensching, eds. *Reaching and Teaching Diverse Library User Groups: Papers Presented at the Sixteenth National LOEX Library Instruction Conference Held at Bowling Green State University 5 and 6 May 1988.* Ann Arbor, Mich.: Pierian, 1989.

Library of Congress. "Accessibility Home." www.loc.gov/access (15 March 2011).

Liu, Mengxiong, and Bernice Redfern. "Information-Seeking Behavior of Multicultural Students: A Case Study at San Jose State University." *College and Research Libraries* 58, no. 4 (1997): 348–54.

Lockwood, Deborah L., comp. *Library Instruction: A Bibliography.* Westport, Conn.: Greenwood, 1979.

Loe, Mary, and Betsy Elkins, "Developing Programs in Library Use Instruction for Library Learning: An Overview." In Brottman and Loe, *The LIRT Library Instruction Handbook*, 7–8.

Longstreet, Wilma S. *Aspects of Ethnicity: Understanding Differences in Pluralistic Classrooms.* New York: Teachers College Press, 1978.

Longworth, Norman. *Lifelong Learning in Action: Transforming Education in the 21st Century.* London: Kogan Page, 2003.

Lord, Barry, ed. *The Manual of Museum Learning.* Lanham, Md.: AltaMira, 2007.

———. "What Is Museum Learning?" In Lord, *The Manual of Museum Learning*, 13–19.

Lubans, John, Jr. *Educating the Library User.* New York: Bowker, 1974.

———. "Library-Use Instruction Needs from the Library Users'/Nonusers' Point of View: A Survey Report." In Lubans, *Educating the Library User*, 404–5.

———. "Nonuse of the Academic Library." *College and Research Libraries* 32 (September 1971): 362–67.

———, ed. *Educating the Public Library User.* Chicago: ALA, 1983.

Machlis, Gary E. "The Social Organization of Family Camping: Implications for Interpretation." In Machlis, *On Interpretation*, 75–87.

Machlis, Gary E., and Donald R. Field, eds. *On Interpretation: Sociology for Interpreters of Natural and Cultural History.* Rev. ed. Corvallis: Oregon State University Press, 1992.

Madden, Susan B. "Learning at Home." *School Library Journal* 37, no. 7 (1991): 23–25.

Mahaney, Michael C. "Client-Centered/Situational Bibliographic Instruction: A Mouthful That Need Not Always Be Said." *Bookmark* 46 (Fall 1987): 36.

Mancall, J. "Educating Students to Think: The Role of the School Library Media Program." *School Library Media Quarterly* 15, no. 1 (1986): 18–27.

Manning, M. Lee, and Leroy G. Baruth, eds. *Multicultural Education of Children and Adolescents*. 5th ed. Boston: Pearson, 2009.

Maricopa Community College Library. *How to Be a Webhound*. www.mcli .dist.maricopa.edu/webhound (12 March 2011).

Markgen, Susanne. "Reaching Out to Generation Y: Adapting Library Roles and Policies to Meet the Information Needs of the Next Generation." In Kennedy, Vardaman, and McCabe, *Our New Public, a Changing Clientele*, 46–54.

Marquam, Tamara. "Fable and Fact: Serving the Homeschool Population in Public Libraries." *Indiana Libraries* 27, no. 1 (2008): 12–18.

Martin, Charity K., et al. "Closing the Gap: Investigating the Search Skills of International and US Students: An Exploratory Study." *Library Philosophy and Practice* 11, no. 2 (2009): 1–17.

Maslow, Abraham H. *Motivation and Personality*. 2nd ed. New York: Harper and Row, 1970.

———. "A Theory of Human Motivation." In Maslow, *Motivation and Personality*, 35–58.

Massachusetts Initiative to Maximize Assistive Technology (AT) in Consumers' Hands (MATCH). www.massmatch.org (15 March 2011).

McCarthy, Cheryl. "Progress in School Library Media: Where Have We Been? Where Are We Now? And Where Are We Going? *Advances in Librarianship* 30 (2006): 271–97.

McClure, Charles R., ed. *Planning and Role Setting for Public Libraries: A Manual of Options and Procedures*. Chicago: ALA, 1987.

McCook, Kathleen de la Pena, ed. *Libraries: Global Reach, Local Touch*. Chicago: ALA, 1998.

———. "Public Libraries and People in Jail." *Reference and User Services Quarterly* 44, no. 1 (2004): 26–30.

McCook, Kathleen de la Pena, and Peggy Barber. "Public Policy as a Factor Influencing Adult Lifelong Learning, Adult Literacy, and Public Libraries." *Reference and User Services Quarterly* 42, no. 1 (2002): 66–75.

———. *Chronology of Milestones for Libraries and Adult Lifelong Learning and Literacy*. Prepared for the ALA Committee on Literacy, 2002. ERIC ED 458888.

McGahey, Michelle. "Hosting a Family Literacy Night at Your School." *Teaching Librarian* 13, no. 1 (2006): 52–59.

McKenzie, Walter. *Walter McKenzie's One and Only Surfaquarium: I Think . . . Therefore MI: Multiple Intelligences in Education*. http://surfaquarium.com.

McLaren, Peter, and Noah De Lissousky. "Paulo Freire (1921–1997)." In *Encyclopedia of Education*. Vol. 3, 900–3.

McLaughlin, John A., and Gretchen B. Jordan. "Logic Models: A Tool for Telling Your Program's Performance Story." *Evaluation and Program Planning* 22 (1999): 65–72.

McNicol, Sarah, and Pete Dalton. "Broadening Perspectives on the Learning Process in Public Libraries." *New Review of Libraries and Lifelong Learning* 4, no. 1 (2003): 27–43.

Meier, Deborah. *The Power of Their Ideas: Lessons for America from a Small School in Harlem*. Boston: Beacon, 1995.

Mellon, Constance A. "Attitudes: The Forgotten Dimension in Library Instruction." *Library Journal* 113, no. 14 (1988): 137–39.

———. *Bibliographic Instruction: The Second Generation*. Littleton, Colo.: Libraries Unlimited, 1987.

Mental Health America. www.nmha.org (15 March 2011).

Mi, Misa. "Cultural Competence for Libraries and Librarians in Health Care Institutions." *Journal of Hospital Librarianship* 5, no. 2 (2005): 15–31.

Michigan State University. *American Sign Language Browser*. http://aslbrowser.commtechlab.msu.edu/browser.htm (15 March 2011).

Misunderstood Minds. www.pbs.org/wgbh/misunderstoodminds/ (15 March 2011).

Molz, Kathleen. "The 'State of the Art' of Public Library Orientation." *Maryland Libraries* 34 (Winter 1968): 10–17.

Montgomery County Public Libraries. *Disability Resource Center*. http://montgomerycountymd.libguides.com/disabilityservices (15 March 2011).

Moore, Raymond S. *School Can Wait*. Provo, Utah: Brigham Young University Press, 1979.

Moyer, Jessica E. "Learning from Leisure Reading." *Reference and User Services Quarterly* 46, no. 4 (2007): 66–79.

Multiple Intelligences for Adult Literacy and Education. http://literacyworks.org/mi/home.html.

Mundava, Maud C., and LaVerne Gray. "Meeting Them Where They Are: Marketing to International Student Populations in U.S. Academic Libraries." *Technical Services Quarterly* 25, no. 3 (2008): 35–48.

Murray, Jennifer S. "Library Psychiatry." *AALL Spectrum* 14, no. 2 (2009): 10–13.

Mustain-Wood, Janice R. "Library Instruction: The Public Library." *Colorado Libraries* 9 (June 1983): 34–36.

Nassiimbeni, Mary. "Adult Education in South African Public Libraries: A Profile of Activities." *South African Journal of Library and Information Science* 72, no. 1 (2006): 12–26.

National Association for Interpretation. www.interpnet.com.

National Association of Councils on Developmental Disabilities. http://nacdd.org (15 March 2011).

National Commission on Excellence in Education. *A Nation at Risk: The Imperative for Educational Reform: A Report to the Nation and the Secretary of Education, United States Department of Education.* Washington, D.C.: Author, 1983.

National Consortium on Deaf-Blindness. www.nationaldb.org (15 March 2011).

National Council on Disability. www.ncd.gov (14 March 2011).

National Down Syndrome Society. www.ndss.org (15 March 2011).

National Easter Seal Society. http://easterseals.com (14 March 2011).

National Home Education Network. www.homeschool-curriculum-and-support.com/national-home-education-network.html (13 March 2011).

National Home Education Research Institute. www.nheri.org. (13 March 2011).

National Information Center for Children and Youth with Disabilities. www.nichcy.org/InformationResources/Documents/NICHCY%20PUBS/bp2.pdf (14 March 2011).

National Institute of Mental Health. www.nimh.nih.gov (15 March 2011).

National Institute on Deafness and Other Communication Disorders. www.nidcd.nih.gov/ (15 March 2011).

National Library Service for the Blind and Physically Handicapped (NLS). www.loc.gov/nls. www.loc.gov/nls/reference/circulars (15 March 2011).

———. *Assistive Technology Products for Information Access.* Comp. Carol Strauss. Washington, D.C.: NLS, 2000.

———. *Learning Disabilities: National Organizations and Resources.* www.loc.gov/nls/reference/circulars/learning.html (15 March 2011).

———. *NLS: That All May Read.* www.loc.gov/nls/reference/index.html (15 March 2011).

———. *Accessibility: A Selective Bibliography.* www.loc.gov/nls/reference/bibliographies/accessibility.html (15 March 2011).

———. *Physical Disabilities: Information and Advocacy Organizations.* www.loc.gov/nls/reference/circulars/physical.html (15 March 2011).

———. *Physical Handicaps: A Selective Bibliography* www.loc.gov/nls/reference/bibliographies/awareness.html (15 March 2011).

———. *Deaf-Blindness: National Resources and Organizations.* www.loc.gov/nls/reference/circulars/deafblind.html (15 March 2011).

———. *Learning Disabilities: National Organizations and Resources.* www.loc.gov/nls/reference/circulars/learning.html (15 March 2011).

National Organizations on Disabilities. http://nod.org (14 March 2011).

Natowitz, Allen. "International Students in U.S. Academic Libraries: Recent Concerns and Trends." *Research Strategies* 13 (Winter 1995): 4–16.

Neely, Teresa Y. *Information Literacy Assessment: Standards-Based Tools and Assignments.* Chicago: ALA, 2006.

Neely, Teresa Y., and Jessame Ferguson. "Developing Information Literacy Assessment Instruments." In Neely, *Information Literacy Assessment*, 153–71.

Neely, Teresa Y., and Katy Sullivan. "Integrating the ACRL Standards." In Neely, *Information Literacy Assessment*, 6–18.

Neill, Alexander Sutherland, and Albert Lamb, eds. *Summerhill School: A New View of Childhood*. New York: St. Martin's, 1993.

Nelson, Sandra, for the Public Library Association. *Implementing for Results: Your Strategic Plan in Action*. Chicago: ALA, 2009.

———. *The New Planning for Results: A Streamlined Approach*. Chicago: ALA, 2001.

———. *Strategic Planning for Results*. Chicago: ALA, 2008.

New England Assistive Tecnology (NEAT). *The NEAT Center at Oak Hill*. www.neatmarketplace.org (15 March 2011).

Newman, Ruth T. "Instructing the Out-of-School Adult in Public Library Use." In Lubans, *Educating the Public Library User*, 62–67.

Newton, Angela, and Debbi Boden. "Information Literacy Development in Australia." *Library and Information Update* 5, no. 1 (2006): 42–43.

Norlin, Dennis. "Helping Adults with Mental Retardation Satisfy Their Information Needs." In *Information Services for People with Developmental Disabilities*, ed. Linda Lucas Walling and Marilyn M. Irwin. Westport, Conn.: Greenwood, 1995, 181–95.

———. "We're Not Stupid, You Know: Library Services for Adults with Mental Retardation." *Research Strategies* 10, no. 2 (1992): 56–68.

North, Sue. "Catching Them in the Cradle: Family Literacy Programs." *Aplis* 16, no. 2 (2003): 66–71.

North Carolina State University. Center for Universal Design. www.design.ncsu.edu.

Norton, Alice, ed. *Your Public Library: Standards for Service*. Prepared for the Promotion of Standards Committee of the Public Library Association, a division of the American Library Association. Chicago: ALA, 1969.

Norton, Melanie J. "Effective Bibliographic Instruction for Deaf and Hearing-Impaired College Students." *Library Trends* 41, no. 1 (1992): 118–50.

Norton, Melanie J., and Gail Lukovalik, eds. "Libraries Serving an Underserved Population: Deaf and Hearing-Impaired Patrons." (Special issue) *Library Trends* 41 (Summer 1992): 1–176.

Nye, Robert D. *What Is B. F. Skinner Really Saying?* Englewood Cliffs, N.J.: Prentice-Hall, 1979.

O'Beirne, Ronan. "Raising the Profile of Information Literacy in Public Libraries." *Library and Information Update* 5, no. 1 (2006): 44–45.

Oberman, Cerise, ed. *Theories of Bibliographic Education: Designs for Teaching*. New York: Bowker, 1982.

O'Donnell, Ruth. "Planning to Implement the ADA in the Library." In Foos, *How Libraries Must Comply with the Americans with Disabilities Act*, 32–69.

Ohio Library Foundation. *Marketing the Library.* www.olc.org/marketing/ Index.html (12 March 2011).

Ohio State University. net.TUTOR. http://liblearn.osu.edu/tutor (12 March 2011).

———. Nisonger Center. *The Next Chapter Book Club* www.nextchapterbook club.org (15 March 2011).

Oldenburg, Ray. *Celebrating the Third Place: Inspiring Stories About the "Great Good Places" at the Heart of Our Communities* (New York: Da Capo, 2002).

———. *The Great Good Place: Cafes, Coffee Shops, Bookstores, Bars, Hair Salons, and Other Hangouts at the Heart of a Community.* New York: Marlowe, 1999.

Olson, Edward E. *Survey of User Policies in Indiana Libraries and Information Centers.* Indiana Library Studies Report No. 10. Bloomington, Ind.: The Center, 1970.

Online Asperger Syndrome Information and Support (OASIS). www.asper gersyndrome.org (15 March 2011).

Overall, Patricia Montiel. "Cultural Competence: A Conceptual Framework for Library and Information Science Professionals." *Library Quarterly* 79, no. 2 (2009): 175–204.

Palmour, Vernon E., and Marcia C. Bellassai, eds. *A Planning Process for Public Libraries.* Chicago: ALA, 1980.

Paperboy. www.thepaperboy.com (14 March 2011).

Patterson, Thomas. "'Idea Stores': London's New Libraries." *Library Journal* (May 1, 2001): 48–49.

Pearl, Nancy. *Book Lust.* Seattle: Sasquatch, 2003.

Pellowski, Anne. *The World of Children's Literature.* New York: Bowker, 1968.

Perkins Braille and Talking Books Library and the Minnesota Braille and Talking Book Library. *Info Eyes Information Service* (virtual reference service). www.infoeyes.org (15 March 2011).

Perry, William G. "Cognitive and Ethical Growth: The Making of Meaning." In Chickering, *The Modern American College*, 76–116.

Perry, William G., and Harvard University Bureau of Study Counsel, eds. *Forms of Intellectual and Ethical Development in the College Years: A Scheme.* New York: Holt, Rinehart and Winston, 1970.

Perspectives Network. www.tbi.org (15 March 2011).

Phoenix Public Library. *Accessibility Center.* www.phoenixpubliclibrary.org/ pageView.jsp?id=6027 (15 March 2011).

Pinellas Public Library Cooperative. *Literacy Services in Pinellas County.* www.pplc.us/literacy/index.shtml (15 March 2011).

Pond, Patricia. "Development of a Professional School Library Association: American Association of School Librarians." *School Media Quarterly* 5, no. 1 (1976): 12–18.

Postsecondary Education Programs Network (PEPNeT). *About PEPNeT.* www.pepnet.org/about.asp (15 March 2011).

———. PEPNeT Dissemination Center. www.pepnet.org/pdc (15 March 2011).

Powell, Sara Davis. *An Introduction to Education: Choosing Your Teaching Path.* Upper Saddle River, N.J.: Merrill, 2009.

Presley, Lauren. "Educating the Millennial User." In Kennedy, Vardaman, and McCabe, *Our New Public, a Changing Clientele,* 104–13.

Press, Nancy Ottman, and Mary Diggs-Hobson. "Providing Health Information to Community Members Where They Are: Characteristics of the Culturally Competent Librarian." *Library Trends* 53, no. 3 (2005): 397–410.

Public Library Association (PLA). Goals, Guidelines, and Standards Committee. *The Public Library Mission Statement and Its Imperative for Service.* Chicago: ALA, 1979.

———. Standards Committee. *Minimum Standards for Public Libraries.* Chicago: ALA, 1967.

Public Library of Cincinnati and Hamilton County. *Outreach Services.* www .cincinnatilibrary.org/main/outreach.asp (15 March 2011).

Quezada, Shelley. "Nothing About Me Without Me: Planning for Library Services for People with Disabilities." *Public Libraries* 42, no. 1 (2003): 42–46.

Rader, Hannelore B. "Information Literacy 1973–2002: A Selected Literature Review." *Library Trends* 51, no. 2 (2002): 242–48.

———. "User Education and Information Literacy for the Next Decade: An International Perspective." *Reference Services Review* (Summer 1996): 71–75.

Rapaport, William J. *William Perry's Scheme of Intellectual Development: A Journey Along the 9 "Perry Positions" (as Modified by Belenky, et al.).* www .cse.buffalo.edu/%7Erapaport/perry.positions.html (12 March 2011).

Rayner, Stephen, and Richard J. Riding. "Towards a Categorisation of Cognitive Styles and Learning Styles." *Educational Psychology* 17, nos. 1–2 (1997): 5–27.

Ready, Sandy, et al. "Library Instruction in Academic Libraries, Including Graduate Four-Year and Two-Year Institutions." In Brottman and Loe, *The LIRT Library Instruction Handbook,* 25–28.

Reenstjerna, Frederick R. "Developing Statewide Library Instruction Standards: Rationale and Preliminary Steps." In *Teaching Library Use Competence: Bridging the Gap from High School to College: Papers Presented at the Eleventh Annual Library Instruction Conference Held at Eastern Michigan University, May 7–8, 1981,* ed. Carolyn A. Kirkendall. Ann Arbor, Mich.: Pierian, 1982: 87–107.

The Reference Librarian. New York: Haworth, 1982.

Reference Services Review (RSR). Ann Arbor, Mich.: Pierian.

Rehmer, Julie. "Family Reading Night: A How-to Guide." *Library Media Connection* 25, no. 7 (2007): 16–17.

Reid, Rob. *Family Storytime: Twenty-Four Creative Programs for All Ages*. Chicago: ALA, 1999.

Rice, James R. "Library-Use Instruction with Individual Users: Should Instruction Be Included in the Reference Interview?" *Reference Librarian* (Spring/Summer 1984): 81–82.

Rochester Institute of Technology (RIT). National Technical Institute for the Deaf (NTID). *What Is NTID?* www.ntid.rit.edu/ntidweb/about_ntid.php (15 March 2011).

———. Wallace Memorial Library. *Deaf Studies Internet Resources*. http://library.rit.edu/guides/deaf-studies/internet-resources/deaf-studies-internet-resources.html (15 March 2011).

Rogers, Carl R., and H. Jerome Freiberg, eds. *Freedom to Learn*. 3rd ed. New York: Merrill, 1994.

Rose, Colin. *Accelerated Learning*. New York: Dell, 1985.

———. "Learning Styles." *Accelerated Learning*. http://chaminade.org/inspire/learnstl.htm (12 March 2011).

Roy, Loriene. "Circle of Community: The Freezing over Moon Month or Gashkadino-Giizis." *American Libraries* 38, no. 10 (2007): 6.

Rubin, Rhea Joyce. *Planning for Library Services to People to Disabilities*. Chicago: ALA, ASCLA, 2001.

Rubric Module. *Guidelines for Rubrics Development*. http://edweb.sdsu.edu/triton/july/rubrics/rubric_guidelines.html.

Rush, Michael D. "Community College Libraries, Learning Resource Centers Meet the Generation Y Challenge." In Kennedy, Vardaman, and McCabe, *Our New Public, a Changing Clientele*, 161–72.

Sager, H. "Implications for Bibliographic Instruction." In *The Impact of Emerging Technologies on Reference Service and Bibliographic Instruction*, ed. G. Pitkin. Westport, Conn.: Greenwood, 1995.

Salony, Mary F. "The History of Bibliographic Instruction: Changing Trends from Books to the Electronic World." *Reference Librarian* 24, nos. 51–52 (1995): 31–51.

San Antonio Public Library. *Special Needs Services*. http://guides.mysapl.org/content.php?pid=46718 (15 March 2011).

San Francisco Public Library. *Deaf Services Center*. http://sfpl.org/index.php?pg=0200002001 (15 March 2011).

San Francisco State University. *Outline Advancement of Student Information Skills (OASIS)*. http://oasis.sfsu.edu/chapters (12 March 2011).

Sannwald, William W. *Checklist of Library Building Design Considerations*. 5th ed. Chicago: ALA, 2009.

Schanze, George. "A View from a Library Phobic." *Colorado Libraries* 14 (June 1988): 23.

Schiller, Anita R. "Reference Service: Instruction or Information? *Library Quarterly* 35 (January 1965): 52–60.

Scotch Plains Public Library and Fanwood Memorial Library. *Libraries and Autism: We're Connected.* www.thejointlibrary.org/autism/ (15 March 2011).

Seattle Public Library. *ADA Special Services.* www.spl.org/default.asp?page ID=audience_specialservices (15 March 2011).

Seeholzer, Jamie, Frank J. Bove, and Delmus E. Williams. "What's Old Is New Again: Library Services and the Millennial Student." In Kennedy, Vardaman, and McCabe, *Our New Public, a Changing Clientele,* 241–54.

Selden, Timothy David. "Montessori, Maria (1870–1952)." In *Encyclopedia of Education.* Vol. 5, 1675–80.

Shalinsky, Audrey. "Culture Shock." In *Encyclopedia of Anthropology.* Vol. 2. 2nd ed. Ed. H. James Birx. Thousand Oaks, Calif.: Sage, 2006, 682–83.

Shapiro, Beth J., and Philip M. Marcus. "Library Use, Library Instruction, and User Success." *Research Strategies* 5 (Spirng 1987): 60–69.

Shapiro, Jeremy J., and Shelley K. Hughes. "Information Literacy as a Liberal Art." http://net.educause.edu/apps/er/review/reviewArticles/31231 .html (12 March 2011).

Sheesley, Deborah. "The 'Net Generation: Characteristics of Traditional-Aged College Students and Implications for Academic Information Services." *College and Undergraduate Libraries* 9, no. 2 (2002): 25–42.

Shirk, John C. "The Library Learning Inventory: A Process for Understanding the Adult Learner." In Lubans, *Educating the Public Library User,* 57–61.

Shonrock, Diana D., ed. *Evaluating Library Instruction: Sample Questions, Forms, and Strategies for Practical Use.* Chicago: ALA, 1996.

Shores, Louis. "The Library Arts College, A Possibility in 1954?" *School and Society* 41 (January 26, 1935): 110–14.

"A Silver Anniversary: 25 Years of Reviewing the Literature Related to User Instruction." *Reference Services Review* 28, no. 3 (2000): 290–96.

Simmons, Peter. "Studies in the Use of the Card Catalogue in a Public Library." *Canadian Library Journal* 31 (August 1994): 330–35.

Skinner, B.F. *Walden Two.* Indianapolis: Hackett, 2005.

———. *Beyond Freedom and Dignity.* Indianapolis: Hackett, 2002.

Skov, Annette. "Information Literacy and the Role of Public Libraries." *Scandinavian Public Library Quarterly,* no. 3 (2004): 4–7.

Slattery, Ann. "In a Class of Their Own." *School Library Journal* 51, no. 8 (2005): 44–46.

Snavely, Loanne, and Natasha Cooper. "The Information Literacy Debate." *Journal of Academic Librarianship* 23, no. 1 (1997): 9–14.

Snell, Kim. "Ready to Read Grant: How Columbus Metropolitan Library Got It and What They Learned." *Children and Libraries* 6, no. 2 (2008): 45–48.

Snowman, Jack, Rick McCowan, and Robert Biehler. *Psychology Applied to Teaching*. 12th ed. Boston: Houghton Mifflin, 2009.

Soltis, Jonas F. "Dewey, John (1859–1952)." In *Encyclopedia of Education*. Vol. 2, 577–82.

Soren, Barbara J. "Audience-Based Measures of Success: Evaluating Museum Learning." In Lord, *The Manual of Museum Learning*, 221–51.

St. Lifer, Evan, and Michael Rogers. "Library Offers Master's Degrees." *Library Journal* 119, no. 15 (1994): 16–17.

Stevens, Dannelle D., and Antonia Levi, eds. *Introduction to Rubrics: An Assessment Tool to Save Grading Time, Convey Effective Feedback, and Promote Student Learning*. Sterling, Va.: Stylus, 2005.

Stevens, Richard. *Erik Erikson: An Introduction*. New York: St. Martin's, 1983.

Strauss, William, and Neil Howe, eds. *The Fourth Turning: An American Prophecy*. New York: Broadway, 1997.

——. *Generations: The History of America's Future, 1584–2069*. New York: Morrow, 1991.

Stripling, Barbara K. "Quality in School Library Media Programs: Focus on Learning." *Library Trends* 44, no. 3 (1996): 631–56.

Studies in Media and Information Literacy Education (SIMILE). http://utpjournals.metapress.com.

Stueart, Robert D. *International Librarianship: A Basic Guide to Global Knowledge Access*. Lanham, Md.: Scarecrow, 2007.

Taggart, Germaine L., ed. *Rubrics: A Handbook for Construction and Use*. Lancaster, Pa.: Technomic, 1998.

Teacher Visions. *Creating Rubrics*. www.teachervision.fen.com/teaching-methods-and-management/rubrics/4521.html (12 March 2011).

Terzian, Sevan G. "Rousseau, Jean Jacques (1712–1778)." In *Encyclopedia of Education*. Vol. 6, 2079–81.

Texas School for the Blind and the Visually Impaired. *Overview of Assistive Technology*. www.tsbvi.edu/resources/21–technology/1004–overview-of-assistive-technology (15 March 2011).

Thornton, Glenda A., Bruce Jeppeson, and George Lupone. "A Traditional Library Meets Twenty-First Century Users." In Kennedy, Vardaman, and McCabe, *Our New Public, a Changing Clientele*, 183–205.

Tiefel, Virginia. "Evaluating in Terms of Established Goals and Objectives." In *Evaluating Bibliographic Instruction: A Handbook*. Chicago: ALA, 1983.

Tilden, Freeman. *Interpreting Our Heritage*. 3rd ed. Chapel Hill: University of North Carolina Press, 1977.

Toffler, Alvin. *The Third Wave*. New York: Bantam, 1989.

Tough, Allen. "Interests of Adult Learners." In Chickering, *The Modern American College*, 296–305.

Tucson Public Library. *Disability Services*. www.library.pima.gov/services/
disability/ (15 March 2011).

Turnbull, Ann P., and Michael L. Wehmeyer, eds. *Exceptional Lives: Special
Education in Today's Schools*. 5th ed. Upper Saddle River, N.J.: Pearson/
Merrill/Prentice Hall, 2007.

United Methodist Church. General Board of Discipleship (GBOD). "Lectionary Planning Help for Sundays. www.gbod.org/site/c.nhLRJ2PMKsG/
b.3879973/k.9C35/Lectionary_Planning_Helps_for_Sundays.htm.

United States Department of Education. National Institute on Disability
and Rehabilitation Research. *Abledata*. www.abledata.com (15 March
2011).

United States Access Board. www.access-board.gov (15 March 2011).

University Centers for Excellence in Developmental Disabilities Education, Research, and Service (UCEDD). www.workworld.org/wwwebhelp/university_
centers_for_excellence_in_developmental_disabilities_education_
research_and_service_ucedd_.htm (15 March 2011).

University of Hawaii. Archimedes Hawaii Project. http://archimedes.hawaii
.edu (15 March 2011).

University of Illinois. Illinois Online Network (ION). "Learning Styles and
the Online Environment." www.ion.uillinois.edu/resources/tutorials/id/
learningstyles.asp (12 March 2011).

University of Maryland, Baltimore. Health Sciences and Human Services Library. "Consumer Health." http://guides.hshsl.umaryland.edu/consumer
health (12 March 2011).

University of North Carolina, Asheville. North Carolina Center for Creative
Retirement. www2.unca.edu/ncccr/.

University of Rhode Island. Disability Services for Students. *Emerging Schol-
ars, Students with Disabilities: A Handbook for Faculty and Administrators in
Rhode Island Public Institutions of Higher Education*. Kingston: University of
Rhode Island Disability Services for Students in cooperation with Paul V.
Sherlock Center on Disabilities, Student Life Office Rhode Island College,
2004.

———. *Disability Services for Students*. www.uri.edu/disability/dss (15 March
2011).

University of South Carolina Beaufort Library. *Bare Bones 101: A Basic Tutorial on Searching the Web*. www.sc.edu/beaufort/library/pages/bones/
bones.shtml (12 March 2011).

University of Washington. *Disabilities, Opportunities, Internet Working, and
Technology (DO-IT)*. www.washington.edu/doit/ (15 March 2011).

———. *Resources on Accessible Web Design*. www.washington.edu/doit/
Resources/web-design.html (15 March 2011).

University of Wisconson Extension. *Enhancing Program Performance with
Logic Models*. www.uwex.edu/ces/lmcourse (12 March 2011).

———. Program Development and Evaluation. *Logic Models.* www.uwex .edu/ces/pdande/evaluation/evallogicmodel.html (12 March 2011)

Van Fleet, Connie, and Karen E. Antell. "Creating Cyber Seniors: Older Adult Learning and Its Implications for Computer Training." *Public Libraries* 41, no. 3 (2003): 149–51.

Vavrek, Bernard. "Struggle for Survival: Reference Services in the Small Public Library." *Library Journal* 108 (May 15, 1983): 966–69.

Velleman, Ruth A. *Meeting the Needs of People with Disabilities: A Guide for Librarians, Educators, and Other Service Professionals.* Phoenix, Ariz.: Oryx, 1990.

W.K. Kellogg Foundation. *Logic Model Development Guide.* www.osswa.org/ pdf/kellogg.pdf (12 March 2011).

Wagner, A.B., and Cynthia Tysick. "Onsite Reference and Instruction Services." *Reference and User Services Quarterly* 46, no. 4 (2007): 60–65.

Walling, Linda Lucas, ed. *Information Services for People with Developmental Disabilities: The Library Manager's Handbook.* Westport, Conn.: Greenwood, 1995.

Web Accessibility in Mind (WebAIM). *Evaluating Cognitive Web Accessibility.* www.webaim.org/articles/evaluatingcognitive/#principles (15 March 2011).

Wedgeworth, Robert, ed. *World Encyclopedia of Library and Information Services.* 3rd ed. Chicago: ALA, 1993.

Wellness Information Zone. www.wellzone.org (12 March 2011).

Whelan, Debra Lau. "The Equal Opportunity Disorder." *School Library Journal* 55, no. 8 (2009): 30–34.

Wikel, Nancy. "A Community Connection: The Public Library and Home Schoolers." *Emergency Librarian* 22, no. 3 (1995): 13–15.

Witkin, Herman A., C.A. Moore, D.R. Goodenough, and P.W. Cox. "Field-Dependent and Field Independent Cognitive Styles and Their Educational Implications." *Review of Educational Research* 47, no. 1 (1977): 1–64.

Woods, Kathleen G., Helen T. Burns, and Marilyn Barr. "Planning an Instruction Program in a Public Library." In Brottman and Loe, *The LIRT Library Instruction Handbook*, 49–50.

World Wide Web Consortium (W3C). Web Content Accessibility Working Group. *Web Content Accessibility Guidelines.* www.w3.org/TR/WAI-WEB CONTENT/#loc (15 March 2011).

Wright, Kieth C., and Judith F. Davie, eds. *Library and Information Services for Handicapped Individuals.* 3rd ed. Englewood, Colo.: Libraries Unlimited, 1989.

Xie, Bo, and Paul T. Jaeger. "Computer Training Programs for Older Adults at the Public Library." *Public Libraries* 47, no. 5 (2008): 52–59.

Yucht, Alice. *Alice in InfoLand: FLIPit!* www.aliceinfo.org/flipit (12 March 2011).

Zarsky, Terry. "Instruction for the Business Community." *Colorado Libraries* 26, no. 4 (2000): 38–39.

Zoe, Lucinda, and Diane DiMartino. "Cultural Diversity and End-User Searching: An Analysis by Gender and Language Background." *Research Strategies* 17, no. 4 (2000): 291–305.

Zurowski, Paul. *The Information Service Environment: Relationship and Priorities*. Washington, D.C.: National Commission on Libraries and Information Sciences, 1974.

Index

About the Author

Donna L. Gilton earned a bachelor's degree in history and elementary education from Simmons College, a master's degree in library science from Simmons, and a Ph.D. in library science from the University of Pittsburgh. She served as a children's librarian at the Boston Public Library, head librarian at the Belize Teacher's College, and business reference librarian at Western Kentucky University and Pennsylvania State University. She is now a professor at the University of Rhode Island, where she has taught reference and information services, information literacy, multiculturalism in libraries, comparative and international librarianship, the history of the book, and courses in business, humanities, and social sciences reference. Gilton started the first course related to library instruction at the University of Rhode Island, one of the first courses in this field in the country. She has published several articles on information literacy and created the website Teaching About Information. She is also the author of *Multicultural and Ethnic Children's Literature in the United States*.

CPSIA information can be obtained at www.ICGtesting.com
Printed in the USA
BVOW071550080312

284748BV00003B/1/P